FOUR FOR THE CORPS

THE EDUCATION OF A PEACE TIME MARINE

BY WILLIAM J. K. BEAUDOT

© 2019

Ⅱ GEMINI RISING

Beaudot, William J.K.

Four for the Corps: The Education of a Peace Time Marine

Published 2019 by Gemini Rising

Milwaukee (Wis.) – 20th Century – History — Fiction

Wisconsin – History – 20th Century – Fiction

Marines – United States – Fiction

United States Marine Corps – Fiction

Adak, Alaska – 20th Century – Fiction

Naval Air Station, Adak, Alaska – Fiction

Whidbey Island, Washington – 20th Century – Fiction

Naval Air Station, Whidbey Island, Washington – Fiction

Camp Pendleton, California – 20th Century – Fiction

Bildungsromans

813.54

c.2019

*T*able of Contents

Also by William J. K. Beaudot .... *iv*
Dedication: Jerome "Jerry" Litke .... *v*
Acknowledgment .... *vi*

Daughter's Expectation
    "Once a Marine…"

CHAPTER 1
    CAMP PENDLETON
    "Every Marine a Rifleman"

CHAPTER 2
    NAS WHIDBEY ISLAND
    Garrison Marine

CHAPTER 3
    INTERREGNUM
    Briefly Back Home

CHAPTER 4
    NAS WHIDBEY REDUX
    "Brig Rats"

CHAPTER 5
    NAS Adak Island
    "Playground of the Bering Sea"

CHAPTER 6
    OSCAR COMPANY
    "Short Timer"

Daughter's Reflection
    "…always a Marine"

Also by William J. K. Beaudot

A Kid to the Corps: A Midwestern Boy's Life with Movies and the Marines (Gemini Rising, 2016)

The 24th Wisconsin Infantry in the Civil War (Stackpole Books, 2003)

In the Bloody Railroad Cut at Gettysburg, co-author. (Savas Beatie, 2015)

An Irishman in the Iron Brigade, co-author (Fordham University Press, 1993)

Dedication: Jerome "Jerry" Litke

Jerome ("Jerry") Walter Litke

Born, Milwaukee, September 28, 1947

PFC, Company C, 1st Battalion, 9th Marines

Killed in Action, Quang Nam Province, June 6, 1966

Vietnam Veterans Memorial

Nearly 50 years have passed since your death in Vietnam, Dear Brother. It doesn't seem that long ago that you and your pals were hanging out at Litke's Old Place in Milwaukee. You were taken from us too early in life.

There was so much you missed. Many nieces and nephews were born after you were gone who never got to know you. Our sister Kathy went into labor at the news of your death; she named her son, Jerry. Our dad, a World War II veteran, died not long after the news of our loss; he was heartbroken.

You are missed every day by family and friends. Beloved brother, you live in our thoughts and hearts. We will love you always. Your little sister, Bev.

*A*cknowledgment

First and foremost, to Chellie Beaudot, my first-born daughter and editor who helped coax the manuscript into life. And to my good son Andre Beaudot for his work on my first Marine narrative, *A Kid to the Corps*.

I thank my younger daughters, too – Corinne and Renée – for their encouragement and friendly ears. And to my grandchildren – Mary, Collin, Jarett, and Camden; Lauren and Katherine; Fonsi and Xavi; and great-granddaughter Layla, too. I also mention daughter-in-law Traci, and sons-in-law Paul and Alfonso, and Maggie. And, of course, thanks to Bev for her patience and forbearance when I spent endless hours on the keyboard.

Once again, without Rod Holloway, the incomparable camera artist and compositor, this manuscript would never have been transformed from mere type-written pages to a book.

Much esteemed gratitude to Dina Merz, my brilliant editor who corrected numerous faulty constructions, and ferreted out a myriad typos, grammatical errors and more. More, her encouragement was essential and unstinting. Thanks, too, to Nancy Cline.

And gratitude to my bosom pard, mentor and former Marine, Ron Schiessl, that citizen of the State of Jefferson who waded through many foul papers, providing invaluable counsel. And thanks to my old traveling companion and bunkie, Art Tyszka, who's now on heaven's firing line; his family tales have gravitated to these pages. And to Gerald Duane Coleman who will recognize many of his experiences transfigured in this narrative. I always warned him and others to be careful around me because some of their stories might be used in what I deem a "creative" memoir. Or is it an autobiographical novel?

I thank, too, friends in Salvador, Brazil who continually prodded me to finish writing the story, and mention especially Antonio Moraes Ribeiro.

To others I have inadvertently failed to mention, thank you, too.

Finally, I again salute Jerry Litke, brother-in-law and young Marine whose name is high on the Vietnam Veterans Memorial.

Wm. J. K. Beaudot 2019

Daughter's Expectation

"Once a Marine..."

"Yeah, I read it, man," began the brief handwritten note he showed me a few years back. It was from Heissen, an old Marine Corps buddy who'd shared the trial and travail of Boot Camp those many decades before. Our Dad had mailed the buddy a few manuscript chapters, little more than foul papers, he called them, of what became *A Kid to the Corps*.

"Did a good job writing about those grueling hours on MCRD's [Marine Corps Recruit Depot] 'Grinder,' learning close order drill — actually, one of the best accounts I've ever read." While our Dad thought the comment generous, his old buddy mentioned nothing else about the narrative of recruit training under the San Diego sun in the early 1950s. "Perhaps he's damning with faint praise," our Dad grumbled.

Our Dad rarely used the verb "published" when referring to his work. He'd actually paid to get it into print — compensated an artist friend to cast the manuscript into electronic form, and paid a vanity press to produce a physical book. But he hadn't engaged a copy editor to ferret out numerous typographical and grammatical errors that lingered in the finished product. Thus, his mortification when a myriad mistakes glared at him from the printed pages.

Years later, he smilingly showed me an e-mail from a friend in Germany who'd read the book after Dad sent one of the scores of copies that collected dust on a closet shelf. It hadn't been long, Dieter commented, before he'd been "captured" by the narrative, and liked nearly all of it. "Your story shows an author with skills." He'd enjoyed especially the tales of our Dad's family, youth and the back stories of the Marine Corps characters who peopled the Bildungsroman.

As the pitiful few others who fully read A Kid to the Corps may remember, my brother had taken it upon himself to assist our Dad in that endeavor. After our Dad had published several respected books of non-fiction about Wisconsin in the Civil War, he wanted to try his hand at fiction. But neither father nor son was patient or disciplined enough to ferret out the voluminous mistakes — egregious grammatical errors and clunky constructions that plagued the book. "We just didn't see the trees for the forest," my brother admitted, sharing our Dad's mortification at the flawed first experiment in fiction.

I disagreed when my brother took hold of the raw manuscript and intruded his own subjective observations in the narrative. While these were meant to clarify and correct some of what my brother regarded as outright inventions and misstatements, my sibling should have permitted our Dad's words to stand on their own, as I will do in this sequel.

I'm the oldest of four, and despite occasional differences, our Dad and I had a loving relationship, especially in our latter years. I think he sometimes used me as a "daughter confessor," admitting to commissions and omissions in life that he hadn't revealed to my sisters and brother. But none of us ever detected that one of us was favored over the others — by him or our mother.

So, a word or two about the father *I* knew: He preferred balance, harmony, and subtlety in life and in the arts (much to the consternation of our brother's avocational pursuit). He was a man of probity for the most part who honored commitments and was loyal to his family and friends as well as to his country. Our Dad also valued efficiency and dependability in himself and others. He often delayed gratification, thinking more of the future than the present — although this seems to be contradicted by the amount of time he spent on this and the earlier narrative. He confessed to a lack of quick-wittedness, and wasn't adept at thinking well on his feet. He often fussed over old discussions – even back to youth — discomfited that he'd not cast assertions differently or with more supportive evidence. Perhaps that's why he preferred writing, for it gave him an opportunity to reconsider, edit and polish.

He regretted that he should have been smarter after more than eight decades of life, of being more analytical, insightful and incisive, persuasive and certainly more accomplished overall. As he aged, he worried about things he'd left undone and unsaid as much as of things done and said badly. Patience was certainly not a virtue that could be applied to him. But then, he was an only child – one key to his character, I suppose.

I think our Dad should have been pleased with his achievements, overcoming disadvantages and deficiencies of early life to register at least modest academic and professional successes. But he declared these were due solely to favorable fortune and circumstance.

Our Dad was an agnostic if not a reluctant atheist unsuccessfully bent on sloughing off remnants of religious dogma that still clung from early life. In this, he told me, he was especially reacting to the rise of what he called America's evangelical Taliban — contemptuous of those who misused Christian Scriptures, selecting only blasphemous, self-serving interpretations.

He was man of books, as his ultimate profession will attest, and of the performing arts. He maintained a life-time "romance" with jazz and the American songbook. He'd been transfixed by the first play he'd ever seen, in second grade, when older classmates served as toga-clad Romans on the school "boards" in "Julius Caesar." Later, at age 12, he'd been captivated by Moira Shearer's tragic performance in Michael Powell and Emeric Pressburger's lush screen interpretation of "The Red Shoes." He'd sat alone in the undistinguished and uncrowded North Milwaukee theater, presumptuously named the Ritz, mesmerized through three showings in as many days, and decades later every time it was broadcast on Turner Classic Movies. We all now share season seats at the Milwaukee Ballet.

He lamented that he'd been far less than successful during our childhood as a husband and father. Back then, we sometimes felt like Marine Corps recruits. But after our parents divorced, he became better at both callings – or shall I say, improved as a former husband to our mother, and father to us. Our parents had parted when I was about 15; my sisters were then 12 and four, and my brother was ten.

"I'm from the on/off switch generation," our Dad often proclaimed, indicating, I think, his aversion to our world's devil-may-care embrace of binary code technology. Still, he wasn't a Luddite, and accepted technology as vital in fostering communication and efficiency. It certainly aided his creativity. He used e-mail but always wrote in complete and grammatically correct sentences, eschewing silly social media acronyms and detestable emojis. He resisted our encouragement to submit to social media and use a cell phone, considering the latter a devil's device.

His formative years occurred against the backdrop of constant war in the world. He retained clear recollections from radio, newspapers, and especially movie newsreels of the dastardly attack on Pearl Harbor, traumatic to our maternal grandparents (both immigrants), and to our paternal grandfather. Too old for military service, he'd volunteered as a hometown Air Raid Warden. He and our grandmother toiled tirelessly in Milwaukee's defense industry.

Our Dad's childhood disquiet over the rise of Nazism in Germany and elsewhere in the last century, especially its industrial obliteration of millions of Jews, gypsies and marginalized "others" was recently reawakened by the dangerously divisive politics of American reactionaries, particularly one scurrilous president and his party of duplicitous sycophants.

Our Dad's memories of hated Axis villains – Hitler, Tojo, Mussolini and their murderous ilk – burned white hot in his childhood and as cautionary portraits in later life. The roll of battles, armies and the panoply of war were ever etched in his memory, thanks largely to Hollywood. Guadalcanal, Tarawa, D-Day, Iwo Jima, VE-Day and revelations of the Nazi's Final Solution, the atomic bombing of Japan and VJ-Day, Korea. More recently, he thundered against the renewed rise of racism and white supremacy.

He was deeply influenced by more than three-quarters of a century of watching movies, as many as six or more in a week during childhood and youth, and on television as an adult. "They comprised my doctorate," he mused.

His boyhood heroes and models were larger than life – screen portrayals by Errol Flynn, Tyrone Power, Stewart Granger and John Wayne, among others, of characters like Robin Hood, Pedro De Vargas, Walter of Gurney, Scaramouche, and, especially Marine Sergeant John Stryker. Others like Burt Lancaster, the "Swede" in "The Killers," Humphrey Bogart as Philip Marlowe in "The Big Sleep" and Sam Spade in "The Maltese Falcon," provided flawed but more humane examples of strength.

"Since war hung like a pall over my generation, we anticipated military service after high school, to volunteering in our turn," he told me. "I just enlisted a year earlier than most." Of course, potential benefits that accrued – the federal G. I. Bill that permitted financial assistance for college – a prime argument to convince our grandmother to agree to his enlistment at 17.

Our Dad never experienced combat that he'd craved in youth. Thus, his memoir focuses upon standing on that wall, as proposed by the Jack Nicholson's Marine Colonel Jessup in "A Few Good Men." "We live in a world that has walls, and those walls have to be guarded by men with guns," he scowled. And so, that was our Dad's job — to protect America when a hot war with the Soviets turned cold. For one-quarter of his service, he'd stood with fellow Marines, sailors and SeaBees just 500 miles from Soviet Russia.

Decades later, he was fond of quoting the replicant Roy Batty, from "Blade Runner:" "I've seen things you people wouldn't believe.

Attack ships on fire off the Shoulder of Orion. I watched C-Beams glitter in the dark near the Tannhäuser Gate. All those moments will be lost in time like tears in rain." He hoped his grandchildren might understand.

While my siblings and I thought little of what we regarded as his silly scribblings, our Dad worked and reworked his manuscript fitfully over a many years. "It kept me focused and interested as a dotard," he said. "I thought of it as some kind of *Picture of Dorian Gray* that kept me going."

I think he wrote these books primarily for us — his kids and grandchildren, and to leave a little record behind of how he'd passed this way.

I won't testify that every event, every scene, every character in our Dad's fictional memoir is accurate or even factual. There are some characters that I suspect were transposed from his later life. He took creative liberties, as readers will see, to cast this narrative in fictional form, needing to use artifice and literary license to fill fallible gaps. You know what Mark Twain said in late life: "When I was younger I could remember anything, whether it happened or not; but my faculties are decaying now and soon I shall be so I cannot remember any but the things that never happened."

Then, there was Charlotte Bronte's Jane Eyre that I like: "I was tormented by the contrast between my ideas and my handiwork, in each case I had imagined something which I was quite powerless to realize."

What's more, to paraphrase a character in Louis de Bernieres' novel, *Captain Corelli's Mandolin* there's this: "[He] would want to be beside each reader in order to answer their objections, and tell them not to skip any sections...."

Yet, I think our Dad dutifully captured the life of a volunteer, non-combat Marine. I know because I served in the peacetime military and know a thing or two.

These days, our Dad bristled when hearing the glib toss-off, "Thank you for your service." He also scowled at "the bone spur deferment brigade, from presidents on down, who didn't and don't have the guts to render service to our nation or even to stand on America's peacetime wall. Yet, they ungratefully accept all of the freedoms and benefits our country provides," he thundered. "Patriotism's earned by more than mere slogans and flag waving."

"Once a Marine, always a Marine," our Dad often said. As proud as he was of having been a Marine, he felt his service paled in comparison to that of his brother-in-law. "Like me, Jerry Litke enlisted in the Corps before he'd finished high school. He was killed in combat in 1966, not yet 19. Name's etched on the Vietnam Veterans Memorial – an example of selfless service to our nation."

Chapter 1

CAMP PENDLETON

"Every Marine a Rifleman"

Garson scrunched down, a mole in his fighting hole — a three-foot gouge in the semi-arid scrub — his mind stuporous, crowded with an ill-formed image of a phalanx of furry tarantulas scuttling toward the Baker Company MLR, the main line of resistance. The real night was pitch black, not a speck or glow of light, neither moon, star or planet daring to defy the darkness.

Then, a sound split the silence — the muffled *"CHRUMPF"* of an enemy mortar launched from a distant ridge. Garson twitched awake, imaginary arachnids dispersing before an equally unreal skirmish line of Aggressors who charged toward the Marine position.

Within expectant seconds, the mortar shell burst in the inky sky, a blinding Fourth of July explosion. But it wasn't July; it was April. "Willie Peter" — white phosphorous – flashed overhead, dazzling magnesium sparks showered from the shell that dangled from a tiny parachute as it lazily descended, bathing the battlefield for hundreds of yards in weird, tremulous illumination, flickering like a silent movie at the vest pocket Ritz Theater back home. The burning shell hissed menacingly in its descent. Such sentences, Garson mused as he wrote them decades later, were better suited to British writer Bulwer-Lytton, he of the "It was a dark and stormy night."

"Look away from the light 'cause it'll steal your night vision," Garson remembered an instructor admonishing. He squinted, tipping his head and helmet forward to shade his eyes, simultaneously fingering the M-1 rifle trigger safety. He was uncertain whether to unlock the safety and force a round into the chamber. In minutes, the mortar shell exhausted its pyrotechnic fuel and winked out, shrouding the battlefield once more in impenetrable blackness.

"Say, Boondocks," whispered Tino from the neighboring fighting hole several yards away, using Garson's Pendleton sobriquet. "Think I see something to the left," his voice seemed to point. " There!" A climactic scene from the war movie, "Bataan," flashed in Garson's mind. It was one of the survivors of a doomed army squad defending the Pacific Island, perhaps Leonard Purckett portrayed by baby-faced Robert Walker who spoke. Garson couldn't be sure of such details from the World War movie he'd seen ten years before. As Jap soldiers stealthily probed the unit's perimeter under a blanket of Hollywood ground fog, Purckett whispered to Robert Taylor's Sergeant Dane.

"Hey, Sarge, Sarge! I think them trees an' bushes're movin'." Japs always employed such dastardly tactics in Hollywood's version of war in the Pacific: Sniping or bayoneting under cover of darkness or other obscurity instead of manly stand up and fight in daylight tactics. Newsreel commentators had long avowed the truth of those assertions when they spoke about Guadalcanal, the Solomons, Tarawa, and Iwo Jima. Sneaky little yellow bastards! The Aggressors to Garson's Baker Company front employed similar tactics.

Suddenly, thirty yards to the left of Garson's fighting hole, a rifle shot cracked in the night. His heart jumped. Then one or two more shots rang out until what sounded like an entire platoon opened up. Crimson muzzle flashes from a BAR barked in the dark. This might become a full-blown fire fight, Garson feared. He nervously clicked off the trigger safety, and swung his M-1 toward the tempest.

"Cease firing!" An angry voice growled. "Cease fuckin' firing, you dumb fucks!" It sounded like one of the Baker Company Troop Handlers. Firing sputtered and stopped. Silence prevailed once more, but Garson's spine prickled in the pregnant atmosphere. His nerves were trip wire taut, and he was unable to calm himself. Then a voice, amplified from a far ridge:

"Hey, Gyrene, we're gonna fuckin' come get you soon!" The speaker's words were raw and raspy, like a man suffering from the night's dews and damps, a verbal saw cutting through the unsettling blackness. The enemy may have been 50 yards out there, as far as Garson could discern, somewhere beyond no man's land. Then, the disembodied voice cackled before changing tone to one of teasing enticement:

"Hey, *Maline*, wanna fuckey-fuckey? We got *ichi bon* pussy over here. Hot coffee. Lucky Lager Brew for you. All ya' gotta do is come on over." The voice feigned a curious accent, artificial, like those American movie actors who portrayed Japs and Chinese, or someone like the despicable Richard Loo, Hollywood's favorite Asian villain. But Garson had heard from some vets who'd fought in Korea that Gooks and Red Chinks actually did this sort of thing in combat.

Minutes later, horns howled and flutes twittered, drums thumped in an eerie, unharmonious musical concoction that wafted across the battlefield – stabbing at nerves. Garson trembled in his earthen depression, feeling more like a fox hiding in a hole than a Marine prepared for battle. Soon, he was certain, the enemy would begin advancing on the MLR in earnest, probing for weaknesses among Marines drowsy or sleep deprived after three days in the field.

"They say fuckin' Aggressors'll sneak into our lines to snatch guys," was a recent claim. Wide-eyed Garson, of course, soaked up such scuttlebutt, certain that captives were stripped to their skivvies, abused, throttled and cuffed. One knowledgeable Baker Company buddy had heard that prisoners were confined at length to tiny four-by-four tiger cages, ridiculed, spat at, even pissed upon. Worse, after release, Garson concluded, a captive would be labeled like a forehead tattoo as untrustworthy, without courage and lacking combat readiness. He feared such moral failure.

During Garson's four years in the Corps, it was his life-long lament, that the three-day Camp Pendleton training exercise would be the closest he'd ever come to actual combat.

Months before, Garson had been among the last of his Boot Camp buddies to depart the Marine Corps Recruit Depot at San Diego, after having completed the 13 weeks of recruit training. He'd considered that he'd been mostly successful in this initial endeavor of a four-year enlistment, having earned his stripe as a private first class (not every member of Platoon 023 had done so), winning a Sharpshooter medal with the M-1 rifle (missing Expert by a mere two points) and excelling with the .45 pistol. Garson had only been a few months past his seventeenth birthday, after all, a high school drop-out with limited prospects. He still fussed that recruit Platoon 023 had not won the company's Honor Platoon award. He blamed Fletcher for the shortcoming because of the goggle-eyed Detroiter's inability to mind the step in close order drill competition.

Garson had bid farewell to the two buddies with whom he'd enlisted – tall, handsome and angular Preston and squatty, fiery-haired Rusty, whose coloration connoted his personality. Back in Milwaukee, they'd been known as the Three Musketeers, having bonded for more than a year before their decision to quit school and find adventure. Their hometown pals, Toby and Chet, had seen California's Seven Cities of Cibola, Los Angeles, the summer of 1953, and returned with golden tales of magical travels along Route 66 and concupiscent conquest in Mexico, leaving unsaid that the latter came at a price.

Having grown to near manhood in the World War environment, the Musketeers had agreed that the Marine Corps would fulfill the nascent sense of duty and desire for adventure. It was the finest fighting force on earth. Garson hoped only that the summer truce called in Korea would not hold, and provide them a fighting arena to prove their worth.

After recruit graduation from MCRD, Preston and Rusty held orders to Marine Air Wings, the former to El Toro, California, and the other to Cherry Point, North Carolina where they'd spend their entire enlistments.

That's "pogue duty," Garson scowled, using the derision derived from "pogey bait" or candy, implying easy duty. More galling was that his pals had signed papers for only three years while he'd been designated as a basic infantryman, a 0300 "grunt," for four.

Garson had also said his farewell to several other Platoon 023 buddies with whom he'd become close, notably Liska and Jensen, the Detroiters, fellow Badger Stater Heissen as well as Hupner, the burly, blue-eyed Texan, appointed platoon mail clerk after it was discovered by Right Guide Barker that he was unable to read or write, an infirmity kept secret from Drill Instructors. Garson and others had helped read letters from home and write responses.

What was more, he'd worried about the heavy-footed Priech, whose Teutonic name was invariably corrupted by drill instructors and others as "Prick." Garson would also miss Ridley, the Southern Cal college boy and mentor who'd imparted knowledge and insights about movies that impressionable Garson valued. Of course, there was inimitable Hal Faltschaft, Platoon 023 gadfly and raconteur who always had an ear for the latest MCRD scuttlebutt, and distracted fellow recruits with inexhaustible repartee.

"Know what *déjà vu* is?" Faltschaft asked following graduation, preparing to depart MCRD.

"Well, yeah, that's a feeling you been at some strange place before."

"Then, do ya know what *vuja dé* is?" Garson and others returned quizzical stares.

"That's the feeling that you never want to come back to this fuckin' place ever again." The speck of silver filling flashed from his right front tooth. "Semper fuckin' Fi, Jarheads!" With that, Faltschaft shouldered his seabag and walked out of the quonset hut door. Garson would never again meet him or any other MCRD buddies.

Since Garson's lower partial denture hadn't been fashioned by the time of graduation, he'd been transferred to temporary duty in Casual Company, an amorphous collection of Marines awaiting discharge, assignment to further training or orders to permanent duty stations. Here, Garson and other transients spent mornings in police duty, cleaning vacated quonsets and heads. To Garson's delight, they'd been assigned to the elite Sea School mess hall with crockery plates and cups, and jars of peanut butter and jelly on each table; he paid a gastric price for overindulgence in those near forgotten delicacies.

As a PFC, he drew the princely sum of $40 a payday on the first and fifteenth of each month, as determined by the Navy Department, to which the Marine Corps owed begrudging fealty. Since college boy Ridley had, in smarmy detail, described the dens of debauchery that lay only a 99-cent streetcar ride south of San Diego in Tijuana, Mexico, Garson, with liberty pass carefully clenched in his fist, and others made a hasty run to the border town. There, Garson was bilked out of a third of his cash by a gorgeous Copacabana Club bar girl who convinced him of her ardor.

Thus, it came down to a dreary and shabby whore house where a comely doxy claimed his virginity and unceremoniously introduced him to the marvels of coupling; in his afterglow, Garson convinced himself that his stamina had somehow won her heart. In the pre-dawn hours of the following day, the small band of "seasoned" Marines strode across the long concrete bridge to the border gates, singing the Corps's version of the "Colonel Bogey March," refraining, "Horse shit, what makes the brown grass green. Horse shit, what a good Marine!"

Finally, dental appliance fitted, Garson was handed orders for advanced combat training at Camp Pendleton between San Diego and Los Angeles. He was generously accorded a half-day travel time to make the 40-mile transit. Watching from the Greyhound bus, he noted a sign for the beach community of Torrey Pines, past which, during Boot Camp, Platoon 023 had slogged en route to the Camp Matthews rifle range. Other beach towns along Highway 101 passed — Del Mar, Selena, Encinitas and Carlsbad. Finally, that afternoon, he stepped down on the main street of Oceanside, a collection of garish commercial fronts that obviously catered to the Marine base.

During his wait at the transit station, he meandered past the aggregation of retail fronts, including a liquor store, haberdashery guarded by a pair of chipped and dusty manikins adorned in civvies, a pinball arcade and a tattoo parlor whose walls were adorned with typical Marine designs – the distinctive eagle, globe and anchor emblem, a fanged and helmeted First War Devil dog, a blood dripping blade with an unfurled banner proclaiming "Death before Dishonor," and hundreds more. Garson was familiar with such stereotypical images from the ink emporium in downtown Milwaukee – voluptuous pinups, Betty Boop, Chinese dragons, black panthers and more. Arms akimbo, a seedy looking "sentinel" wearing rumpled trousers and gaudy luau shirt glared from the doorway.

From Camp Pendleton's Mainside, the base's headquarters area, Garson was assigned to fourth platoon of Baker Company, headquartered at Las Pulgas — no matter that the name meant "sand fleas" — one of the several disparate camps scattered over thousands of acres of rolling coastal highlands. He'd not been interested at the time to investigate anything beyond the near horizon, but the Marine training base had been developed only a decade before, the Defense Department having purchased several adjoining ranchos to constitute the sprawling facility. In the immediate area – at about the center of the base, north to south — the undulating, bluffed semi-arid landscape bore little more greenery than anemic ground cover, occasionally interrupted by sage and chaparral, small woodlots and lonely copses of trees.

When setting down his impressions of those days at long remove, Garson sadly compared his poor descriptions of Pendleton's landscape with that of a more accomplished writer like Ian McEwan, the richly lauded British novelist, who likely would have observed this about Camp Pendleton as he did of wild southern France: "Everything was tough, scrubby, prickly, hostile to the touch, preserving its fluids in the bitter cause of survival."

One of a hundred thousand young Marines who tramped over the inhospitable hills during the Korean era, Garson was relieved to be among the first trainees billeted in new single-story concrete barracks; these had replaced the ranks of peaked four-man tents of an earlier time. After five weeks in the dusty and drafty Camp Matthews canvas camp the past November, he'd had enough, now reveling in modernized accommodations with commodious heads and showers. Crappers were even separated by partitions and outfitted with lids; his testy bowels could settle down.

But Baker Company was still gathering, and to Garson's chagrin he was assigned another week of mess duty. Every private and PFC was required to annually perform a week of this onerous duty. He breathed relief only because he wasn't assigned to scrubbing heavy pots and scouring pans similar to those in Boot Camp; burly Marine cooks everywhere, it seemed, would never be confused with chefs. A constant refrain was that the Corps received the best foodstuffs in the military, but its cooks ruined every menu. Garson had seethed when he literally chipped away at crusted residue of fried eggs and burned chocolate pudding, like swabbies removing paint from warships.

"Say, ever been to Maxwell Street in Chicago?" Asked Constantino, one of Garson's first Pendleton acquaintances that spring of 1954, after he'd learned Garson's home town. Called "Tino," of course, he was of moderate height and proportions with dark blue eyes, untended blonde hair and calm demeanor. A year or two older than Garson, he'd graduated from high school and worked in a shoe store before enlisting.

"Yeah, been there," Garson replied. "My cousin took me one time." But he'd seen no more than a block or two, jostled amid the commercial throng of what was said to be the largest open air market in America. Bob had warned that much of the cheap merchandise was shoddy, counterfeit or goods likely stolen by gangsters. Tino also recalled Negro performers on the street, playing "hot" jazz music along the concourse.

Another trainee Garson met during mess duty was Skuda, a 20-year-old from Cleveland, unusual in that most enlistees from east of the Mississippi who graduated from Parris Island were assigned to combat training at Camp Lejeune, North Carolina.

"Musta been some kinda fuck up," he groused. Short, barely above the Corps's minimum height, round headed and sturdy, in certain situations he brought to Garson's mind the movie actor, Elisha Cooke, Jr., famously the "gunsel" Wilmer in "The Maltese Falcon." Often surly and haughty, he had a penchant for lousy jokes and anecdotes. With him, the never-ending debate among Marines was rekindled, about which Boot Camp experience, MCRD or Parris Island was more brutal. Such discussions invariably ended with Skuda proclaiming, "See Parris and die!" Garson's relationship with him would occasionally be testy.

Mess duty ended and Baker Company finally assembled, Garson

and others were issued M-1 rifles (his had obviously been badly handled, although its bore was unblemished) bayonet and scabbard, helmet and 782 gear pack, metal mess utensils and shelter half – impedimenta necessary for the months ahead.

"Ya' don't have ta say 'sir' here anymore," one Baker Company Troop Handler chided Garson early on, "'cept to officers, a'course." He was a trim and tall three-striper, one of the junior NCOs assigned to guide the unit through advanced combat training. When in dress uniform, his chest bore a row of combat ribbons from Pacific War service and Korea. In looking back from decades-old perspective, Garson couldn't recall the sergeant's name. No matter, for he, like other superiors, couldn't measure up to that paragon of Marines, Garson's MCRD senior Drill Instructor, Staff Sergeant McQuade, who would always stand foremost in memory.

Virtually all Troop Handlers and instructors were junior NCOs – corporals and sergeants – so-called permanent duty personnel, enlistees or draftees from the Pacific and Korean wars, now biding time until discharge. To Garson, their duties seemed easy, as he would learn firsthand in later years. They were responsible for maintaining unit discipline and cohesion, close order drill and fitness, leading their companies on long conditioning marches in Pendleton's arduous, undulating landscape, often setting blistering paces. While trainees were burdened with the rifles and the full panoply of combat equipment, Troop Handlers carried only themselves.

"Gonna meet that fucker on liberty one day," one trainee bitterly complained *soto voce* during a particularly brutal march, "an' we're gonna have a *talk*." More, when Baker Company bedded down uncomfortably in the field overnight, only one Troop Handler remained with the unit; other NCOs rode back to normal billets, rejoining the company the following morning.

Discipline during training, less stringent than Boot Camp, wasn't precisely slack. Some superiors permitted a degree of familiarity, but most maintained distance between themselves and their subordinates.

"Every Marine first and foremost a rifleman" was a recently introduced Marine maxim. Everyone – basic 0300 like Garson, cook, clerk, airdale or artilleryman — no matter the MOS (military occupational specialty), all were trained to become infantrymen, building blocks of Marine fighting units, learning skills necessary for combat readiness and survival. Proficiency with small arms was coupled with instruction in maneuver and tactics – fire team, squad, platoon and company. Combat marksmanship included proficiency with use of grenades, heavy and light .30 caliber machines guns, and mortars. There were lessons in land navigation, mapping and compass reading, anti-tank tactics, first aid and hygiene.

"Classrooms" were open air in the "boonies" so the daily regimen included physical conditioning – slogging in Pendleton's precipitous hills, some summits rising above 3000 feet, a landscape cut by canyons, draws and dry river ravines. Trainees also scrambled through obstacle courses more arduous than those MCRD, Garson's legs and lungs told him. He'd added pounds to his enlistment weight of 125, and his underwhelming muscles were growing sinewy. Still, his visage, cheeks and chin devoid of whisker, face without crease or line, was that of an adolescent. To his chagrin, he remained to himself and others, one of the baby Marines.

"After you're through here, y'all'll know how to fight, survive and win in combat," more than one instructor intoned. Garson hoped so, images of Wayne, Wallace Beery, John Garfield, Richard Widmark and other Hollywood Marines ever clear in mind. One twilight after evening chow in the field, Baker Company watched the John Ford documentary, "Tarawa," depicting the ill-planned 1943 Marine landing on the Pacific atoll of Betio. The film, projected on an open-air screen, remained gripping for Garson; as a school boy, he'd watched it at the Ritz, troubled by the graphic color images of the disastrous assault that, in three harrowing days, claimed over a thousand Marines with double that maimed. Tidal pools ran crimson, dead bodies in faded Marine dungarees floating in the surf like flotsam.

The Corps, of course, remained wedded to the tactic of amphibious assault. It had later proved successful, although costly for Marines, most famously at Iwo Jima and Korea's Inchon of more recent vintage. For reasons Marines like Garson did not know, the practice of actual mock landings from ships along Camp Pendleton's 17 miles of beaches had been curtailed.

During Baker Company's days, amphibious assault training consisted of a mockup of a two-story tall "vessel" and a sham Higgins landing craft — both ludicrously "moored" in the semi-arid California landscape miles from the Pacific. Called dry-net training, the exercise required trainees, laden with full complement of weapons and gear, to swing over the port gunwale of the wooden shipside, clutch heavy rope nets and descend into the unrealistic boat below. Garson and others joked about the ludicrous simulation, like a cowboy gunfight in a make-believe town of faux facades, like a Trojan Horse vacant of warriors. No sea swells pitched or rolled beneath the vessels, no ropes swayed or twisted, no Marine lost his grip and plunged into surging sea. There was talk that the Corps planned to develop a special aircraft to facilitate the revolutionary tactic called vertical envelopment – but that was another war away.

When squads hunched low in the landing boat, Garson, Walter Mitty like, pretended he rode to the imaginary beach, plunging into wave troughs, salty spray in his face, stomach-churning odor of cordite and vomit, buddies murmuring prayers, the shriek of fighting planes roaring toward the beach. Then the boat ramp dropped with a thud. The company Troop Handler shouted "Charge!" Two dozen Marine trainees growled on cue like rabid animals, rifles and BARs at high port, sprinting into the imaginary semi-desert "surf," fanning out and flopping down on the scrub carpet of anemic grass and prickly plants. Garson thought he'd been better served by boyhood war games in which he'd formed assault teams with Toby, Larry and other Milwaukee pals.

A visual record remained in Garson's photo album decades after those days, several snapshots taken on a Sunday between paydays when only a few inadequate dollars remained. Garson and three other Baker Company buddies decided to hit the boonies, and pose for photos, a combat safari as it were. He, Tino and Skuda were joined by a Negro pal from the third platoon, a trainee from Kansas City.

"Name's O.D.," he said, thrusting his hand forward when they met. "Some call me 'Odd'." Garson snorted. It was short for O'Donoghue, "with a 'who' at the end," he said. "Black Irish." Tall, wiry with coal black skin, narrow lips and tiny ears, he was sociable and nonthreatening. When he occasionally mimed the screen routines of the bug-eyed Negro movie actor Stepin Fetchit, a Hollywood caricature, Garson laughed with the rest; but in time, he grew uncomfortable with his buddy's antics.

More than a dozen black and white photos depicted that impromptu outing. Outfitted in full combat gear and carrying weapons, they tromped to the obstacle course and dry net training venue, posing like real Marines with fearsome expressions on the wooden shipside and in the "beached" Higgins boat; several images depicted feigned bayonet fights, hand-to-hand combat – all intended, Garson later supposed, to impress girlfriends and folks back home.

During Pendleton training, Garson rarely extracted from a lower recess of his footlocker the thick, paper-backed tome he'd dutifully carried in his rear pocket in Boot Camp, the Corps's "bible." Only occasionally these days did he consult the pages of the *Guidebook for Marines* to amplify what Pendleton instructors had propounded in the field.

"This here's the only good book you'll ever need." He recalled the pontifical words of Staff-Sergeant McQuade as he held the red-covered tome aloft. "It's got all the information you need to become a combat Marine — to protect yourself and your buddies, to stay alive in combat and keep up the fight, to survive and succeed. This book's more important, more sacred to this man's Corps than even the *Bible*." Garson no longer considered such assertions blasphemous.

When Baker Company fully assembled, Garson began his exposure to trainees from diverse backgrounds and life styles, from different racial, ethnic and cultural groups. At MCRD, Platoon 023 had no Negro recruits and only a few Mexicans and Puerto Ricans. During childhood and youth he'd "known" only two Negro kids – one, a tiny and largely silent girl named Salomea in his kindergarten class. The other was a tall very dark boy, the only Negro in Holy Redeemer Grade School, who'd protected Garson from playground bullies. Charles Hill was the smartest student in the school, and the nuns doted on him. After the war, when Garson's father rented a commercial front for his new confectionary business, Garson encountered two giggly Mexican girls, sisters by the look of them, with creamed coffee skin, dark eyes and flashing white teeth who seemed to take a fancy to him. He was seven or eight at the time.

He confirmed that, as in Boot Camp, most Baker Company buddies were urban youths, in their late teens or early twenties; several, like him, school drop-outs or recent graduates – under- or ill-informed about history or salient events of the day, culture or the arts. Politics was rarely a topic contention, many still adjusting, after a lifetime of Democrats in the White House, to the two-year-old presidency of General Eisenhower. They knew one thing: The Cold War was on, and the red Commies presented a clear and present danger to their country and democracy around the world.

Most barracks conversations meandered down tangential pathways, touching topics real and speculative, mundane and inane, but rarely insightful. Discussions often sprung from the latest scuttlebutt. New Marines, as a way of introduction, shared hometown experiences; some like Garson, puffed them to out-sized proportions. They also offered impressions about movies – a virtual *lingua franca* among most urban enlistees. But paramount focus was of cars and, most urgently, girls.

"Ever been to Cal City?" Tino asked when he learned of Garson's hometown.

"Cal City?"

"Yeah, Calumet City, Indiana, right around the corner of Lake Michigan from Chi-Town." The infamous Lake Michigan shoreline town had a reputation as wide open and wild. Garson's Cousin Bob had boasted of frequenting bars and strip clubs that lined the garish main street – to hear his cousin tell of it, a northern Tijuana. Merchant seamen, servicemen and rough-neck workers from the sprawling fuel and gas works availed themselves of the cheap licentious offerings in innumerable boozy dives and "cat" houses that flourished with the protective collusion of cops and politicians who augmented meager salaries with kickbacks and bribes. Occasionally, good citizens were shocked by a headline about under-the-table dealings, but those press sensations quickly faded.

Worse, perhaps, Cal City's skies were alight in ghastly glows from gas and petroleum crackling plants of nearby Gary that hugged the lower Lake Michigan shoreline. Both towns were choked in a perpetual sulfurous haze that, if the wind was right, might waft as far north as Wisconsin, leaving in their wake rheumy eyes, grating lungs and shortened lifespans. Tall rigs spewed flames skyward, a Hellish vista that director Ridley Scott would later recreate in his dystopian movie, "Blade Runner."

Tino, the Chicagoan and, of course, an ardent and long suffering Cubs fan, agonized about his team's futility in getting to the World Series. (Garson never knew if he lived to witness the incredible event more than six decades later.) He and Garson shared views about historic developments in the majors, particularly the surprise departure of the Braves from Boston to Milwaukee. It would provide a natural National League rivalry with the Cubs.

"Yeah, we got some good pitchers like Warren Spahn and Lou

Burdett now, and that young hitter, Hank Aaron," opined Garson, flashing only recently acquired expertise. Truth be told, he'd only briefly found favor with the sport, at first frowning at the hullabaloo and hoopla surrounding the first Negro in the majors — Jackie Robinson, the flamboyant Brooklyn Dodger. But Garson had been more fascinated with the first American League Negro player, Larry Doby, a humble and composed center fielder for the Cleveland Indians; the team had won the 1948 World Series. Garson's mother might still have retained his bubble gum baseball card collection.

Over time, Garson and Tino conversed more about their respective cities. As a boy, Garson's remembered visits to dapper Uncle Hervé and his second wife, the voluptuous, platinum-haired Bacia whose wet, plummy kisses he disliked. Cousin Bob took him to Chicago's Brookfield Zoo, Soldier Field stock car races, and the magnificent Riverview park with its sprawling north side midway and assembly of daring, twisty rides and tacky amusements. As an early teen, Garson had been enamored with his cousin's gleaming convertible with its brassy fender-mounted air horns; older by several years, Bob often displayed photos of beautiful, well-coiffed and endowed girlfriends. But it was that 1949 lemon yellow Mercury convertible that Garson most envied; he could still recall the thrill of riding in that car on the final day of his *Journal* newspaper route.

In Baker Company's fourth platoon, Garson was designated Assistant BAR-man, whose duty was to aid the buddy primarily assigned to carry and maintain the heavy and cumbersome Browning Automatic Rifle.

"Short rounds like you hump BARs because you're small targets." Garson remembered that Boot Camp dictum, wincing that in combat he'd have a bullseye on his back. The BAR was the foundation of the four-man fire team and basis of the Corps's combat organization; three teams composed each squad. The quartet of infantrymen was the basis for Marine Corps firepower and maneuver. Garson hated the cumbersome weapon, twice as heavy as his M-1, particularly because he was required during some marches to relieve the burden from Skuda, the BARman — too often he thought.

"Fuck, man, I'm tired of takin' care of this fuckin' thing!" Garson doubly grumbled while helping disassemble and cleaning the weapon after firing exercises. Skuda glared at him. Its parts were numerous, and powder residue and dirt coated the barrel, grit penetrating its every recess. He attributed this antipathy to life-long ineptitude with things mechanical – this despite his father's jack-of-all-trades expertise. For Garson, the only pleasurable aspect of the heavy weapon was watching crimson tracer bullets arcing toward enemy positions. It was tempting to let loose with an entire clip-full of rounds with a single trigger squeeze.

"Short bursts! Short fuckin' bursts! Easy on that trigger there," one weapons instructor admonished. Even with its steadying front feet, it was difficult to hold the BAR consistently on target. Garson had watched many movie Marines accurately firing them off-hand at strafing fighter planes; he now knew that was but Hollywood fancy.

Tino was named fire team leader, or scout, of the unit. The final fire team member was Cortes from East Los Angeles, specifically Montebello, where, he crudely put it, he lived among "Wetbacks." Of medium height, he had jet black, spiky hair, his hairline drooping nearly to his heavy eyebrows; his skin was like parchment and eyes the color of milk chocolate. He claimed to be an "*Españolo*," not Mexican at all, because his forebears had settled in Los Angeles for generations, even before the Bear Flag Republic. Cortes's English was clear and correct, but Mexicans complained that his Spanish language cadences and word inflections were archaic.

Garson, his new buddies and acquaintances had been in combat training for several weeks. Now, with exceptions for overnight camps, trainees were free from duty evenings and weekends. Occasionally, some Baker Company trainee could be coaxed for a few dollars to don dress greens (the Corps didn't permit undress uniform or dungarees to be worn off base) to board the Camp

Pendleton shuttle into Oceanside and return with grease-stained bags of tacos, tortillas loaded with beef or chicken, cheese, lettuce and tomatoes spiced with savory sauce. Like pizza before, the repast was new to Garson.

It was perhaps early March when the payroll officer counted out two crisp ten-dollar bills and four fives one payday. The Las Pulgas Slop Chute had limited offerings – over-done hamburgers, Lukewarm hot dogs, limp fries, Cokes, etc. – antidotes to mess hall fare. Neither Garson nor his new buddies were of age, so even 3.2 percent Slop Chute beer was unavailable. The Camp Pendleton movie theater, a large, stark and featureless quonset, with uncomfortable seats and screeching sound system, was located at Mainside. Garson, who'd once watched as many as six movies a week back home, was disinclined to ride a jarring jitney for uninspiring third- and fourth-run features several years old.

For those like Skuda who were unable to husband cash for liberties and other needs, Marine barracks loan sharks were anxious to reap usurious interest rates. The rascally entrepreneurs demanded two dollars for a $3 loan, due on the next payday; a seven-dollar advance required $10 in repayment. Garson recalled observing desperate Boot Camp pogey bait hounds paying a dollar for a few vending machine coins.

"Say, let's take a liberty to 'Dago,'" Tino suggested. Cortes demurred because he'd long planned to visit his family in Montebello. Thus, after the initial Camp Pendleton payday, Garson, Tino and Skuda boarded the Greyhound from Oceanside for the day-long "Cinderella Liberty." They'd need to return to the main gate before midnight. Garson had a vague recollection of downtown San Diego after Boot Camp weeks before. He and others had quickly boarded a trolley for the 99-cent ride to the Mexican border. The foray had been taken by thousands of young Marines like Garson over the decades. The lone token of that T-Town evening was a tiny, overpriced photo of him embracing a smoldering bar-girl. He'd failed to recognize the falsity of her promise of a purple evening and was left with an expensive bar bill. Afterward, however, he'd breathlessly given up his virginity to a whore house tart who he'd name Catana after the Jean Peters character in "Captain from Castile."

"Wow, what a great town," Skuda marveled when the liberty Marines departed the bus station from Camp Pendleton to begin their trek along San Diego's main street. Harrisburg, his home town, obviously couldn't boast of such perfect climate. After nearly four months, Garson had become acclimated to such balminess, remembering that Milwaukee at this time waited to welcome stubbornly resistant springtime. Temperatures were ten to 20 degrees colder.

"You Jarheads'll piss 'n' moan about anything, even heat here," Skuda groused. "Parris Island's like a steam bath. And talk about sand fleas, we got poisonous snakes, giant spiders and other critters." Garson's toes curled in his shoes.

From his authorial perspective of nearly many decades, Garson was unable to recall whether the trio of trainees sauntered along Hawthorn or Grape Street, Second Avenue or other downtown thoroughfares. It was clear, however, that principal commercial streets were awash in a sea of liberty sailors from nearby San Diego Bay naval installations. Enlisted men had already changed dress uniforms from winter blues to summer whites. It reminded Garson of Great Lakes "swabbies" who'd invaded his hometown during the war — waves of white blouses, bell-bottomed trousers and Dixie Cup caps, like Gene Kelly and Frank Sinatra in "On the Town." Garson imagined he and his Pendleton buddies meeting Vera-Ellen's and Ann Miller's, trim, leggy girls who'd provide companionship or perhaps more.

Garson looked disdainfully at the sea-going servicemen. Despite the Marine Corps's subservience to the United States Naval Department, antipathy always marked the sister services. Marines were pejoratively called "Sea-Going Bellhops" for their shipboard duties, particularly running brigs where incarcerated miscreants were reputed to be treated with heavy hands. In Marine eyes, only navy corpsmen assigned to the Corps were worthy of respect.

"You can kick the ass of any two Deck Apes," was a Boot Camp proposition. Garson had almost been convinced that he could handle them back then, but now he wasn't so certain.

"Say, they got a Little Italy section in town here," said Tino. "Let's get us a pizza or somethin'." Chow seemed to be a paramount item of interest. The liberty Marines agreed, even though Garson had never tasted such "foreign" delicacies. His mother was a pure meat and potatoes cook who'd prepared beef swimming in grayish gravies and a paucity of vegetables. Milwaukee's thriving Italian community was predominantly composed of swarthy Sicilian immigrants who'd congregated in the city's east side ward near Lake Michigan. Garson's bachelor uncle, Vin, who'd sometimes entered those environs, had long warned his nephew about the dark dangers abroad there. That did not square in Garson's mind with images of entertainers like Tony Bennett, Dean Martin, Hal Martino and others, handsome balladeers enamored by his childhood friend, Lana, and other North Milwaukee girls.

The trio of liberty buddies stepped into the gloomy confines of Pepi's Pizza Parlor, said to be San Diego's favorite. Dark woods, gingham table cloths, empty wine bottles coated in congealed wax and sprouting candles, statues of saints and a shimmering stained glass portrait of the Virgin and her son were prominent décor features. With assurance, Tino selected the toppings – olives, mushrooms, peppery sausage slices and a frisky sauce layered on thick pale cheese. But the waiter wasn't convinced that any of the fresh-faced Marines were old enough for alcohol, refusing to pour even a bottle of Lucky Lager beer for Tino, the most mature looking. Garson came away with an unenthusiastic endorsement for the Italian staple, finding the crust the consistency of cement. Afterward, the liberty Marines continued reconnoitering of varied commercial areas, still hoping to meet some comely California blondes.

"Say, did I tell you about the babe I saw in downtown 'Dago' one time," Tino opened as they sauntered along, elbowing through the unending parade of white-clad seamen; only a few Marines seasoned the military mélange. "Yeah, she was a real looker, hot, on the opposite side of the street. Spiky high heels, tight skirt, sweater. We got stopped by a corner traffic light, I looked over at 'er and smiled. She smiled back, real fuckin' nice." This, as Tino's story continued, occurred several times as they kept pace with one another.

"So, I says to myself, she looks promising. Maybe she'll jump. I picked up the pace, got ahead of 'er and crossed Second Avenue. We was walking together now. Up close she was gorgeous – red hair swept up in back, great body, bulging tits, pulpy lips achin' ta be kissed, mouthful of beautiful teeth. Wow!

"So I says to her, 'Hi! Would you go to bed with a Marine for twenty bucks?' After a minute or two, she smiles and says, "Sure." So we walk a little ways further. At the next light, I ask her, 'Would you go to bed with a Marine for a fin – five bucks?' She stops short right on that sidewalk, puts hands on both hips, gets all huffy with me. 'Say, whadya think I am?'

"'Well, ma'am' says I. 'We already established that. So would you go to bed with a Marine for that fiver?' An' she walks off." Garson, ever the naif, guffawed, but Skuda, was unimpressed. Tino reminded Garson of the Platoon 023 raconteur, Hal Faltschaft, the recruit outfit's perennial jokester and gadfly.

Midday chow at Pendleton during combat training was almost always in the field. Marching Baker Company – three platoons of about 60 trainees each – to outdoor instruction areas was time consuming — three dusty and sinuous ranks strung out more than 30 yards in those torturous boonies. Noonday chow was hauled by four-by trucks. A water trailer dispensed warm, metallic-tasting water.

"Man, see this fuckin' shit?" Skuda grumbled as usual, pointing to olive drab C-Ration cans dating from an earlier era. "They're probably from the war, maybe Korea, maybe the First War." He claimed he'd once deciphered the coding on a can, dating it to 1943, but Garson failed to credit that. No true cooks came into the field. In those impromptu kitchens, canned meals were simply dumped into charred steel barrels set upon gas-fired flames; boiling water heated the containers. Often, when trucks didn't arrive early enough, food was only lukewarm. There were about a half dozen different canned concoctions, but trainees were not permitted to select from the "bill of fare." "Eat what you fuckin' get!" A hard-eyed mess-man spewed.

"Can't stand this shit," Garson groused when he was handed a can of Lima beans and hamburger patties. To no avail, he attempted to trade the selection for something more consumable. The putative meat and vegetables swam unpalatably in gravy as dark as old motor oil. His stomach churned as he poked his fork at the noonday repast, washing it down with gritty coffee. A packet of ossified caramel crackers as pliable as Civil War hardtack served as dessert. The offering also included a green box containing four Camel cigarettes, but few dared smoke them, fearing that the chaff-dry tobacco would blacken their lungs.

At one field chow during the first month, the key opener broke as Garson twisted it. He withdrew his bayonet, wedged the blade between lid and partially opened can, and banged the edged weapon with the heel of his left hand. After one or two blows, he felt a sharp pinch in his left palm. Blood spurted like the wounded Moby Dick. Garson clapped his right hand over the wound and staggered to the knot of Troop Handlers, who looked up at him in unison.

"What's a matter with you, Marine?" Garson lifted his covering hand, and the wound spouted anew; blood dribbled between his fingers and dripped onto the ground. His knees were weak. "Corpsman!" One Troop Handler yelled immediately.

"JEE-sus fuckin' Christ!" The seaman second class shouted,

eyes bulging. Save for his naval rank, his dungarees were identical to that of Marines. "That's a real good one," he commented, quickly calming himself. He extracted a hypodermic from his haversack. Even in his already woozy state, Garson thought the needle was better suited to a horse. He was made to sit on a camp stool as the corpsman inserted the dagger-like syringe into the gaping, L-shaped wound that Garson later measured at over an inch. Pain ebbed only slightly as the seaman methodically sutured the ugly gash, like some immigrant New York City garment district seamstress, pulling jagged skin edges together.

"Well, you ain't gettin' any Purple Heart for this," the corpsman offered in an unconvincing attempt at levity. He dropped a handful of pills into Garson's right palm. "Take two of these every four hours. If the bleeding doesn't stop by tomorrow, go to sick bay. Skuda gathered up Garson's rifle and gear, and loaded them into a six-by truck that returned to the barracks; he was relieved of duty for the next day.

"Folks round here call 'em 'Devil Winds,'" Cortes said ominously, crossing himself three times before touching his right thumb to his lips. "People think Santa Ana comes from Saint Anne. Mexicans called it *Los Vientos dos Santana* – from Satan. They usually arrive later in the year, fall, maybe, and winter. But this year, they're here now, I think." He went on to explain that these bone-dry winds howled from the high Mojave Desert, roaring down coastal mountain slopes, scouring southern California. "Sometimes they fan tiny brush fires into infernos from Hell." Spring weather, Garson noticed lately, was uncommonly warm.

Baker Company had settled into makeshift wooden bleachers set up in the lee of a wide hillock, listening to the drone of an instructor about squad maneuver and fire. The brisk breeze carried a whiff of smoke, Garson thought.

"Fire!" Someone shouted. Garson craned his neck to see a phalanx of flames charging up the little hillside behind the bleachers.

"Outta them fuckin' seats!" The instructor yelled. "Let your gear behind!" Trainees already enveloped in a haze of gray smoke scrambled to the ground. Garson's eyes teared and his throat burned as he legged it up the slope, over charred sage grasses, stomping on isolated fingers of flame abandoned by the swift wind-borne surge. When he reached the summit with the others, wind tore the dungaree cap from his head. All he saw ahead was the blackened landscape, the line of flames already swelled into a fiery wave, crackling over the long swale to the next ridge. Not one delicate blue flower remained. Much later, he mused, that his grandmother must have witnessed similar scenes as a child when she'd survived the devastating Wisconsin Peshtigo Fire of the last century.

He ran with his buddies, breath coming hard in the choking pall. Several in Baker Company pulled off dungaree jackets to beat lingering patches of fire. The company swiped and sweated for what Garson took to be an hour, until the shriek of Las Pulgas fire trucks was heard; the red and yellow vehicles bounced across the scorched landscape to attack the blaze. Baker Company was relieved from its futile effort to head off the flaming carpet that ultimately blackened hundreds of acres.

As Baker Company trudged doggedly back across the blackened plain, every footfall puffed up ash that swirled about ankles and knees. Garson could feel the earth's warmth through the sole of his boots. The only sound was a concert of coughing, sneezing and spitting. When they later returned to the outdoor classroom, they looked like an ashen army, eyes reddened, mouths parched, noses draining mucous. But before they arrived, Garson had a nightmare experience.

"Hey, what's 'at?" He gasped. He'd spotted something moving in the carpet of ash.

"Fuck, tarantulas – lots of 'em," replied Cortes. There were scores, no hundreds of the furry brown creatures driven by flames to abandon their burrows that now scuttled to safety. Garson's mind reeled, his fear manifest. Since childhood, he'd been gripped by a phobia to any species of arachnid, from cellar spiders to Daddy Long Legs. These tarantulas were the size of quarters, some larger. His toes threatened to curl inside his boots. The sight of the creatures created fearful nights when the company slept in the field, Garson's mind conjuring the sequence when Hollywood's Sabu fought a giant bulbous orb spinner in "The Thief of Baghdad."

During those Pendleton months, Garson received only a handful of letters; he wrote only a few in response. Magdalena, who now insisted upon being called Lana, wrote once or twice. They'd been acquainted since childhood, but while he'd been enamored of her before enlisting, she considered Garson no more than her "little brother," and, like Jane Austen's Emma, matching him with putative girlfriends. He received a missive or two from her in Boot Camp (including photos of provocative poses in dance togs), and now at Pendleton; she was a few years younger than Garson, and wrote much about senior year events and triumphs at Custer High.

His mother wrote once or twice in those months, short notes in her careful cursive; his father sometimes scrawled a few labored lines at the end. Their relationship had been a rocky one at times. His father's disappointment at his enlistment was pronounced; he'd long hoped that his son would in time take over the confectionary business. Now, that endeavor was proving financially problematic. In a recent letter, his mother asked him to telephone, collect if necessary; it was important.

"Hi, Ma," Garson began one Saturday morning, after standing in line at the lone outdoor phone. "I mean, Mom." She hated being called "Ma." They passed pleasantries, Garson asking about his favorite cousins and neighborhood pals. She told him what little she knew of the latter, not having contact with them since Garson departed the preceding fall.

"You remember that insurance policy I opened for you?" Garson assented. The insurance agent who lived across the street had coaxed her into the plan shortly after Garson's birth. She dutifully handed him $1.25 every week for all these years; at maturity on Garson's 18th birthday, the policy would pay Garson $2000, money to be used for college, she'd insisted.

At war's end, the mortgage on the North Milwaukee house purchased before the Depression had been paid, and a metal cash box on a closet shelf contained thousands of dollars in war bonds. But Garson's showy, fast-talking Uncle Hervé came to town after the war and convinced his brother to quit the welding trade and join him in a commercial venture — the ABC Popcorn Company. Overcoming his wife's resistance – she'd never trusted her flashy brother-in-law or warmed to his brassy, bejeweled second wife – his father had purchased a franchise. Indicative of Hervé's bent, he hadn't offered his brother a reduced price for the territory.

For Garson, about nine or ten at the time, the new occupation had been novel, even exciting. Despite his natural gregariousness, Garson's father, a garage tinkerer at heart, wasn't a salesman, didn't have the looks, demeanor or patter of his younger brother; he couldn't coax customers to buy more popcorn than they needed or wanted. Thus, in less than a decade, bonds had been cashed to buy a commercial building and mortgages hung over both properties. Monthly payments had become overwhelming, and a foreclosure on Garson's childhood home was imminent.

"If I send you these papers on your insurance policy, would you sign and return them so we can cash it in? Your dad wants to at least save the Galena (Avenue) building." Her voice quavered, and Garson could see her eyes welling. Without saying so, she blamed her husband for failure and loss of her cherished house. She loved that little bungalow and it would break her heart to leave it. Garson dutifully signed the documents and mailed them home.

"See you got a pocket book there," said Skuda, peering into Garson's footlocker. "Civil War?" The paperback cover depicted a charging Yank soldier, gripping an American flag, almost an artistic rendering of Audie Murphy in "The Red Badge of Courage." Garson had spotted the little book at the Oceanside Greyhound station, and recalled that a high school history teacher, Sister Assunta, he thought, had recommended it to him. But while he exhibited some interest in American history that she tried to encourage, his enthusiasm had been insufficient to read more than a chapter or two of Fletcher Pratt's *Ordeal by Fire*, a popular account of the sectional conflict. Perhaps he'd finally finish in the weeks ahead.

"Yeah, you know my great gramps had a farm near Gettysburg back then — when the Rebs came north to Pennsylvania. Story goes that they grabbed his pigs, and handed over a worthless Confederate ten-dollar note to him in payment. He gave it to me when I was little. That wasn't all."

In one of his loquacious moods, Skuda went on to explain that the invaders shackled the family's hired field hand, a freedman who'd escaped from slavery ten years before.

"The Rebs, a Mississippi bunch, I think, said they was taking the man back to his real owner in the South. 'If your Yankee army can capture our niggers as contrabands,' one said, 'we're takin' your'n'." The Skudas never discovered the freedman's fate.

Fifty years later, when Skuda's father was a little boy, hundreds of gray-haired former Johnny Rebs and Billy Yanks gathered at Gettysburg to celebrate the battle's anniversary. Garson thought credibility threatened Skuda's concluding episode.

"This one old codger wearing a grayback uniform and kepi limped into our farm yard. Pa was a kid back then. Said he remembered that old soldier talking to gramps who showed the man that old Confederate ten-dollar note — all worn and raggedy by then. They talked for a bit and shook hands afterwards. 'Save your Confederate money,' the raggedy Reb said, departing. 'The South'll rise again!'"

It was after April Fool's Day now, and Garson's pockets bulged with cash from the month's first payday.

"Whadaya, say we go to T-Town. Get our ashes hauled. Relieve our blue balls," Tino proposed. Skuda immediately agreed, almost salivating at the prospect. Mac, the Negro buddy as usual, demurred as usual. Cortes was, as always, bound for Montebello. Garson was reluctant because he'd seen that Mexican elephant; his desire was for love beyond the cash nexus. What was more, he often preferred his own company, an only child's penchant, he thought, and determined to spend the day rummaging around Oceanside, perhaps purchasing some civvies and an AWOL bag, as it was known, a small weekend gripsack for carrying a change of skivvies, socks and toiletries. Pendleton combat training was coming to an end, and he'd soon need to travel to his "permanent" duty station.

He wandered the main street of the military town, spending most of his cash on planned purchases, eating at a local hamburger joint, then picked through the Greyhound station's commercial fronts. He plugged nickels into two pinball machines in the cramped arcade, then straggled to the tiny tattoo parlor. Through the open double door, he perused the ceiling to floor wall of designs, most familiar to him from Milwaukee's lone ink emporium in downtown where bored Great Lakes sailors roamed. Once more, he viewed familiar designs — wide-faced, chinless Betty Boop and an array of voluptuous World War pinups flashing stockings, generous thighs and perky breasts. The Oceanside parlor also exhibited the "mandatory" eagle, globe and anchor icon with a ribbon proclaiming "First to Fight" along with other common designs seen on tattooed Pendleton Marines. A Chinese dragon snorting flames and a black panther with bloody claw marks caught his eye.

"Lookin' for a tattoo?" It was the same scruffy man wearing wrinkled gray trousers and an audible luau shirt he recalled from his arrival at the Greyhound terminal the month before.

"Naw!" Garson shook his head.

"Got good prices here. Best in Oceanside. Got time right now," the man persisted. Garson hesitated. But the sharper was canny and detected an easy mark.

"Well, now, if you was to have one of these skin art designs, what would you get?" Garson's eyes surveyed the vast wall-to-wall collection, finally answering that he liked the panther. 'Eight bucks."

"Don't have that much."

"How much you got?" Garson reached into his pocket and counted his crumpled bills – six singles. The man replied that he could ink the black cat tattoo in short order, well, a smaller version anyway, for that amount. Garson almost immediately found himself in a barber chair, and the buzz of an inking machine beginning the outline of the wild cat. A putative Marine, he tried to disguise wincing from the needling sensation as the animal began to take shape, blood oozing slightly from his left bicep. It took less than half an hour for the image to emerge, his skin puffy and sore under a bandage.

"Careful now," the tattooist warned as he accepted the cash. "Make sure you don't knock off them scabs or they'll pull out the ink. You'd have to come back for re-inking. That'll cost you more." Garson, proud of the manly body artifact, was careful in every shower.

Skuda's other personality, the better half, emerged during a weekend liberty to Los Angeles with Garson. He was like Olivia deHavilland in "The Snake Pit," one of those provocative movies Garson's Milwaukee pals had eschewed and he sat through alone one night. He'd been mesmerized by the actress's portrayal of a woman with two personalities, having been accustomed to her portrayals as the beautiful and virginal Maid Marian and Arabella Bishop opposite his screen idol, Errol Flynn. But, Skuda, sometimes caustic, haughty and demeaning, was on his best behavior in Los Angeles.

Cortes had long regaled buddies about the wonders of his amazing city, mentioning the LaBrea Tar Pits where fossils and bones of woolly mammoths, saber-toothed tigers, other animals and insects that lived thousands of years before had been entombed in asphalt-like sediment. Skuda and Garson shook their heads in disinterest.

"We got something called Watts Towers just off The 110," Cortes went on. "Some weird guy's collection — rusty pieces of junk steel he set in concrete, raising a dozen or more towers – some near a hundred feet high, I guess. Wrapped 'em in wire mesh. Decorated the place with broken pottery and bottle glass. Calls it *'Nuestro Pueblo.'* Man, bet you can't believe what you're seein'," his eyes lighted like a tour guide. "There's also talk around town about Walt Disney. Bought a big chunk of land in Anaheim. Building some kinda huge amusement park." That piqued Garson's interest, but he and Skuda were more intent on concupiscent adventures downtown; Cortes confirmed there were strip joints there, some that featured completely naked girls.

"Watchin' naked babes prance around on stage is like fuckin' with a rubber – a lot of the sensation is missing," opined Tino. He and O.D. were bound for another sprint to Tijuana to get their ashes hauled again.

Garson retained a vivid memory of his lone foray below the border, especially his breathless half hour or so with the whore he would name Catana. But the recollection of his elemental deflowering long remained as less than satisfying; he'd yearned for love and sex freely given.

During the Greyhound ride from Oceanside to Los Angeles – about a two hour nonstop run — Garson watched the picturesque locales pass: San Clemente, at the northern extremity of Camp Pendleton, and location of San Onofre, a training area with which he'd later become familiar. Then, the highway jutted east to San Juan Capistrano famed for its returning swallows; the beautiful beaches and marinas at Laguna, Newport and Huntington followed.

"Heard Milwaukee's got a lotsa Polacks," Skuda said during the journey. Garson responded that his city's Slav south side was the home to thousands of those European immigrants, including Bohunks, Bohemians and Serbs who'd flooded neighborhoods beyond the industrial river valley that separated two halves of the town.

"They even got the only basilica in Wisconsin, St. Josephats. Never been there but they say it's beautiful, like in Europe. You kin see the top of the dome from downtown." Even the north side featured a bronze equestrian statue to the Revolutionary War hero from Poland, General Pulaski. But Milwaukee's strongest heritage remained German, he explained; tens of thousands from the pre-Bismarck states had flooded Milwaukee in the last century. Every brewery bore a German family name, the faded signs of Tröstle, Pfister and Vögel tanneries still visible on riverside factory buildings. The magnificent and ornate Pabst Theatre on the same river bank remained the crown jewel of opera and symphony.

"Hey, we're here, in Los 'An-ga-lees.'" Skuda persisted in pronouncing the city name with a hard "g" and double "e's." Highway 101 arrowed into downtown on a broad boulevard, Figueroa Street. After a hurried bus station lunch of hamburger and fries, the pair strolled along a few downtown thoroughfares, marveling at the magnificent Los Angeles Theater on Broadway, with its soaring, multi-story façade. It might be baroque architectural style. He recalled the grade school nuns describing the decorative features — fluted white Corinthian columns bordered a tall arched recess. The belated addition of the movie marquee, Garson thought, detracted from the theater's magnificence.

"Cortes said they got a place in a park here called Pershing Square, where anyone, nuts and crazies an' all, can stand on a soapbox and spout any kinda fuckin' bullshit you can imagine." But it wasn't architecture or orations that attracted the liberty pair. On one of the side streets they found a utilitarian venue, the box offices flanked by framed photos of the renowned strippers of the day – platinum Lili St. Cyr, flame-haired Blaze Starr who reminded Garson of Rita Hayworth, and Ann Corio with her dusky skin and dark tresses. As a boy, he'd eyed similar tempting images outside the Empress, Milwaukee's lone burly house; he'd often been shooed away by a man with a boxer's punched-in nose, prominent brow ridges and dingy teeth.

The odor of smoke and bad breath ushered the liberty Marines into the seedy theater, its seats nearly filled with sailors and Marines in uniforms and civvies. Garson had learned to spot fellow military by the way they wore clothes and their manner. The audience hooted at stale jokes and disjointed repartee of the opening comic, and laughed at the juggler who repeatedly dropped balls and batons. The master of ceremonies returned.

"Ladies and gentleman and honored service members, let me introduce for your appreciation and pleasure one of the sexiest ecdysiasts working today." A murmur of impatience greeted his introduction. "She's the one and only Dixie Lee Dix!" No applause welcomed the performer, who strutted out from the stage left in an oval of light which often lost contact during her movements. She wore an ankle length gown slit on two sides to reveal dark stockings and garter belt. Even though Garson and Skuda had failed to purchase front row seats, it was immediately apparent from the tenth row that the stripper was beyond her prime; she'd played too many low-rent venues. Her upper thighs were loose, her waist thick and hips wide; her breasts, though generous, sagged almost to a slack stomach that trembled like Jell-O with each move. Unseen musicians below the level of the stage – snare drum and sad saxophone – dissolutely accompanied her movements. Dixie slipped off long, elbow length gloves, twirled them in the air above her head like a rodeo cowgirl before tossing them aside. She strutted, crouching in deep knee bends, arising to gyrate and pump her pelvis. Skuda complained afterwards that he hadn't been titillated in the least; Garson agreed.

"Come'on, babe, take it off! Take it *all off!*" Several arose from their seats to hoot derisively. In ten minutes, the sad dancer had disrobed, clothing items scattered carelessly about the stage. Gypsy Rose Lee need not fear this competition, Garson mused silently. Finally, she stopped mid-stage, spreading her legs wide apart as a drum cymbal crashed a beat or two early. Triumphantly, she flung her arms aloft. Her beasts drooped, opaque pasties obscuring tiny areola. A glittery black g-string hid her pudenda, although Garson swore afterwards that he'd spotted stray gray pubic hairs curling from the covering.

"What a fuckin' gyp," Garson groused. Despite having paid five dollars for admission (the servicemen's discounted price), the young Marines, suspecting more of the same from the program to follow, determined to vacate their seats in a strategic retreat.

"Thought Cortes said there was burly houses here that had strippers – wha' did that guy call 'em – ekthy-something? — who took everything off. This g-string and pasty stuff is fuckin' crap." That evening, they reconnoitered the downtown area for real nude show lounges, asking locals and other Marines. They were informed that those sorts of spicy show houses served beer and booze, and demanded IDs; more, tickets were said to cost double what they'd paid before. And after a dinner of inedible veal cutlets, mashed potatoes with gravy, and sliced carrots, their funds were running low. They boarded a Greyhound back to Pendleton.

In those Camp Pendleton days, Garson never attempted to parse his fascination with carnivals, amusement parks, seaside boardwalks with their thrill rides, sideshows and often seedy attractions. Wisconsin's State Fair, primarily an annual showcase for livestock, agricultural products and crafts was scheduled in August. But the sprawling grounds featuring midway rides, games and other tawdry diversions remained open the entire summer; schools slated excursions in June. With much anticipation, Garson had ridden the rattling yellow street cars to fair grounds where he'd boarded most rides, tried his hand at games and purchased useless trinkets.

Most, he was mesmerized by the gaudy, seductive atmosphere, the seedy operatives and muscular roustabouts who, like gypsies, took their nightly ease in shabby trailers. Local girls, it was said, were sometimes attracted to these environs, to glib male attendants with shiny black hair, wearing sleeveless tee shirts to display tattoos; a few even wore earrings. It was occasionally rumored that some girl disappeared when the carnival packed up and moved away, leaving behind only wind-blown detritus and debris.

Garson had contrasted all of this with his own life of certainty, stability and permanence, relieved, even as a child, that his lot was so much better. He'd sometimes awakened from nightmares about being carried off by carnies and vagabonds, away from Milwaukee, predictability, never again to see his parents or pals.

Following the first April payday, Garson and Skuda traveled north again, this time stopping at Long Beach. Their destination was The Pike, the popular amusement park in the curve of San Pedro Bay. They spent the day roaming amid hundreds of rides and attractions amid roiling crowds of servicemen and civilians. It all brought back to Garson's mind his trips to Chicago's Riverview that featured numerous stomach-churning coasters and daunting vertiginous thrills. The Pike was said to be rough locale, but Marines and sailors somehow served as guardians of peace.

They were in uniform, their thought to better attract local girls. During a strolling reconnoiter, Garson mentioned that he'd been considering another tattoo, to balance the underwhelming panther on his left bicep. They'd passed two or three ink parlors, before selecting one that wasn't particularly busy. The operator looked young, but had the same scruffy look as the fellow at Oceanside. Tino wasn't interested in marking himself. Garson quickly pointed to the Chinese dragon among the myriad designs on the walls; its price was double that of the panther. About halfway through the inking process, two girls poked their heads through the open doorway.

"Don't do it!" They pleaded in duet. "Please don't get that tattoo!" One mewed. Both had dark hair – one stick straight, the other wavy. Their creamed coffee skin and bright teeth reminded Garson of those giggly little Mexican girls back home over whom he'd fawned when he was a boy. They were now nicely grown up. When the girls stepped away from the shop doorway, Tino followed, leaving Garson to bear the biting needles alone. When he departed the shop after his ordeal, his buddy had corralled the girls, and was talking animatedly. He clandestinely steered one of them toward Garson, the prettier of the two, as luck would have it. She offered her hand, and Garson reached out. But he immediately drew back almost as if burned by her heat.

"Wow! You okay?" He asked.

"Oh, that," she smiled. "My body temperature's naturally higher. Lots of people think I'm sick or somethin'." Thirty years later, her comment came to mind when he saw the movie "Body Heat" with Kathleen Turner whose character, Matty Walker purred: "My temperature runs a couple of degrees high, around a hundred. I don't mind. It's the engine or something."

"Thought it was 'cold hands, warm heart,'" Garson said.

"No, with me it's warm and *warm*." Her girlfriend laughed. Garson hoped she intended the innuendo. Immediately he yearned for a real date with her.

When Garson wrote of the encounter on The Pike decades after, he thought to use an appropriate name, one that reflected his romanced image of the girl. Perhaps she'd be Luna, or Lolita, even Paloma. He exhibited a penchant for that sort of thing, playing with names a la Charles Dickens, when he'd written his Boot Camp recollections.

"Name's Karen," the girl said that day, "Karen Sisko." The quartet chatted, Karen observing at one point that Garson and Tino weren't from "around here." Perhaps she detected the flat character of his speech. No, they were from the Midwest, thousands of miles away, he said.

"Say, want to get some chow, er, lunch or something? Burgers? Hot dogs? Beer?"

"Not old enough," Karen's friend Maria said. "You ain't either." Garson detected a Latin inflection in some words.

"Just a joke," Skuda harrumphed.

Karen's lightly inflected voice was dusky; Garson always found such lower register female voices enticing. Her eyes were chocolate brown, luminous, narrow under perfectly arched brows; ruby lips were full, kissable, Garson thought. Her hair, the same shade as her eyes, was thick, wavy and coiffed, falling to the nape of her neck. She stood a few inches shorter than Garson. The short coat she wore on the spring seaside day obscured her upper body, its hem about to her waist; narrowly cuffed jeans hugged her buttocks snuggly. In the photo booth image for which they later posed, her expression seemed tentative, perhaps guarded. It was as if she'd hoped to be Skuda's date. But she later warmed to him a bit when she considered that a charcoal sketch of Garson that had been rendered by a midway artist didn't do him justice.

The quartet spent the afternoon and early evening on amusements, the girls screaming mightily at every precipitous coaster plunge, at every lurch and swirl of whirling rides. Garson gritted his teeth, pretending to enjoy the dizzying experiences. He and Tino tried their hands at games; he won a Teddy Bear for Maria, but Garson was unable knock over a single cigarette pack with an air rifle loaded with tiny corks. They eschewed side shows displaying canvas banners of a bearded lady, a five-legged pony, dog-faced boy and two-headed fetus. The girls occasionally exchanged words in Spanish, and Garson worried that Karen's impression of him remained inconsequential. They lived in Montebello, Karen said, in east L.A.

"Say, we got a buddy from there, name' a Cortes?" Skuda asked.

"Know him?" Garson put in. "Says he's a Spaniard not Mexican." Neither girl knew the Camp Pendleton buddy.

When they parted late in the evening, Karen jotted her phone number on a slip of paper. She'd assented when Garson asked if he might call sometime. He yearned for a date with the pretty *chiquita*. She and Maria boarded one of the large red interurban cars, waving goodbye as the conveyance lumbered off. Garson and Tino had a Cinderella Liberty, and needed to return to base before midnight.

Only weeks of Pendleton training remained – a few more long slogs as the daylight grew longer and coastal temperatures rose. Baker Company began its preparation for the final phase of training – three days of continuous maneuver and mock battle against the dreaded Aggressors.

"You Wisconsin *Wisenheimers* are, like, some kinda big-time deer hunters, I hear," Skuda needled, obviously from the black half of his personality.

"Deer hunter?" Garson paused as his mind tumbled. He recalled old pictures from his dad's youth, images of scores of animals dressed out and hanging from a cable strung between trees, of hunters in woolen knickers and high laced boots. He also remembered the yarns his old childhood pal, Mellish, had spun about hunting all kinds of game in the open fields on the city's fringe.

"Yeah, I've hunted, ducks and birds mostly, with my dad."

"Kill any deer, then? Bucks?" Garson hesitated again, considering a response. Skuda seemed to be testing and appraising him when in those dark moods.

"Yeah, I got a six-pointer once," Garson muttered. Skuda widened his eyes, and asked what kind of gun Garson used.

"Oh, a four-ten." Skuda scowled, and Garson knew immediately his buddy was conversant with guns and hunting. His neck caught fire, and a bead of sweat dribbled down his spine.

"Four-ten shotgun? That's for birds and small game, not deer."

"No, no, I mean a 12-gauge, yeah, 12-gauge Remington pump." Garson said no more, not wanting to be caught in his fabricated web. In fact, he'd only once killed an animal, and that was a common sparrow with a .22 rifle on his uncle Essig's farm. Holding the tiny limp body in his hand, and gazing into the bird's dead milky eyes, he'd felt a wave of guilt and fought back tears. He'd obviously lacked manliness. He never killed another animal, and deflected future conversations with Skuda about the sport.

When Garson penned his memoir of Boot Camp, he erroneously credited the concussive final firepower showcase of the Corps's arsenal – small arms, automatic weapons, mortars, tanks, rockets and more, all targeted upon a Roman arena of rusty vehicle hulks, bunkers and ersatz enemy installations – to MCRD's Camp Matthews. But on more careful reflection, he assured himself that he'd witnessed the deadly extravaganza at Camp Pendleton in those final weeks.

The final booming fusillade featured the squatty, tracked vehicle, the "Ontos," Greek for "The Thing" that carried a chugging .50 caliber machine gun and four recoilless rifles manned by a three-man crew – driver, loader and aimer. Garson's chest puffed when an instructor noted the anti-tank weapon had been developed in Milwaukee, at the city's sprawling west side machine works, Allis-Chalmers.

"Hey, who're those guys?" Garson asked as the platoon trooped toward the huge quonset that served as Las Pulgas supply. They were turning in rifles and 782 gear. A truck stopped in the field about 30 yards away, and a group of a dozen men milled about. Their attire was bizarre – unkempt uniforms of strange cut and color, helmets crowned fore and aft by an odd protrusion like something out of a Gilbert and Sullivan operetta or the Marx Brothers' "Freedonian army." More, the men's faces were swirled with green and black paint, making them appear sickly and dangerous.

"Hey, man!" grunted Skuda, "those're the fuckin' Aggressors. You know, those guys who we 'fought' out there in the boonies, who kept us up all night with all that Willie Peter, hollerin', music an' shit." So that's what they looked like, Garson thought; must be good duty.

At the close of his Pendleton days, Skuda was headed for cold weather training in the Sierra Nevadas at Pickle Meadows; Tino held orders for Twentynine Palms, "the Stumps," it was called, near San Berdardino, California; Garson hadn't known that his buddy was artilleryman. "O.D." O'Donoghue drew the best assignment to Eighth & I, Marine Headquarters in Washington. "Maybe State Department duty. You know, 'dress blues, tennis shoes and a light coat of oil,'" he smirked.

Garson opened orders to his so-called permanent duty at the Naval Air Station on Whidbey Island, Washington, in the Puget Sound – said to be the largest island in the United States — over twelve hundred miles up the coast. The small Marine Barracks there was designated exclusively for guard and security, for the Navy's anti-submarine airwing. He was accorded three days travel time.

Days before his departure he phoned Karen. Could they meet in downtown L.A., tomorrow?

"Just a sec," she said in that soft voice. He overheard her conversing in Spanish with someone, her tone pleading, he thought. His heart sagged as minutes passed. Finally. Yes, she would meet him the next afternoon. Garson exalted silently, his body flushed with joy.

When he arrived downtown on Broadway, he spotted Karen standing near the theater box office, small against the tall, gray Beaux Arts building in which the theater was located. Her radiant smile beckoned. They hadn't made specific plans, only agreeing to meet.

"How 'bout the pictures," she smiled, her voice lilting; "we're right here anyways." Garson failed to note the movie titles, uncommon for someone who'd spent thousands of boyhood hours in movie houses. The colorful marquee was alight in the clouded afternoon, like Milwaukee's Riverside downtown that seated two thousand. The interior décor was similarly elegant — brocade, velvet, faux marble, dazzling chandeliers, ceiling frescos, terra cotta accents.

They passed the secondary concession stand but Karen requested nothing. They'd obviously not come to see a movie, Garson concluded, heart fluttering. He followed her light perfume, a pheromone, in the dimness. On the final landing, he hesitated, looking back: The screen was small from this perspective, almost like a television set; the final flight of stairs was precipitously angled. She grabbed his hand and tugged him upward, impatient. The theater's roof lowered to meet them. Garson's fallible recollection later convinced him that each row in that theater eyrie contained a double seat constructed without a dividing armrest, a feature with which his date was apparently familiar.

Karen set aside her jacket in the topmost row, revealing a silken pink blouse, contrasting prettily with her tawny skin; only her lower calves were visible below a long, dark skirt that hugged her buttocks — "Apple Cheeks" his mother would call them. They were barely settled when house lights dimmed and the screen came alive. Karen gently pulled Garson's hand over her shoulder.

"What's this," she pulled his left hand closer, tracing the still vivid, pink scar below his thumb.

"Oh, that." Garson thought at first to inflate the story of the wound, spinning it into something dramatic, heroic. But his usual proclivity for truth pressed him to minimize the disfigurement as only an accident. So, Karen nestled against him. He thought fleetingly of his first teen girlfriend, Leora, and their date at the Riverside – "ancient" history now. Back then, despite sensing her expectations, he'd been too intimidated to do more than drape his arm over her shoulder. After a double feature, the limb was needlingly numbed. Leora had dated him only that once.

Neither Garson nor Karen paid heed to the "Coming Attractions," he, the hardened Marine, intent upon living up to this girl's expectations. He nuzzled her ear and chastely kissed her cheek, recalling Lana's detestation of boys who opened their slobbering mouths to kiss. He castigated himself for such distracting thoughts. Karen responded, turning her face to his. He sensed more than saw her pulpy lips purse. She fixed them on his, and Garson wrapped both arms about her.

To his amazement, her lips parted and the tip of her tongue

wriggled between his lips, into his mouth, exploring. Momentarily startled, he paused before widening his mouth to permit deeper access, teasing his tongue with hers. He'd never kissed like this before – wetly, hungrily. She murmured lowly. It was his first French Kiss, a seductive sensation — primal, vertiginous. His breath seized and pulse pounded at his temples. His genitals stirred.

"*Cariño*," Karen whispered several times as his hands fleetingly pressed the front of her blouse, brushing the flat of her stomach until she gently pushed his hand away. But she didn't resist his tight embrace, their bodies like puzzle pieces. At intervals, they paused for breath, and she straightened her blouse. How was this possible, he pondered? He'd already had the ultimate carnal experience, but it hadn't been freighted with overwhelming emotional undertow like this. That afternoon in the Orpheum balcony passed too quickly.

The memory of that erotic experience remained vivid for the remainder of Garson's life. He convinced himself then that he'd found real love at last. But there was no way to pursue this intoxicating encounter to its conclusion, no place for them to realize what they'd kindled. When he walked her to the trolley late in the evening, he pledged love and fidelity; at the least, he promised to write from his permanent duty station. His throat twitched when they pulled apart from a final embrace. He thought her eyes misted when she boarded the scarlet interurban car.

Perhaps both sensed that they might not see one another again, at least not soon. He would exchange letters afterward, for years actually, until the time he betrayed her. Much later, in his life's long course, he wondered how her life had turned out, and if she even fleetingly thought of him as he did of her.

Chapter 2

NAS WHIDBEY ISLAND

Garrison Marine

It didn't take long before Garson recognized that the thickset corporal at Marine Barracks, Naval Air Station, Whidbey Island would be troublesome. And when Garson wrote about him those many decades later, he burdened the NCO with loathsome attributes, even a telltale name. But, then, his narrative wasn't objective. He'd determined to shape it to his purposes.

The superior's head was outsized, larger than it should have been, even fitted on a nearly neckless blocky corpus, an intimidating mass. Dominating large facial features, cheek bones jutted sharply above cheeks cratered like moonscape, pocked with ugly acne scars.

Garson clandestinely smirked at the corporal's sandy hair, crowned by a cowlick made unruly by regular Marine trimmings; it reminded him of a noxious weed, even a burdock. As if perpetually sleepy or disaffected, the NCO gazed at everyone from the lower half of his eyes, intensely pallid like those of the silent movie actress, Brigitte Helm in "Metropolis." The NCO's eyes pinioned listeners with withering, unblinking stares. Threatening, too, was the two-striper's penchant for standing nearly nose-to-nose when conversing, assaulting Garson and others with fetid pipe tobacco breath. When Garson backed away, imperceptibly, he thought, the distance between was invaded anew.

Most irritating to Garson was the corporal's penchant to begin clarifications and reiterations with the words "I'm just sayin'," a phrase that Garson found repugnant.

While most staff sergeants and above bore airs of deserved superiority, no other Marine Barracks corporal struck such a self-exalted pose. Junior NCOs – two and three strippers — shared the main squad bay with privates and PFCs, after all. Certainly, the corporal deserved respect for his Far East service, chest ribbons attesting to duty in Korea, Japan and the Philippines. But, he'd not seen any actual combat, at least to hear one detractor's scuttlebutt, which Garson chose to accept.

During Garson's first few days at NAS Whidbey Marine Barracks, he'd flopped into a guardhouse bunk after the midnight to four main gate watch. Not having showered since morning, yes, his socks were a bit gamey. The duty Corporal of the Guard and another NCO ambled through the squad bay of sleeping Marines.

"That new fucker looks like a real 'crud'," he muttered. "Crud" was one of the most scornful aspersions one could level against a fellow Marine. When setting his recollections to print in due course, Garson at first thought to identify his superior with an obviously odious name – Sikes, Magwich, or Quilp, anything to register rank detestation. But he ultimately settled on Judson (even though Garson's character could not rightly be called "Fatso") the name of the brutal stockade guard who killed Maggio, Frank Sinatra's character in "From Here to Eternity."

Months before, perhaps even a year (Garson's memory when he wrote of those days was often hazier than he liked) he'd hoisted his seabag onto his bony shoulder at the Oceanside Greyhound bus station adjacent to Camp Pendleton, orders in hand to his "permanent" duty station. He was headed north, up the coast over a thousand miles to the Puget Sound west of Seattle, to serve with a small company of Marines guarding the naval air station there. A sparingly educated, 17-year-old high school drop-out, Garson likely could not have readily pinpointed the Pacific Coast location on a map. A Camp Pendleton buddy informed him that the Southern Pacific's Coast Daylight train traveled to San Francisco where he could transfer to the Cascade Line across the Bay in Oakland for the run to Portland.

The journey could be completed aboard the Union Pacific to Seattle, "Rain City," a Baker Company buddy from Washington called it. Somewhat later, the metropolis became known as Emerald City for the lush verdure of forests that framed it.

"After a while," he smirked, "you'll get webbed feet just like the rest of us!" Garson had enjoyed train travel well enough, recalling the long journey from home to San Diego and MCRD after enlistment the autumn before. But even as he carried almost $40 from the most recent payday, the rail journey would consume a considerable part of it. Besides, he had been accorded three days travel time, and the Greyhound would get him to the Pacific Northwest cheaper and with time to spare. His buddy mapped the route for him.

Decades later, he'd lamented having paid scant attention to the ocean and mountain vistas north of Los Angeles. During much of the journey he lulled and slept. But years later he fancied a recollection of a breathtaking passage across the Golden Gate Bridge (the two ends had been joined in the year of his birth) with a view of Alcatraz Island, "The Rock" of movie fame. He'd also hoped to view majestic Sequoias and giant redwoods farther north, and the famed Bernard DeVoto cedars he may have recalled from one of James A. Fitzpatrick's ten-minute film travelogues screened between Ritz Theater feature movies. The towering and massive trees were ancient; they had germinated from seeds more than a thousand years before. But such scenes and vistas were impossible on that bus journey he chose.

Garson's recollection seemed to be more certain when the Greyhound rumbled across the state line into Oregon where a few crude billboards proclaimed a curious peculiarity — "State of Jefferson." He'd not read about that in school history books. The highway thereafter threaded between the coastal ranges along the edge of the Pacific, the soaring Cascades particularly crowded with vibrant verdancy – ancient arboreal stands of conifer and pine shared the landscape with deciduous forests. Here was the forest primeval, Garson supposed.

At the Seattle terminal, he changed to a local bus, one of those narrow, slightly shabby conveyances he recognized from old movies. Spewing clouds of black diesel exhaust, it trundled along the eastern shore of Puget Sound to the dock at Mukilteo, one of the many native-named towns and geographic features such as Puyallup, Enumclaw, Snoqualmie and others. After a churning 45-minute ferry ride, the vintage bus landed at Port Clinton on Whidbey, an elongated amoeba said to be the longest island in the continental United States. Then a twisting hour-long rumble along a snaking highway that passed through shaded shoreline hamlets, most no larger than a general store and gas station, to the seaside town of Oak Harbor near the island's northern limit whose main street curved about a picturesque shoreline named Crescent Harbor on Skagit Bay.

Dropped off on the principal thoroughfare, Pioneer Way, Garson shouldered his seabag, and trudged toward the naval air station's main gate. As he reached midpoint, a gray liveried Jeep with canvas and isinglass sides rattled up behind him and stopped. The passenger door was opened by a Negro sergeant who identified himself as Coleman; he drove up to the guarded base entrance to NAS Whidbey's Ault Field. A stern-countenanced, polished and pressed Marine gate sentry scrutinized Garson's ID card and orders. He wore dress greens, a white helmet liner, braided brassard; he was armed with a .45 automatic pistol protected by a polished leather holster. Garson would quickly become familiar with that livery. Waved through the gate, in minutes, the NCO driver stopped at an unadorned two-story concrete building, the base's main administration center, where Garson was directed to Marine Barracks on the top floor.

"Welcome to Whidbey," the sergeant said with little effusion. Garson recalled scenes from war movies in which recruits received only lukewarm welcome into combat outfits, old veterans aware that the new men would be early casualties. But his judgment of the Negro sergeant was premature.

Almost two centuries past, even before the Declaration of Independence, the Marines Corps, according to oft-touted legend, was organized at Tun Tavern in Philadelphia. Red-uniformed Marine contingents, wearing leather collars to protect against saber and cutlass cuts were assigned as shipboard boarding and landing parties; they'd fought in high seas battles against the British and piratical bands off the North African coast, and later won fame fighting against the Mexican army at Montezuma. During the Civil War, Admiral David Farragut was quoted saying that "A ship without Marines is like a uniform without buttons." Dashing actions in Cuba during the Spanish-American War, in Central American incursions in the new century, and during the First World War were overshadowed by the storied landings and harrowing sacrifices of the Pacific war.

The new World War newsreels and movie Marines like John Wayne had imprinted indelible images on Garson's boyhood mind. While, the stalemated conflict on the Korean peninsula lacked the "romantic" heft of Tarawa or Iwo Jima, it had promised the possibility of personal glory, perhaps even fame. Garson and his two pals had grown bored with school and chafed by their unremarkable Midwestern lives. That summer of 1953 a truce was negotiated before any of the boys – for mere boys, they only were — came of age. But they enlisted all the same, hoping the cessation of war wouldn't hold.

Still, following arduous months of Boot Camp and advanced combat training at Camp Pendleton, Garson believed himself prepared for real duty, fit for the Fleet Marines, the FMF, combat ready units honed by mock landings along Mediterranean coasts, or occupation forces in Japan, Korea or elsewhere; even U. S. State Department duty in which Marines in classic dress blues protected embassies in foreign capitals and climes would have provided adventure. But he was deflated with orders to his "permanent" Pacific Northwest duty station, thinking perhaps his early achievements had not sufficiently distinguished him. Duty at a mere Marine guard and security company in Washington State was far below his expectations.

Naval Air Station Whidbey encompassed a large swath on the northwest coast of the narrow amoeba-shaped island. The base, once home to famed Navy Catalina PBY "flying boats" that had scoured the Pacific for enemy vessels and aircraft during the recent World War, was still primed for contemporary combat. The base's runways had been expanded to accommodate new P2-V Neptune's, heavily-armed hunter-killer bombers whose jutting stinger tails were packed with sophisticated electronic detection devices.

"Sometimes, navy pilots fly right under Deception Pass Bridge that connects Whidbey to the mainland," one future buddy would describe. "Paid the price for their derring-do with court martials," he claimed. At Whidbey's northern extremity, he said, a magnificent double cantilever span linked the island to the mainland, soaring 200 breathtaking feet above the Puget Sound. Garson would need to wait for months before driving across the scenic quarter-mile.

The former Japanese enemy, of course, had given way to Communist Russians whose submarines, it was reputed, prowled from Soviet bases near Alaska. Six squadrons of the sleek, dark blue Lockheed aircraft were deployed at Ault Field, the droning sound of their engines a constant reminder of NAS Whidbey's Cold War mission. Pilots, naval personnel and base-housed dependents were billeted in barracks or single family units proximate to aircraft facilities.

NAS Whidbey headquarters, administration and support functions as well as fuel and ammunition storage areas were a few miles distant from shoreline runways that faced the Strait of Juan da Fuca. Marine Barracks was the lone billeting on the base's eastern side, perhaps more than a mile from hangars and runways, and other base housing. Marine Barracks squad bay, with high ceilings and tall windows, was undivided, a center bank of wall lockers and rifle racks aligned between double bunks positioned along the unshaded windows. Some 40 privates, PFCs and junior NCOs bunked in the main squad bay while staff NCOs shared double rooms. "RHIP – Rank Has Its Privilege" was the watchword. The Marine command's captain and lieutenants were billeted separately, with navy officers at the Seaplane Base. Enlisted Marines enjoyed their segregation from two thousand ordinary airdales — swabbies assigned to the air wings.

Whidbey Island Marines, like their shipboard counterparts, were primarily responsible for complete security on the sprawling base; they manned two main exterior entries and controlled the brig around the clock. In addition to sentry duty, Marines were responsible for security at the fuel and ammunition "dump," its internal portal open only during daylight hours. Garson recalled studying various official lading documents to insure that heavy tanker trucks carried the proper fuels and explosives to the seaplane base. That duty, Garson would soon learn, was indeed dull, with only sporadic traffic. Daily four-hour watches dragged interminably.

Marine Barracks enlisted men were divided into three watches – each 24 hours on guard duty and 48 off. Two Ault Field entry gates were manned round the clock in four-hour shifts. The brig was likewise secured permanently. On-duty watches of about 12 to 15 Marines were billeted in the second story guard house adjacent to Main Gate One, sharing space with the brig.

Brig population was typically small, normally less than ten, the majority enlisted sailors penalized for minor offenses such as short-term AWOL or insubordination that drew sentences of 30 days or less. Each prisoner wore a dungaree jacket or shirt emblazoned with a conspicuous white "P" on his back. Occasionally, a fellow Marine was incarcerated, and he was invariably designated as Right Guide to lead prisoner details during their movements about the base. More, imprisoned Marine buddies actually were invariably treated leniently, avoiding the incessant physical and verbal harassment meted out to navy miscreants, abject swabbie fuck ups, as Garson and his buddies considered them, who deserved all the mistreatment they could dispense. He quickly came to understand the long history of antipathy between the two military services that sometimes led to near sadistic abuse meted out by brig guards.

Called "prisoner chasers," guards were armed with 12 gauge "riot" shotguns loaded with devastating scatter shot, and .45 automatic pistols. Garson found that the designation was misnomer because Marines never actually "chased" anyone; none had even heard of an escape attempt by these minor offenders. Few Whidbey inmates were hardened criminals, and none with long sentences were jailed there. Instead, hard core inmates were quickly transferred and incarcerated in the navy's infamous Mare Island, California facility that bore a reputation equal to Alcatraz or Sing Sing.

The confined were assigned daily work chores, cleaning away weeds and debris from base walk- and roadways, sweeping streets, painting buildings and many make-work assignments. Brig details, prisoners and chasers, sat apart from normal mess hall diners and when attending Sunday worship services. Garson always suspected prisoner piety was only a ruse to avoid Marine harassment. He found such daily duty deadening, guarding and observing activities, shifting foot to foot, cradling the deadly shotgun that could reputedly cut a man in half with one blast. He dreaded an unlikely escape attempt. Indirectly, one brig assignment would lead to a confrontation with the menacing martinet, Judson, ending in traumatic consequences.

Off-duty Marines daily policed Marine Barracks, and attended refresher classes and lectures on Corps history, combat tactics and strategy, and more. Guard and security Marines were also required to annually qualify with the M-1 rifle, like their infantry counterparts, as well as the .45 pistol, and prove competence with the 12-gauge shotgun.

For the majority of the Marine company, Whidbey was either the first or ultimate "permanent" duty station. Late Korean era draftees completing mandatory two-year tours, anxious to return to normal life, shared billeting with late war enlistees and newer volunteers like Garson — unwashed "fresh fish," in Civil War parlance, who lived largely on expectations and imaginings. Many had either joined following high school graduation or, like him, after prematurely terminating formal education. It was a polyglot company.

"He's just a '*chooch*,'" opined Sergeant Coleman, the Negro NCO Garson had met on his first day at Whidbey, commenting on Judson's officious superiority.

"*Chooch*?"

"Yeah, *chooch*. Means asshole, something like that among some Chicago folks." When Garson set down his recollections from the remove of decades, he found "*chooch*" to be the colloquial Chicago corruption of the Italian word *ciuccio* meaning a dummy. But he meant more.

"Call me G. D.,'" the smiling three-striper had said early on — "short for Gerald Duane." When they came to know each other better, Coleman said his Mississippi grandmother called him "*Jay-ree*" instead of Jerry or Gerald. Their wall lockers abutted. It was readily evident that Coleman didn't demand the same deference to rank as Judson. In fact, Coleman became a veritable confidant and mentor, among the first, to Garson in those early NAS Whidbey days.

Coleman' s appearance was always impeccable, and Garson found the sergeant's even temper and self-controlled manner, and his affable and gregarious demeanor refreshing. Yet, he never considered his new buddy handsome, his skin was dark mahogany, nose flat and broad with outsized nostrils; ears were tiny, and eyes the color of root beer. The sergeant's voice was comfortably modulated and words measured, and Coleman was not given to an overabundance of scatology or profanity, as Garson remembered, even eschewing the Corps's preferred four-letter explicative – at least under most circumstances.

Coleman and Garson became an unlikely pair of buddies, the former five years older, a wounded combat veteran wise to the ways of the world. But, to Garson's later lament, their friendship rarely extended beyond Marine Barracks and Oak Harbor. There had been no Negroes in his Boot Camp platoon, and he'd become acquainted with only a few at Camp Pendleton, "O.D." O'Donoghue was the exception. Shared off-base liberties were unusual among white and Negro Marines except in groups, the latter understandably finding the closest comity among their own race, Garson thought. While integrated for a half dozen years already, the Corps, long dominated by Southern sensibilities, had resisted President Truman's 1948 order to the last.

On Main gate duty, Marine guards wore dress green uniforms accented with red "M.P." armbands, braided brassards and dangling brass whistles threaded through their epaulets. They wore polished white helmet liners accented in fore and aft red stripes and the classic brass Corps emblem. A spit-shined pistol holster and .45 automatic completed a sentry's livery.

"Check every vehicle comin' in here for proper windshield

decals," Coleman instructed during Garson's orientation. "Red's fer enlisted. Gotta check pedestrians for proper IDs and valid liberty passes, too. Most important, when you spot that yellow sticker for officers, ya gotta render proper courtesy." Garson learned to bark his heels together audibly, like Cary Grant in "Gunga Din," waving officer vehicles through with a snappy salute, the well-practiced Corps "highball" — right hand fingers and thumb welded together, touching helmet brim before smartly cutting the gesture away. Every gate sentry affected his own distinctive variation of the crisp gesture.

"Even officers' wives and civilian personnel are rendered this courtesy," the NCO advised. "Give 'em all a neat highball." In time, Garson adjusted the stern set of his lips and softened his eyes into a welcoming expression for pretty dependents and civilian secretaries. But, of course, his nearly adolescent appearance contrasted sharply with hardened demeanor of combat Marines. His uniform jacket bore no emblems of serious duty stations, only the pitiful "Fire Watch" ribbon designating him as little more than a recruit.

Contrasted to Garson, Coleman displayed more than a row of ribbons – Korea combat, Japan and Okinawa service, Good Conduct and the highly respected Purple Heart. Garson in time asked about the circumstances of his wounding. He envied his superior's uniform issue, especially the battle or "Ike" jacket (Garson disliked his long, thigh length dress blouse) and the dark green wool dress shirts handsomely accented with red-trimmed chevrons and khaki tie. More, Coleman's combat boots were polished to perfection, to veritable mirror finishes, a task only the Negro sergeant had mastered.

Garson and Coleman were initially drawn together by Chicago, like Garson's Pendleton buddy, Tino, the sergeant's home town. Not that Garson was totally conversant of the Lake Michigan metropolis, but his dandified Uncle Hervè, affectionate Aunt Bacia, and revered cousin Bob had occasionally invited Garson down to their home in

Cicero, feting him to outings at the sprawling Riverview amusement park, Balboa Zoo and even stock car races at Soldier Field.

Garson's recollections of those Chicago summers were vivid, as was his mother's antipathy toward her brother-in-law and his brassy blonde second wife, she of the moist, pulpy kisses, generous bosom, gleaming gold and gems and heady floral perfumes. Uncle Hansel had changed his given name to William, after all, and somehow fraudulently used his brother's stellar credit report to borrow money, or so Garson's mother always claimed. Garson couldn't recall his uncle, who sported a Gilbert Roland pencil mustache, wearing casual clothes; he invariably dressed to the nines in glen plaid suits, eyelet collar shirts and cufflinks, flamboyant ties and pocket poofs, set off by two-tone wingtip shoes and, in season, dapper summer straw boaters worn at jaunty angles.

"Ever been to Maxwell Street?" Garson asked Coleman in an early conversation, hoping to learn more about his superior.

"Naw, they wouldn't let us coloreds hang out over there. But cousin a mine – well, he wasn't a cousin really; we just called him that — had a basement full a stuff — suits, shirts an' ties, trousers an' belts, all hanging from basement water pipes, shoes in boxes. Said they 'fell' off'a trucks somewheres.' Sold to kin, neighbors and folks who came to his barber shop. Complete suit'd cost ya' a saw buck; shoes fer five, ties fer 50, maybe 25-cents." Coleman said his cousin also sometimes sold steaks and chops out of the back door of his shop.

"Been to that big museum with the coal mine?"

"Museum of Science an' Industry, you mean?" Coleman nodded. Garson's cousin Bob, the idol of his youth, had taken him there during a summer week's visit. He distinctly remembered that mine.

"Tried to go there once when I was a kid," Coleman replied. "Me 'n my cousins, three or four, I think. Couple'a museum guards wouldn't let us in. One held up his hand like a traffic cop. 'You dark clouds better just go on home now,' he told us. He really meant 'coloreds'...." Coleman paused to consider his next word, Garson thought, hesitant to use the foul fighting word, "niggers." He didn't. Garson swallowed almost audibly. "Never went back after that."

"What about the art museum on Michigan Avenue?" Garson queried.

"You kiddin'?" Coleman countered. "They didn't like us coloreds there either. And I wasn't all that much interested in most of that stuff." He was warming to Garson's queries. "Don't think they show any art by black folks anyways."

"Knew a kid on the block once," he offered, "fought all the time. Gray eyed – not unknown among us coloreds, a' course – but other kids called him a 'trick baby,' meanin' his mama consorted with a white man — that's where he got his light eyes an' skin. That made him really mad, an' his fists was always balled up ready to sock somebody." Coleman went on to explain that his crowd played a game called "the Dozens" when insults were hurled like rocks at one other, often with insinuations about family lineage, even someone's paternity, a mother's depravity, consorting with white men. "Some insults cut to the bone, you had to keep your cool and not react, stay calm. First kid who fired out was the loser."

Coleman mentored Garson on many things: Care and pressing of dungarees and care of uniforms, and spit shining shoes and boots. Garson envied Coleman's, the glossiest in Marine Barracks.

"Gotta look good out there – on those main gates. You're representin' the Mother Marine Corps."

To Garson's initial discomfort, his superior even commented on Garson's personal grooming.

"Gotta get rid'a that mono-brow a yours," Coleman suggested, indicating his disfavor with the hair the bridged Garson's eyebrows. "Looks oafish, Neanderthal even." Garson had frankly never paid attention to such hirsute details. But he scrutinized the collection of Marine Barracks mugshots posted near the captain's office, concluding that Coleman was correct. There would be more to their camaraderie and candor.

Among other duties, Marines were also responsible for raising the national flag onto the towering NAS Ault Field pole every dawn and retiring it each sundown. The three-man detail — flag bearer and two armed guards – marched about 200 yards from the guard shack. As the "National Anthem" reverberated over base loudspeakers, military and civilian alike halted in place, and vehicles stopped as the ensign was rapidly run on high. Military froze and saluted smartly. At daylight's end, the national ensign, to the sound of "Tattoo," was retired — lowered slowly as bugle notes echoed. After Coleman's tutelage, Garson became adept at carefully folding the banner into the prescribed triangular shape, only the blue field and stars visible.

"Carry the colors with reverence," was Coleman's admonition. "They're the symbol of what we fought and died for." Indeed, the bearer carefully cradled the national ensign like a protective mother with child.

When writing of his NAS Whidbey Island days, Garson's hazy recollections, sometimes conflated real with fancied episodes and characters, intermingling the two into a simulacra of what truly occurred nearly seven decades before. But, his memory of the grand Washington mountain vistas was verifiable, ever looming on clear days to the south and west, the snow-capped eminences of Mount Rainier and the Olympic Mountains, shoulders shaggy with dense coniferous forests. Douglas fir, aromatic cedars, white and black spruces, jack pines, tamarack, balsam fir, Garson was told by Marines who knew, that shared these acres with deciduous oaks and maples. Forest floors, he found after a few solo tramps, were carpeted with dank mosses and lichens. The moist Pacific

Coast climate featured hundreds of inches of saturating annual precipitation and the extended growing season pushed trees to lofty heights and all greenery into lush verdancy.

The landscape and its flora contrasted with southern Wisconsin's whose gently rolling rural landscape, were once densely populated with conifers and pines during the preceding century before being voraciously logged over. After Wisconsin's logging "cut-over," the landscape, particularly the northeastern part of the state, was transformed into gently undulating farmland with few extensive forests – a cautionary lesson he remembered from grade school years.

On many Whidbey Island days, Garson felt hemmed in, claustrophobic amid the soaring coastal mountains and white-shrouded peaks that occluded the sun prematurely and spread evening shadows early. Pacific Ocean systems roiled clouds, milking them of rain and nearly incessant mist, creating the all-consuming moist Washington Coast environment.

More, to Garson's pleasure, Washington winters, unlike Wisconsin's, were mild and snows minimal. A simple dusting, to Garson's amusement, sent locals into driving paroxysms. The coldest deep winter days in the Pacific Northwest were 30 degrees warmer than back home. Still, the daylight seemed always to be cast damp blues and greens. His feet, however, had not yet grown membranous webbing.

"How was it out there – in Korea?" Sucking up his courage, Garson asked Coleman one vacant afternoon. He'd been discomfited for several months now, having enlisted to become a combat Marine, as he and his chums Preston and Daily had naively planned, to see the "elephant" and the world, to mature, to become men, to return home with rows of combat ribbons. They'd anticipated upon their return, being hailed conquering heroes and adulated by local girls. Instead, he found himself in the undemanding backwater duty at NAS Whidbey, amid a collection of recent enlistees he considered, like himself, marginal Marines, young men with minimal education, experience and sophistication, of limited potential and prospects.

"Ain' never been warm since Chosin," his new confidant recalled. Garson and others had noted that the sergeant often stood in the shower for what seemed like hours on end. Coleman called it his "scald off." He'd been drafted in the summer of 1950, and after hasty Boot Camp and Pendleton training, been hurried to the Seventh Marines, a unit later surrounded by Chinese forces sent south in November to bolster the faltering North Korean army.

"Was in Fox Company," Coleman reluctantly noted. "You know the story." Indeed, the Marine's fighting withdrawal from Chinese army encirclement of the man-made Chosin Reservoir in northeast Korea was the most storied battle of the entire war, proudly described by Boot Camp and Pendleton instructors who'd been there. Only Garson's persistent queries drew out more details from Coleman's experience.

"Think it was called Hell Fire Valley, somewheres 'round Hangau-ri, they said, when we was battling' our way out of the encirclement," Coleman recalled. Garson detected reticence in his buddy's words.

"Don' remember much, 'cept fer the fuckin' cold and snow. Always below zero, wicked an' windy. Got frostbite. Corps never did get us proper cold weather gear. I was plunked in the left shoulder. December First, a day to remember. Carried out by my buddies" was his terse summary. Marine air power permitted infantry units to batter their way out of the enemy encirclement, making a storied fighting withdrawal. Pride was evident in his words.

"Know fer a fact that our regiment and the Divvie came out with every wounded and dead Marine, every fuckin' weapon, every fuckin' piece of equipment, ammo even," Coleman added. "Left no one er' nothin' behind." Garson thought his buddy's eyes misted.

Over time, Coleman and Garson shared details about their lives before the Corps. For his entire enlistment, Garson was eager to learn about the backgrounds and experiences of buddies with whom he shared lives, measuring his pallid experiences against theirs. When asked in turn, however, Garson was often reluctant to reveal more than the barest of details, thinking his life prosaic and woeful, to admit, for instance, that his father, a war-time welder, had given up a respected trade to enter a decidedly unmanly occupation, the confection business, with his dandified Chicago brother, Hervè, or that his mother was but a restaurant dishwasher. Neither parent had even completed grade school. Garson felt his life had been without moment or merit.

In contrast, Coleman's father had grown up in the Deep South, and as a young man determined to seek fortune elsewhere, initially attracted to teeming New Orleans where Negroes sometimes celebrated Mardi Gras "masked" as Indians, he said. But, Brutus, as he was called then, decided to head north away from lynchings and Jim Crow violence.

"Pap wanted to go north, to New York, where he'd heard Indians worked high iron — steelworkers clamberin' up the skyscrapers, dancin' along steel beams, way above the city, riveting, boltin', weldin'. Changed his name to Coleman to separate hisself ferever from piss-poor Mississippi roots." Garson was struck that Coleman used "Pap" as had Huck Finn. Garson had seen *Life* magazine photos and movie shorts about those workers, Mohawk Indians many of them, if he remembered correctly. Fearful of heights, even in images, he'd shuddered at dizzying newsreels and photos of Indians scrambling along narrow precipitous girders. He remembered turning back, to his father's disgust, when climbing the narrow winding passageway to the Holy Hill Cathedral belltower. It was a church near Milwaukee erected on a high prominence where a Virgin apparition was said to have occurred. His state was noted for several of those putative visitations. Despite his father's cajoling, Garson was unable to calm his wobbling legs higher than a half dozen turns of the spiral staircase. In later years, he would empathize with Jimmy Stewart's character in "Vertigo."

"But they wouldn't hire Pap 'cause he wasn't trained to work steel. He was told he could work underground, buildin' the Holland Tunnel. Workers there were called 'sandhogs' or 'muckers,'" Coleman continued, a pick-and-shovel brigade that labored in a compressed air environment below the river bed. After their shifts, workers entered a decompression chamber to prevent the "bends" — when nitrogen entered the bloodstream possibly causing death.

"Ya know, I saw a movie once when I was a kid," Garson interrupted, "about a tunnel cave-in under the river, water gushing in, hundreds of workers drowning." He vividly and uncomfortably recalled those scenes from one of the many Tuesday "Dish Nights" he and his mother shared, each admission including a gratis piece of common tableware.

"The Ritz was all ladies on those nights," he told Coleman, the usual fare was domestic stories and melodramas – "weepies" they were called. He recalled women sniffling, and his mother daubing a handkerchief to her eyes when tragedy and untimely death intruded on the screen. He still had vivid recollections of "The Five Sullivan Brothers" and "The Clock." Only four or five at the time, Garson slept through most of such films, awaking on that occasion during some Fred Astaire and Ginger Rogers musical number.

"Pap said he worked with Krauts, Polacks, Micks and Guineas," Coleman continued. "'Down there,' Pap said, 'they don't see your black skin.'"

"Ya know, my grandpa worked like that, long time ago, when he first came to America," Garson again interjected. "Ma said he worked with a lot of foreigners, too. He came from the Austro-Hungarian Empire, and worked in a coffer dam in the Milwaukee River. They were laying the foundation for the new Gimbel Brothers Department Store downtown. Said there were lots a' Polacks and Bohunks, even a couple a' Negroes. That was before he went back to Hungary to get my gramma, my Ma and her sisters to bring back to Wisconsin."

"Pap said he hated it down there, underground, out of the light of day. Didn't like subways either. Couldn't see anything out the windows. Heard that Chicago had trains that was elevated so you could ride in the light of day all the time. So he went there as a young man. Met my Ma and married, became a barber and had kids." His Pap, Coleman said, always reminded him of a famous Negro axiom: "Make a way where there is no way."

Despite their affinity, Garson felt too uncomfortable to reveal his kindergarten fascination with a little Negro girl called Sally – "Salomea, from the Bible," she'd told him. She was the first Negro he'd ever encountered. But Garson was reluctant to share the recollection of his beloved immigrant grandfather barring the little classmate from their house. But he permitted them to eat peanut butter and jelly sandwiches on the rear vestibule steps. Neither did Garson mention Charles Hill, the best student at Holy Redeemer Grade School who'd kept playground bullies at bay for him.

As was invariably the case with Garson and others, omnivorous, meandering conversations among Marines invariably focused on movies, an interest common to virtually all save the most rural and insular of buddies. While Garson, of course, listed John Wayne as his favorite Western hero, Coleman spoke of a screen personality Garson had never known.

Called the Bronze Buckaroo and Sepia Singing Cowboy, Herb Jeffries became a hero to Negro kids in cramped movie houses in their segregated neighborhoods — no matter that the actor was a light-skinned, mixed race performer. He began his entertainment career as a jazzman singing with Duke Ellington's orchestra.

"I remember them movies," Coleman explained. "'Harlem on the Prairie' was one of 'em. I think there was also 'Two-Gun Man from Harlem' and 'Harlem Rides the Range.' Jeffries had a great voice. They showed his movies a lot on the southside."

They shared a common fascination with musical movies,

conversing about such dancing stars as Peg Leg Bates, the Nicholas Brothers and Bojangles Robinson. Other conversations focused on music, mainly blues. "Heard a' Muddy Waters? Blues master?" Garson nodded, even though he was not familiar with the musician. "Real name's McKinley Morganfield. Born in Mississippi back in the day, among them crackers an' peckerwoods. But he overcame 'em."

"I like the Andrews and McGuire Sisters." Garson offered weakly. "But I like the Ink Spots and the Mills Brothers, too. They blend their voices so well."

"You mean harmonies," Coleman put in.

"Yeah, harmonies."

"Billie Holiday. Heard a' her? Called 'er Lady Day, you know. Always wore a white gardenia in 'er hair. Blues 'n jazz singer with a voice full of pain – *Black* pain." Coleman mentioned other performers about whom Garson had heard on radio or seen fleetingly in movies – Duke Ellington, Count Basie, Cab Calloway, Fats Waller and others about whom he knew little. There were other topics they shared.

"Don't believe half the bullshit he tells you," Coleman said, warning about a Marine veteran who'd filled the ears of any Marine who'd listen to tales of salacious conquests and derring-do in Far Eastern cities. "Well, don't believe most of it."

The Marine about whom Coleman spoke was mountainous with parchment skin, bulbous eyes framed in faint eyebrows and lashes; his ears flared widely. An untoned body was carpeted orange like an orangutan. All-in-all, he was a decidedly unhandsome Marine. He served with several who called Pacific Islands home, most of whom bore ethnic surnames, tongue-twisters like Tanemahuta or surnames such as Lia'tutufu, even mere grunts like Opu. However, his name was O'Toole, entirely apt to the constant deluge of concupiscent escapades he described. Garson mused about

O'Toole's forbearers, adventurous Emerald Isle seafarers blown off course somehow and shipwrecked in Polynesia. Crude and boorish yet gregarious, his flatulence was legendary, causing Garson to recall his own father's dreadful bassoon-like proclivity.

O'Toole yearned to return to Pago Pago, the principal city of American Samoa. He proudly proclaimed that his island nation had the highest rate of military enlistments in the United States and its territories. "Marines were stationed on Tutuila, the main island, when I was a little kid. They treated us good," he said before returning to his favorite adventures. He often "held court" to impressionable listeners like Garson, sprawled across his lower bunk like a big-bellied potentate, wearing only skivvie shorts, shower shoes and a gap-toothed smile

"Got the clap once or twice but never got syph though, *Ta'aroa* be praised," O'Toole boasted. "But the good ol' corpsmen gave me pills, and I was good to go again in a week, and I went on bangin' them Tokyo Geishas, sometimes two at a time. His yarns were delivered with panache and self-deprecating humor.

Coleman demurred of telling such yarns, clarifying that Geishas weren't really prostitutes, but socially respected girls and women carefully trained in the arts of entertaining men – dance, dining, classical music, conversation and more.

"They didn't engage in sex," the sergeant said. But necessity changed that behavior with the defeat of Japan: The country's staggering economic and social disruption coupled with post-war military occupation forced the former romantic artisans into the tawdry profession.

Garson shuddered at some of O'Toole's recollections, recalling grainy Boot Camp training films about venereal infections with depictions of suppurating sores and chancres, of shuddering, hollow-eyed men in advanced stages of disease, of madness and death. He'd vowed after his lone sexual misadventure in Tijuana to avoid future unprotected congress with girls, professional or other. Still, he was titillated by O'Toole's incessant braggadocio, about his generous physical endowments and sexual stamina during a thousand and one Far East night stands.

"'A course, for a couple of bucks a month, you shacked up with a little *mama-san*. She'll take care of you, get food, cook, wash your clothes, dump the 'honey bucket.' Even give you massages and fuck all day an' night. Liberties're great," he said, eyes bulging. "Bet I even got some half-breed *kamas* — kids a mine, you know — runnin' round over there."

Like most salty Marine veterans, the big Samoan larded his speech with real and bastardized Japanese and Korean words – *konnichiwa* (welcome) *skosh* (a little), *ichiban* (good). He was sometimes given to wearing colorful kimonos and sandals from the Far East. He'd "gone native" in Japan, one critic claimed.

"Some a' them Squint broads get skin cut away from their eyes, makin' 'em rounder, to look more American. Had one once who looked like Sylvia Sidney, you know, the movie actress from way back." O'Toole often rhapsodized about female anatomy.

"Ya know them Oriental cunnies're shaped like X's, not slits like American chicks." Garson grunted in disbelief. His sexual "baptism of fire," as it were, had been in a dimly-lit Mexican brothel where he'd fleetingly glimpsed only the tart's dark pubic triangle. When in due course it became obvious to Garson that O'Toole wasn't particularly observant of female anatomy, most of the islander's concupiscent boasting lost some luster.

"Yeah, seen lots of 'em in Seoul an' Tokyo. Got them fleshy folds under those furry "*padoodas*." He meant pudendum. In evidence, O'Toole proudly exhibited his collection of Asian erotica — illustrations stored in a bottom of his foot locker, reproductions of graphic woodblock prints, scenes of languorous, kimonoed women with bared genitals, their plunging paramours endowed with outsized erections. In time, Garson would discover that the illustrations had been created by popular *shunga* artists centuries before. But now, Garson was fascinated not with the art but the detailed coital gymnastics. O'Toole permitted Garson's repeated perusals; Garson studied them intently. Perhaps at some future Far East duty station he'd acquire his own copies.

O'Toole, like Coleman, wore a Purple Heart ribbon among his other service decorations. Yet he remained only a PFC, indicating perhaps, that during some Far East escapade he'd run afoul of the military police and paid a price of demotion.

"Enlisted when Korea broke out," O'Toole said. "Served in 'Chesty' Puller's First Marines." Colonel Puller was the most decorated officer in the Corps, and his battlefield exploits were storied. "Got plunked right after landing at Inchon," the immense Samoan continued. "Weren't much. Little shrapnel scratch down near my family jewels. Few inches lower, *Ta'aroa* be praised, an' that hunk a metal'd ended my days with them slant-eyed whores and B-girls. " Laughter resonated from the bellows of his belly. He'd seen no further combat action, but spent a year in Japan and Seoul. Still, his Purple Heart ribbon, like Coleman's, marked him as a Marine apart.

Now, O'Toole was a short-timer, only months remaining before his discharge. While his body had given way to paunchiness, un-Marine like to Garson's eye, superiors were loath to pressure him into shape. He stood guard and performed other duties in regulation manner, but without enthusiasm. He obviously missed his *mama-sans* and was anxious to return to his balmy island five thousand miles away.

Oak Harbor, Whidbey's largest town, listed a population of around two thousand featuring, to Garson's recollection, Scandinavian rectitude. Its curved commercial heart along Crescent Harbor contained a two-story hotel, grocery, hardware, haberdashery and other retail fronts, a busy gas station and auto repair, and a miniscule movie house, the Oak, smaller than North Milwaukee's unimpressive Ritz Theater that Garson frequented in his youth.

Also situated on Pioneer Way overlooking Skagit Bay's City Beach was one of the most popular local liberty spots, the Canteen, the town's premier restaurant and bar whose name was chosen to welcome servicemen. It reminded Garson of a similar eatery back home, Shorty's, where he'd worked as a busboy. Because of its distance from navy billeting at the seaplane base, the establishment was unofficially the exclusive province of NAS Whidbey Marines; Garson and a few others even came to call it call it the "E. M. Club" — enlisted man's club. On many Friday and Saturday nights uniformed and civilian-garbed Marines, occasionally including Coleman and a few other Negro buddies, joined the crowd in the banquet area where tables were pushed together. Pitchers of local Olympia and Rainier Beer flowed freely. It was not unknown for Garson and other underage Marines to clandestinely sip brew. He did not recall that glowering Judson had ever joined the revelry.

Overseeing the restaurant was a trim, dark-haired assistant manager and hostess, Flo, a recent graduate from Oak Harbor High. Knowingly, she turned her back on the clandestine imbibing by underage Marines. She also maintained a consistent welcoming demeanor, but firmly resisted ham-handed flirtations and blandishments. The only stern expression Garson ever witnessed in those days was one he accidentally captured in candid photograph.

Garson had for a time attempted to disarm the underlying menace of Corporal Judson, using the Boot Camp tactic of dissembling as well as opening conversations about their shared a hometown. He knew the west side neighborhood where his superior had lived and the Catholic grade school, St. Sebastian's, where he'd studied. The superior, in turn, grunted knowledge of the rough reputation attending to Villard Avenue, called "The Burg" by youthful habitués, where Garson had misspent much of his youth. But just when Garson thought there was an opening, a thaw between them, the door to camaraderie slammed shut and the NCO's typical hauteur returned.

To Garson's recent dismay, Judson exhibited overt fascination with Lana, Garson's putative "sister," having spotted provocative black and white snapshots she'd mailed to her "little brother." Wearing dancer's dark leotards and fishnet stockings, she struck provocative poses, eyebrows arched and lips pursed. Her dark, curly hair was shorter than when Garson had departed Milwaukee the previous year, her calves, thighs and breasts now ampler. She wasn't yet the curvaceous danseuse *a la* Shirley Maclaine or Cyd Charisse, but Garson, visualizing those fetching cobalt eyes, thought that when he returned home, she might disregard her fancied sibling relationship with him. She'd soon be featured in the Custer High musical review, she'd boasted in a recent missive.

"Fuck, man, who's 'at?" the pocked nemesis leered over his shoulder, smoky breath enveloping as Garson shuffled through the black and white images. When Garson replied she was his sister, the bulky corporal loosed a wolfish whistle and growl, widening pale eyes. He daubed a finger onto his tongue, and ran it across both brushy brows.

"Shit, man, I'd like to dip my wick into a lotta that." Garson was affronted. It was as if Lana had been pawed and assaulted by this acned ogre. More would come of this.

Every Marine regardless of MOS, military occupation, of course, was required to annually qualify with the M-1 Garand rifle, the basic shoulder arm of the Marines, the infantryman's boon companion. At the Camp Mathews rifle range during Boot Camp, he'd disappointed himself, falling just short of the coveted Expert medal, scoring 218 of a possible 250 points for a Sharpshooter medallion. He was determined to capture the highest award but was discomfited when he found Judson was among those slated for qualification at the same time.

Garson and a dozen or more Whidbey Marines were relieved of normal security duty for three days, sent to the unimpressive Ault Field firing range to prepare for qualification. There was no need for repeated classroom instruction and familiarization, only reawakening muscle memory because knowledge of the semi-automatic Garand rifle seemed engrained in every Marine. He and others simply practiced "snapping in" or dry-firing from the four basic positions – off-hand or standing, prone, sitting and kneeling, and acquiring the proper sight "dope." Live firing and scoring occurred on the final day of preparation.

The M-1 rifle qualification course was composed of 50 rounds, ten shots at each distance and position: Off-hand and kneeling slow fire at 200 yards; prone and sitting rapid fire at 300, and slow fire prone at 500 yards. Garson, who'd added several pounds and a bit of muscularity in the past year, felt confident he could steady his weapon better than he'd done in Boot Camp.

On the Friday qualification that late summer day, air hung gray and dank, occasional mist borne by winds sliding east from the Olympic Peninsula, defusing light at long distances.

"Shitty fuckin' score," Judson needled, grinning at the woeful 35 points his subordinate had scored in the opening off-hand round. Trying to ignore the comments, Garson gritted his teeth in determination. But the more he bore down, the worse he fired.

"Fuck!" Garson blurted at one point. In the kneeling position at 200 yards, his supporting arm wobbled, and he registered a second dismal score. After dejectedly trudging back to the 300-yard firing line, Garson recovered somewhat in the standing to sitting rapid fire position. He watched Judson survey the chalkboard scores at the center of the firing line.

"You ain' no expert!" the overbearing NCO snorted, bumping Garson slightly as they made their way to far distance for the 500-yard, slow fire prone. Garson recalled how he'd recovered from previous missteps to score a possible 50 points at Camp Matthews the previous winter. If he could replicate that feat, perhaps he might wreck some revenge. At that juncture, Garson noted, Judson's score was barely a handful of points ahead. He settled into the prone position, and tightened the rifle sling onto his left bicep, welcoming the buzz of numbness in his arm.

The bullseye target appeared but a dot over his front sight. The words of his MCRD rifle instructor whispered in memory from the spring before: "Balance the bullseye atop the front sight. Take a deep breath. Release half of it. Squeeze the trigger – 'like squeezing your girlfriend's soft tiny titties." Marine DIs and recruit instructors never allowed for generously endowed sweethearts.

The .30 caliber bullet would exit the rifle's muzzle at 3700 hundred feet per second, he recalled from recruit training, and transit to the target in less than an eye blink. Garson's physicality thrilled when the target stanchion was withdrawn from view and reappeared after each of the ten shots with the scoring white disk waggling ten points over the black center. He'd scored another "possible" – 50 points. Yes, he'd need to replace the Sharpshooter medallion on his uniform with an undistinguished Marksman bar, but disappointment was mitigated when he discovered he'd bested Judson by two points. While privately smug, he said nothing, satisfied that he'd measured Judson.

Later, in more recompense, Garson easily qualified expert with .45 pistol. He recalled the Camp Matthews marksmanship instructor, a salty old gunny, commenting on the size of his hands, making the bulky automatic feel comfortable and easy to fire. Once more he'd defeated his Milwaukee nemesis in what he long afterward regarded as one-on-one competition, and proudly pinned the shiny wreathed medallion on his uniform.

"I'm just sayin'," Judson began. For a man of his bulk, the two-striper's voice was incongruous — highly pitched, perhaps not feminine or falsetto, but above a range Garson considered manly. His invariable opening phrase still set Garson's teeth on edge, reinforcing blinding detestation of the pock-marked superior. He tried to disguise his antipathy toward the NCO, avoiding him as much as possible. But his nemesis shared the watch and served as corporal of the guard. On that fateful morning, Garson had been relieved after four to eight main gate watch. When the jeep had carried him back to the guardhouse, only an hour remained before the morning mess hall closed.

"March prisoners to chow," Judson commanded as Garson entered the duty squad bay. Garson's body deflated. He'd not eaten morning chow himself, having been without sustenance since the half ham sandwich and lukewarm coffee four hours before. Further, he knew that chasers weren't permitted sustenance while guarding prisoners. Moreover, by the time the detail would be completed and prisoners returned to the brig, the mess hall would be closed. He'd be without chow until midday.

"Isn't there anyone else?" Garson mewled. "Just got off a four to eight. Ain't had chow yet."

"I'm just sayin', we don't have anyone else right now." Judson's nasal voice pitched higher. "You're gonna chase prisoners – right *fuckin'* now."

"Aww, *man*," Garson whined. As soon as the words left his mouth, he cringed. He should have addressed him as "corporal," not "man." Most NCOs might let that slide, but not Judson. His caterpillar brows fluttered, and his words fired back in short, sharp bursts. The only things missing were tracer bullets.

"I'm just sayin', you're goin' with Schuster. Cut the fuckin' crap. Grab that .12 gauge. That's a *direct* fuckin' order, *PFC*!" He stood, glaring at Judson for pregnant moments, hesitating just long enough to trigger a cataclysmic response.

"Writin' you up for insubordination!" Judson growled. Bile erupted in Garson's stomach. He turned on his heel, shaking his head. While Schuster gathered the nine prisoners from their cells, and assembled them downstairs, Garson audibly slapped the white helmet liner on his head, tugged on the red armband, adjusted the webbed belt and cinched it to his waist; he loaded the riot gun with a half dozen worn shells, slapped a magazine into the .45 pistol and holstered it. He stepped outside as the detail of miscreants marched off, Garson trailing, riot gun cradled in his left arm. His mind whirled as the prisoners ate; he was tempted to snatch a piece of toast. It was well past nine that morning when he and Schuster returned prisoners to their cells.

While Garson thought that was the end of it, he was shocked, as were others, that Judson had subsequently submitted a "Mast Report Slip," an innocuous looking five-by-eight inch Navy Department form that initiated disciplinary action. A sheaf of such blank forms usually resided harmlessly in the duty NCO's desk; Garson and others paid them scant heed. Now Judson had cited his name, time, date and place of offense, and detailed the charge that his subordinate had abjectly refused an order. One consolation: No one had signed as a witness.

After the charge was officially filed, the specified judicial procedure prescribed by the Uniform Code of Military Justice for minor offenses was triggered. Garson predictably twisted sleeplessly for nights, curious dreams vague, amorphous – silhouettes, improbable scenarios, like some spare Kabuki play. He was even distracted while on main gate duty, waving vehicles through perfunctorily. If superiors accepted Judson's uncontested version of events, he worried, what consequences would result? In his mind, Garson rehearsed a rebuttal. Time passed with aching slowness until the appointed day.

While the procedure did not approach the drama of "The Caine Mutiny," a movie he'd recently seen in Seattle, he feared that the result would mar his early Marine career. Garson sat on the hallway bench outside the office of the Marine Barracks commander, Captain Cathcart. Judson was inside giving testimony. To still his apprehension, Garson repeatedly fingered the knot of his tie to insure it was centered, and brushed away invisible lint from his uniform blouse.

Then, the door opened, and Judson authoritatively stepped out. Like a hitchhiker, he jerked his fist and thumb over his shoulder, indicating Garson was to enter. Garson did not return his antagonist's grimace, but arose, tugged at the hem of his uniform blouse, and thrust out his thin chest. He marched smartly into the office, stopping before the massive mahogany desk, clapping his heels together with a crack. The captain, dour behind his desk, splayed long fingers on either side of several documents. Gunnery Sergeant Stevenson, the unit's top enlisted man, stood to the side. Almost equine in appearance — narrow head, long, crushed nose, down-turned eyes and brows, large ears – reinforced the room's lugubrious air.

"PFC Garson reporting as ordered, sir!" He tried mightily to remain rigid, hoping that the officer and senior sergeant failed to notice the tremor that worried its way up his calves and stuttered at the back of his neck. He gazed at the familiar, imperious portrait of the Marine Corps Commandant, Lemuel C. Shepherd staring at him from the far wall. He tried to dissemble, to maintain a neutral expression, the way he had in Boot Camp to avoid the DI's attention.

Protocols were observed, and the charge against him was read: Insubordination and refusal to obey a superior's lawful command. Garson was asked to explain what had occurred on that fateful Friday in question. He described his four-to-eight morning watch on Main Gate One: He'd had no morning chow, and would not have eaten at all because the mess hall would have stopped serving before the prisoner detail was concluded. He winced, having spoken in a breathless staccato of words.

He'd not been insubordinate, he averred, but simply tried to explain the situation to the duty NCO. He deliberately failed to name the corporal. Ultimately, he pleaded, he'd followed orders. He thought he discerned in Captain Cathcart's demeanor some understanding and sympathy while he spoke. After a momentary pause, he was summarily dismissed and ordered to wait outside; it had seemed so perfunctory, his Marine future hanging in the balance. In the hall, minutes seemed endlessly – 15 or 20 by his estimation, perhaps many more. Time compressed in such pregnant circumstances. Garson tried to hold fast to optimism that Captain Cathcart would concur to the extenuating circumstance that Garson had presented, that no true insubordination had occurred. Yes, he'd spoken when perhaps he should not have, deserving a reprimand, but no more. Then, the Top Sergeant Stevenson summoned him back into the solemn environment.

"PFC, you have been found guilty of the charge of insubordination of a non-commissioned officer," the officer began. "Have you anything to say before punishment is pronounced?" Garson hesitated, but then resigned himself to the inevitable, knowing any mitigating circumstance would be outweighed by Judson's testimony. Garson shook his head. After a pause, he met the Cathcart's steely gaze.

"No, sir!" His modulation was weaker than intended.

"You are to be reduced in rank from private first class to private." Garson's heart seized, but he tried to display no overt physical reaction. "What's more," the captain continued, "you are to perform 30 days of EPD." Insult added to injury.

He was dismissed without further comment, and departed the office with an aching chest. He'd lost his stripe and would be a slick sleeve again, as in Boot Camp, back to where he'd began over a year ago. In the barracks, when snappishly cutting loose the threads that bound his single uniform chevrons in place, his anger rose. He'd been within weeks of eligibility for the promotional exam to corporal. Now he'd be set back from a NCO rank at least another year. Hope of attaining a third stripe before his first enlistment ended was dashed.

He was required to spend a month of extra police duty, after-hours cleaning the Head, administrative office, the common Duty

Room and other public spaces. Where before he'd been known as "Boondocks," he now gained the sobriquet "Warhead," given to kicking chairs, desks and slamming doors and as he swept, swabbed and policed, muttering and growling at his sorry lot. Small comfort that several of Garson's buddies commiserated, quietly cursing the martinet Judson for such chicken shit charges. The final insult was another week of mess hall duty, as obliged annually of every private and PFC – Garson's third chow hall stint since enlisting. In a final fit of pique, when Garson noted that Judson steeped his cratered face in Aqua Velva after shave, he disposed of his partial bottle of that scent and purchased Old Spice in its place.

He avoided Judson as much as possible during ensuing months, limiting the testy relationship to strict military protocol. He detested the sight of that blocky body, the graveled cheeks and colorless eyes. When Judson gave him an order, Garson responded with all of the faux verbal deference he could muster.

"Aye, aye, *cor-po-ral*." When he deliberately drew out the three syllables, Judson glared.

"No need for such formality, Warhead."

"Name's *Private* Garson, *cor-po-ral*." Garson skirted the limits of insubordination. He hoped to make his superior pause, perhaps even to blink. Judson knew it, but failed to take the bait.

"Dismissed, *Private!*"

"Aye, aye, *cor-po-ral*." Thereafter, the relationship was a standoff, a charged armed truce, Garson never permitting an opening he thought Judson was seeking to ease the tension between them. The Milwaukeean mentioned events back home on occasion, but Garson perfected an expression of disinterest.

Later, one off-duty Sunday, Garson sat on his foot locker. He'd received another letter from Lana. Garson sometimes smiled at the memory of her living room instructions for the common waltz and contemporary steps to the Apple Jack, feet twisting in a popular dance craze, readying him for a Custer High "sock hop." Like Jane Austen's Emma, she'd arranged his first real date with her best friend, Franny. That had led to a tenuous relationship. Lana, popular, vivacious and flirtatious, swam in a pool of boyfriends, bouncing from one to another like a late summer firefly. Garson's best pal, Toby, was among them as was Custer's middle weight wrestling champion, muscled Kowalski.

Lana had been a fairly faithful correspondent since Boot Camp, letters composed in careful cursive with news of school and friends but especially of her accomplishments in dance – on the school stage and at proms. He responded regularly.

"Letter from that sweet piece of ass a yours?" Judson's raspy nasal voice startled Garson as he perused Lana's missive.

"My sister!" Garson replied, too unsettled to add his typical disarming "*cor-po-rol.*"

"Shit, man, I'd love to do a horizontal mambo with that sweet liddle cunnie." Garson tried to disguise his repulsion to the affront, Judson's words and lascivious leer seeming to assault Lana. A fleeting premonition of the scarred corporal pawing and kissing her was excruciating in his mind's eye.

"Don't even look like you," the corporal observed as he strode away. Garson thereafter secured the Lana's photos in a dark recess of his wall locker, gazing at them only when he was certain Judson was absent, perhaps on some foray among Seattle B-girls.

Because of his mother's antipathy toward consumers of alcohol like her brother-in-law Hervé, she often scowled even at movie portrayals of drunks. For her, sobriety was one of the measures of manhood. While not what was called a "souse," Garson's father, until dotage, enjoyed beers and jocularity among denizens of local blue collar saloons.

As a result, Garson never suffered drunks gladly. The idea of losing one's self-control in the thrall of alcohol was anathema to manly self-respect. Yes, on one or two youthful occasions he'd sampled beer or wine, but, like his mother, he considered alcohol-induced loss of self-control a weakness, perhaps even a fatal flaw. Even in the late-life era when he penned scenes of those Marine days, he could count on one hand occasions he'd been swamped by over-indulgence.

One night weeks after his captain's mast, well past midnight as ghostly moonlight bathed the squad bay, Garson was awakened from a deep sleep by the sound of someone shuffling toward his upper bunk, lurching from side to side, bumping wall lockers. Squinting sleepily, he spotted Judson wearing disheveled civvies probably returning from Saturday night liberty. When the shadowed figure staggered to Garson's bunk, he closed his eyes as fetid breath – tobacco and booze, and maybe vomit – assaulted him. Hands grabbed at Garson's bunk and shook it, springs squeaking. The Marine expelled a long overwhelming stench.

"Warhead," the graveled nasal voice slurred. "Hey, Warhead." The inebriated NCO, drunk and apparently belligerent, wavered backward, but righted himself. "Wake the fuck up, Warhead, you fuckin' little pussy, you sorry fuckin' crud. Come on down so I can kick your fuckin' ass." Garson stifled his breath and tightly clamped shut his eyes. His heart thumped and temples throbbed. In those seconds Garson had a vision of himself jumping from his rack, punching fists into Judson's cratered face and knocking him cold. Marines in the squad bay cheered. But he knew he lacked the courage or strength to carry out that Walter Mitty movie scene. He cowered like a balled up hedgehog before a predator.

"I hate your sorry fuckin' guts," the superior spewed. "Didn't like you from the first, big nose and all." Judson swayed inches from Garson's face, breathing audibly from his gaping mouth, assaulting

Garson with his flamethrower breath. The corporal shook the rack again.

"Come on down here, you little fucker." The words were louder, more insistent.

"God dammit, Judson, shut the fuck up and hit the rack." The growling voice of Sergeant Coleman barked in the darkness. Garson's mind rose: His buddy had come to his defense. "Some of us want to get to some fuckin' sleep." Judson tottered beside Garson's bunk, hesitating.

"Okey doke! Okey doke, Sarge." The inebriated corporal muttered. "Fuckin' Spook," he whispered *soto voce* under malodorous breath, only loud enough for Garson to hear.

"Okey doke, man," Judson drew out the word, "*m-a-a-a-n*," then released his grip on Garson's bunk. The corporal staggered away, swiping at his nose and snuffling. When he flopped into his bunk across the squad bay, he failed to remove his civvies. Sonorous groans, snorting and muttering continued for hours. In the weak gray Sunday morning light, Judson was undone and unkempt, reeking like a urine-befouled toilet at a low-life saloon.

Within a few months of the incident, Judson received transfer orders to a new duty station, having "shipped over," reenlisted for an additional six years. Garson was relieved.

During incessant gloomy Pacific Northwest days and murky nights, dampness seeped into his every pore and muscle fiber. Garson found tiny electric gatehouse heaters inadequate to ward off the insidious dank invasion. He often stomped about the tiny sentry enclosures trying to coax warmth into his extremities. Nearly two inches of precipitation were registered daily from January to June, lesser amounts during the remainder of the year. Garson found that virtually year-round, maritime temperatures resembled Milwaukee Aprils. Rarely, even in the heart of Puget Sound summers, did temperatures rise to the 70-degree mark.

Garson's conversations with Coleman over those months ranged through a variety of topics, including their plans for the future.

"What'cha you gonna do when you get out?" Garson asked his buddy. Coleman considered for a few seconds.

"Think I'll take the train down to southern Cal, maybe to L.A. or Dago, see if I can find somethin'. Don' wanna go back to Chi-town. Too fuckin' cold and white. Wanna stay warm. You?"

Garson was quick with his patented response, his plan to follow his mother's dream for him.

"Hope to get the G.I. bill and go to college, to Marquette maybe, become a news reporter, a journalist." He thought the latter description seemed more erudite and professional. He mentioned that his hometown university featured a respected school of journalism. Coleman wondered how that had all come about.

"When I was a kid I saw 'His Girl Friday' with Cary Grant and Rosalind Russell." He'd been permanently impressed with the snappy, sharp-tongued newsies, fedoras propped on their heads, press passes parked in hat bands, phones glued to ears, crackerjack dialogue, clacking typewriters and swirl of newsrooms, shouts of "Copy Boy!" and "Stop the Presses!"

"Thought you was a drop-out."

"Getting' my 'sheepskin,' my GED pretty soon. Maybe my high school'll give me an equivalency diploma. They say Marquette likes vets because they're mature and settled. I'll be 21 when I get out."

"So, you got printer's ink in your veins, Warhead. It's *written* all over your face," Coleman laughed. "Get it?" Garson's facial muscles squirreled momentarily until he caught his buddy's meaning.

"Good plan. I'm countin' on you now, to follow through. Gotta make a way where there is no way." Garson long recalled that trenchant aphorism. "But Marquette's got a lousy football team," Coleman grinned at his innocuous aside.

"I'm ready to turn my back on this spit and polish life," Coleman groused. "You know what they're saying about the Corps now: 'If it moves, salute it; if it don't, polish it.' And chooches like Judson're are makin' the Corps totally chicken-shit. They don't know combat. They're only garrison pogues."

Over time, Garson successfully tested for his GED, the military's General Education Development, and he was awarded his "sheepskin." Knowing his mother would be proud of the achievement, Garson buoyed. He also completed correspondence courses in literature, history and other subjects through the United Armed Forces School, and the Marine Corps Institute in D.C. Once, he was honored in the NAS Whidbey's weekly base newspaper, *Prop Wash*, when his photograph and cutline was prominently printed. Never mind that Garson found the studies not particularly challenging.

The weekly's office was proximate to Marine Barracks, and Garson approached the editor, a navy chief petty officer with gold chevrons and service stripes, indicating perfect conduct for 16 years of service. Several of Whidbey's navy departments reported news about their personnel and activities, and, Garson wondered, might he produce an occasional column about Marine Barracks events, previously publically unreported in the weekly.

Using the by-line "Boondocks," Garson wrote monthly, information columns about events on the Marine calendar, men discharged, transferred and arriving, results of intermural sports teams, and chatty anecdotes about sundry Marines. He titled his reportage "Marine Sidelights." With permission to use the company clerk's desk, he produced articles and reports, and gained confidence in his reportorial skills. He enjoyed being known as the voice of NAS

Whidbey Marines.

Gathering confidence, he was further motivated to monitor classes at Oak Harbor High School as a means to improve his academic standing. The school principal and Captain Cathcart granted him permission to attend classes. He was, after all, of an age similar to the school's upper classmen. While the English teacher introduced him as a Marine, he always wore civvies so as not to call attention to himself; he also sat inconspicuously in the rear row. When duty permitted, he attended two or three classes a week. One midday, as he walked away from the two-story red brick building, he heard a voice call from a hallway window above him.

"Hi, handsome!" her voice echoed from above as he strolled beneath. Thrilled, he turned, gazing at the smiling face of the pale-skinned student with short blonde hair; her elbows were propped on the window sill with fists under her chin. Only in the movies had such a scene ever played out for Garson. He'd never been called "handsome" by any girl. He returned her inviting expression and weakly waved in response.

A week or so later, when he attended a Friday night Oak Harbor football game, he saw the girl again. On the stadium sideline in front of him she stood smiling with the cheerleading squad, her taut athletic body and strong, shapely legs visible below the hem of a pleated purple and gold skirt, bulky sweater emblazoned with "O C," each letter clinging strategically. She waved, jumped and tumbled, and burly boys lifted her onto their shoulders and flung her about. He was attentive only to her, not other girls in the squad. At half time, Garson walked to the concession stand. There she was, waiting in line.

"Hi, again!" she said in a soft, breathy voice. Garson was momentarily taken aback as she thrust her hand toward his; reluctantly, he clasped it. Despite the evening's chill, her hand was warm, even a bit moist.

"I'm Nola. Who're you?" Her buttery blonde hair was worn in the teenaged style of the day. As had been his youthful wont, he was immediately consumed by a beguiling smile of perfect teeth. Her skin was creamy, almost without blemish, cheeks and forearms, he later discerned, "dusted" by fine, nearly invisible pappus. A more accomplished author might call her eyes "limpid" — cerulean, evoking frigid fjords and frozen climes of Nordic ancestors, he thought in distant retrospect. She used only a whisper of cosmetics. Mesmerized, Garson judged only a minor impediment — her nose was blunt, ever so slightly large for her face.

"You a sailor?" she queried.

"Naw, Marine. Guard and security for the navy. Run the brig."

"Brig? You mean the jail?" her eyes went wide. "Sounds dangerous."

"Oh, not really. We don't have a lot of prisoners, well, really dangerous ones anyway." He much later explained that the Marines were prisoner chasers even though they chased no one, instead guarding the inmates at chow and on work details.

"See you again sometime?" It was more statement than question — inviting. She passed a backward movie glance as she strolled away.

After that first meeting, they conversed briefly at one or two more games. Then, to his delight she invited him to a junior class bonfire on City Beach after the season's final game. He readily accepted. There, he met her best friend, Dixie Mae, who sometimes seemed overly attached to Nola, a protector of sorts, a bodyguard perhaps. Large spectacles hung on her tiny nose. She wasn't much taller than five feet while her boyfriend, Rollie, an ungainly but affable six footer, towered over her. His natural reticence and half-framed glasses gave him an owlish, scholarly mien.

And, it seemed, in no more than a month that fall, Nola's social orbit opened for Garson, and their friendship blossomed. Since Oak Harbor had no local transit, he cadged rides from Marine Barracks buddies, or sometimes used "shank's mare," walking to events and rendezvouses. Garson occasionally wondered whether her attraction to him sprung solely from his being a Marine, a stranger in school's social whirl. She was popular, an Honor Roll student, and Garson fretted that should she discover his academic and other shortcomings, the bud would prematurely wither.

In time, Nola invited Garson to meet her family. Like Garson, she was an only child, and her parents were predictably protective, doting on her. He was warmly welcomed into the comfortable two-bedroom bungalow on a leafy Oak Harbor street. Grass and low shrubs were well groomed; space behind the house was given to a vegetable plot punctuated with garden geegaws, whirligigs and a wooden glider.

After Nola's parents were more comfortable with him, they occasionally invited Garson to Sunday dinner when he didn't have duty. Nola's mother was round but diminutive with curly graying hair; she was warm and gracious, an interested conversationalist. Garson made note of an assertion sworn to him, that a mothers physical appearances foretold how their daughter would mature. She wanted to know about her guest's life, home and family, but Garson was less than forthright about his parents' true occupations, noting only that his father was a welder while his mother worked at a restaurant. More, he failed to mention he'd been a lackluster student and prematurely dropped out to join the Marines. Nola's mother smiled, perhaps measuring him as her daughter's potential suitor, especially after he announced he planned to attend college and study journalism after the Marines.

"Write a column for the weekly base newspaper, *Prop Wash*, it's called, about Marine Barracks goings on," he boasted. While he was proud of column inches produced, he knew his was an unimpressive authorship.

Nola's father, an effusive thickset man with a prominent nose and loud voice, given to vignettes of youth in old Oak Harbor, queried Garson about his duties, partial as he was to the military because he'd briefly served in the army between world wars. After one Sunday meal, Nola's mother, to her daughter's dismay, displayed family photos, particularly the stereotypical nude bassinette snapshots of her daughter's infancy – nearly colorless hair, nose already a bit prominent, cherubic grin and unadorned, apply cheeks.

One evening, after Nola's parents had turned in, she and Garson settled onto the commodious chocolate mohair sofa, their backs to the living room bay window. After minutes of inconsequential conversation, Nola dimmed the table lamps, raising Garson's expectations. They embraced. While earlier kisses had been chaste – Garson hesitant to impose the "French" expertise learned from Karen that final night in Los Angeles. This night, Nola exhibited decided eagerness, taking pleasure in gently fondling his lips.

"How'd you get this bump on your upper lip?" Nola murmured, touching the tiny disfigurement. Garson guffawed and pulled her hand away.

"Bike accident. When I was a kid," he replied, uncomfortable with the memory.

"Tell me," she whispered. He reluctantly described the incident when he at age seven or eight, riding the old two-wheeler his father had cobbled together from disparate parts; his parents were never able to afford a new one.

"You were poor?"

"Not exactly." Garson replied tersely before continuing the childhood story about the cracked street concrete that had heaved up after years of freezing and thawing, catching his front wheel, wrenching the handlebars from his grip. He'd been literally launched forward, smashing face-first into the pavement. Nola's lips formed an "O," a palm planted on her cheek. Garson thought the gesture overly dramatic.

"Knocked out. Cold. Loosened some teeth and busted my lip. Ma, my mother, wanted to get it stitched up, which I should've..."

"You didn't go to the hospital?" Nola held the feigned expression of pain.

"Naw, hated the thought of needles and doctors. She tried to get me to the hospital, but I screamed and hollered. So, the lip healed with this bump. Does it look bad?" Nola shook her head, and once again pressed a finger to the abused tissue. Unsaid was his recollection of the long healing process, interrupted many times when he laughed at Sid Caesar and Imogene Coca, Milton Berle and other television comics. He'd tried not to laugh too widely, but often failed, breaking open the scab to start the healing process anew.

"Poor baby." Garson had never been called "baby" by anyone before.

Then, with tongue tip visible between slightly parted lips, she renewed her exploration. Garson was startled when her fingers probed inside his mouth, gingerly touching his tongue. He thrilled with an erotic charge. She was way ahead of him, he thought, not merely flirtatious, but seductive. Way back when, Franny, his first girlfriend, would never have been so bold. And his nascent attachment to Betsy back home was limited to written affections in letters. Why, they hadn't even dated before he'd departed for Boot Camp, Garson rationalized. Another image of Karen Sisko fleeted through his mind.

The sound of stirring from her parents' bedroom pushed Nola and Garson apart. She tugged and straightened her sweater and skirt. Her father shuffled down the hall toward the bathroom, clearing his throat. Minutes later, the toilet flushed and he shambled back to bed. But the interruption broke their mood; both pulled back from the precipice. Still, when Garson walked back to base, thoughts distracted him from his stride. It was obvious that Nola, likely still virginal, must have been aware of what they were generating. But Garson was conflicted: He didn't want to become a Marine only on the make, intent on conquest. Fuck 'em and leave 'em was an oft-expressed Marine Barracks sentiment. He obviously couldn't match her purity, having long since busted his cherry with that Tijuana tart he'd named Catana in print – a secret he'd never reveal to Nola. Still, the thrill he'd experienced with her that night was larded with sensual promise whether *she'd* realized it or not. He didn't take her for a tease.

Nola's blonde hair fairly glowed on sunny days. She wore it two ways – short and shorter – and he favored neither. It was sometimes trimmed boyishly close, reminding him of one of his favorite screen dancers, leggy, lithesome Cyd Charisse; nearly everything but her helmeted bob and slightly outsized nose captivated him – her lustrous smile, full lips, taut athletic form, her lightly burnished skin. He'd often study the photos she gave him, one provocatively posed in a tight, one-piece swim suit.

To Garson's delight, he was invited to Thanksgiving dinner that fall, and enjoyed a sumptuous meal, not having sat down to a homemade civilian repast in over a year.

"Your turkey and stuffing are scrumptious, Mrs. Lundegaard, good as my mother's," Garson effused genuinely. "And your pumpkin pie's perfect. I love the crust." She beamed broadly, and her cheeks reddened. Her husband, fortified by two glasses of wine, clapped loudly. Garson was saddened to give his regrets to the invitation for Christmas dinner as he'd be on guard and brig duty.

As Garson and Nola's relationship deepened, seemingly encouraged by Nola's mother, he saw her as often as duty permitted, once weekly at times. They socialized with her close friend Dixie Mae and the girl's tall and awkward, studious boyfriend, Rollie. Watching flames and shadows at the beach bonfire one evening,

Nola invited Garson to the senior prom. He was at first reluctant, and knew he could manufacture an excuse of duty on base to decline. He was unprepared for such a fancy formal event. He'd gathered a small collection of civvies, but needed to "suit up" for the significant spring gala. Before enlisting, he'd never attended more than Custer High informal sock-hops, and then rarely danced, joining pals kibitzing on the gym's periphery.

"*Pink!* Fuckin' *pink* civvie shirt!" one barracks' wag snorted when Garson tried on his new ensemble. He'd worked out a payment plan at Floyd the Haberdasher in downtown Oak Harbor — $10 down and the same amount each biweekly payday. The one-button gray flannel suit and pink eyelet shirt were augmented with a dark, knitted tie, black socks, pocket square and suede wing tip shoes. It occurred to Garson that this was the first suit he'd ever owned, recalling his mortification when homeroom nuns in sophomore and junior years required that he borrow classmates' jackets for class photos.

Garson was anxious when he, Rollie and Dixie Mae rolled up at Nola's house. Rollie had borrowed his father's three-year-old Buick four-door instead of driving the usual dented, rusty old Ford. Garson's pride swelled at first sight of Nola, stunning in an ankle-length patterned pink satin dress underlain by voluminous crinkly crinolines, tight of waist with an over-the-shoulder bodice. They posed for snapshots in the living room that she later enlarged, colorized and matted for a birthday present. That image fairly glowed in Garson's photo album for years.

At the prom, Garson felt he was on display among the students; he could almost hear comments. Most knew Nola dated a Marine now, a worldly Midwesterner they'd met at social outings, and that set her apart. She seemed in a sprightly mood, he thought, during up-tempo dances, especially the Apple Jack that featured rapid foot shuffles and slides but devoid of contact between partners. Garson was grateful that Lana's waltz instructions from years past served him well. He pulled Nola's body tightly, large hands clasping her tiny waist during waltzes, feeling her movements. Afterward, the couples shared burgers and ice cream sodas at The Canteen.

Nola's mother, who'd waited for her daughter's return, conversed briefly about the evening before turning in. Garson planned to walk back to Marine Barracks at evening's end.

"Don't stay up too late now," Nola's mother admonished. "Call Larson's Taxi when Garson goes back to the base. Number's on the fridge."

Sitting on the sofa, his emotional temperature simmered. Nola parted her lips ever so slightly when kissing; she'd never allowed tongues to touch, to entwine with hers like the Montebello girl. Still, she imparted promise, her body tremulous beneath the crinolines, low moans audible.

"Always thought you had awfully big hands," she murmured, withdrawing from a sensual precipice. "Let's see." She held up her left hand, palm toward Garson's. They mated hands, his fingertips extending far beyond hers, dwarfing her hand. Saying nothing, she interlocked her fingers with his, then examined his palm and gently traced the life line and Pendleton scar.

"They're so nice, so strong," she purred. He held his breath, felt his heart flutter. Garson was mesmerized. She's gonna put my hand on her tit, he thought, fleetingly recalling the incident with Franny in the backseat of Toby's old Buick four-door when he'd fondled her brassiere.

When they kissed again, it was a gentle, unhurried connection. Nola parted her lips a bit more, permitting his tongue shallow access. Hers remained curled toward the roof of her mouth, avoiding contact. Still, the shallow kisses were moist, intoxicating. While they kissed, Nola often placed her hand on the back of his head like a canary on a perch, sometimes wriggling a finger at the edge of his ear.

Still, she held Garson at bay, even though he suspected she yearned for more. But her parents were only a room away. Not that night or any other would they proceed beyond the promising portal. On the front porch, they embraced at length, kisses lingering. When he finally walked away, she remained, watching; he turned several times to observe her and wave at the lovely vision of her in the prom dress, until she was out of sight. Garson ached to know if her thoughts matched his. When he walked through Whidbey's Gate One, flashing his identification to a grinning, winking "Ho-Now" Logan, Garson was in full bloom.

Despite Nola, Garson still occasionally traveled to Seattle on liberty, attracted by the city's offerings especially in the central business district. Like Milwaukee, Seattle was a modest-sized city in which he was comfortable. Not yet known as Emerald or Rain City, with its World's Fair and the soaring Space Needle that would later define it, were only then on drawing boards. While the central commercial area was pinched between the Puget Sound and Lake Washington, it had a modest and familiar feel to Garson.

Usually alone, he frequented the blocks of the city's commercial core that contained buildings ornamented with handsome architectural accents — terra cotta panels and cornices and striking marquees. He was especially comfortable amid Seattle's grand picture palaces with their opulent interiors, plush entryways, plush staircases and multiple balconies. Heavily curtained screens were reminiscent of Milwaukee's downtown Warner, Palace and Riverside theaters and L.A.'s opulent central venues.

"You kin watch movies there," a fellow Marine noted, "then curl up in the seats and sleep all night. No need for hotels. They're open all night long."

Three or four shared liberty with Garson during an early foray to Seattle, about a two-hour journey from Oak Harbor: An hour by bus down Whidbey Island's spine to Port Clinton, then 40 minutes aboard a churning steel Washington State ferry across Puget to Mukilteo followed by a ride south into the city. Puget Sound, separating the mainland from the Olympic Peninsula to the west, was crowded with rocky islands and craggy islets, bays and harbors, coves and inlets, rugged fingers of land. He never ceased to be struck by the coastal scenic landscape, the view of the Olympic peninsula and its verdant peaks, and, to the southeast on clear days, snow-capped Mount Rainier rising majestically.

Typically, liberty Marines took in the expected sights – the busy waterfront ferry docks on Elliott Bay, Pioneer Square on Alaskan Way that harkened back to the Klondike Gold Rush era, and Chinatown and Japantown atop the precipitous harbor steps. Streets that descended precipitously to the bay provided vistas similar to San Francisco. Someone suggested seeing Pike Place Market, but the coterie vetoed the idea, determined instead to explore central commercial thoroughfares with the typical collection of department stores, shops, eateries and seamier environs that might be frequented by available girls. They trooped to Pioneer Square and Pike Place Market, rode streamlined streetcars, and prowled seedier environs.

On his solo weekends, Garson ate at dingy diners among hordes of sailors on liberty from Washington State bases. He purchased gaudy paperback books and saucy pinup magazines. It all reminded him of Moroccan bazaars and Middle Eastern souks in the movies where romance, mystery, danger and adventure beckoned from every thoroughfare and alleyway.

But Garson most particularly traveled alone to Seattle to see movies, Oak Harbor's closet venue rarely screening titles he found appealing. Before enlisting in the Marines, he'd routinely viewed a half dozen movies weekly, at the local Ritz and other neighborhood theaters whose daily and weekend programs always offered two features along with selected shorts, cartoons and newsreels. He'd once calculated he'd seen thousands of titles in his youth. Now, in the past year, movie going had been rare. He hungered to renew his habit.

But to his consternation, current film offerings had lost much of their magic and luster, new Westerns, mysteries and action titles lacking convincing stars, production and narrative of earlier Hollywood. New musicals no longer thrilled him, lacking the artistry of the past. "Too much singing," he decried to buddies, "not enough dancing." Former box office heroes now seemed diminished, and he readily dismissed cheap space and horror films that failed to strike menace. He was impatient with youth-oriented pictures, even ballyhooed blockbusters like "The Outlaw" and "Rebel Without a Cause." More, he sniggered at the portrayal of the Marine Corps in "Battle Cry," as it failed to measure up to the Leon Uris novel that he'd read instead of the school-assigned *Huckleberry Finn*. Now he wondered, had movies changed so much during his year in the Corps? Or had he been changed in his new circumstance?

Traveling one Saturday morning for a solo weekend Seattle liberty, the rattling old jitney from Oak Harbor stopped at the Port Clinton dock to await the ferry crossing Possession Sound to the mainland. From the bus window, he glanced at a used car lot where a dozen nondescript vehicles were parked. Among them beckoned one handsome, lemon-yellow Chevy convertible that virtually glowed in the uncommon summer sunlight; its white top was folded down, and a tiny red flag fluttered from the radio aerial. Like an ancient "Argo" boatman, Garson was drawn like an ancient Greek adventurer to the Siren's song, to the car's soft body lines and toothy chrome grille. He stepped from the idling bus and walked to the car lot. Opening the Chevy's driver's side door, he ignored its unseemly metal creak, paint discoloration and incipient rust spots on one wheel well. He also disregarded deep creases in the much-used leatherette upholstery.

As he strolled around the vehicle, admiring the wide white side walled tires and gleaming bumpers, a man emerged from a tiny shack; sauntering toward Garson, he slipped on a gaudy sports jacket, but failed to tighten an outdated florid tie or close the top button of his shirt; he flipped away a cigarette butt and threaded a comb through his shiny, black hair.

"Sharp car, huh?" he said in a dulcet voice. "'47 Fleetmaster." Garson nodded, trying to dampen his obvious interest. Can't trust used car salesmen, he was long warned. The odor of the salesman's after shave lotion wafted almost visibly.

"Low mileage. Runs like a top." Garson nodded again.

"How much?" Garson asked. "Don't see a price."

"That's the beauty of this machine. Boss says to get seven-ninety-nine, but we can talk, negotiate. Make an offer. I'll take it to him. Got a license? You kin take 'er for a spin right now." Garson said he had, but wasn't asked to produce it. "Keys're in the ignition. Go ahead."

"Can't right now. Ferry's comin' over. I'm headed to Seattle. How long're you open?"

"Six tonight." He pulled a business card from his top pocket, and thrust it at Garson with two fingers.

"Name's Roister." Garson wore civvies. "You a sailor?"

"Naw, Marine at the seaplane base."

"Jarhead, huh? Semper Fi!" Roister returned. "Only fifty bucks'll get you into this clean convert!" He meant as the down payment, of course. Garson reboarded the bus as the ferry backwatered to the dock. Garson took one backward glance at the car as he returned to the bus.

"I kin be here most anytime you want. Come on back, and let's talk."

Like a diamond, the image of the sharp Chevy sparkled in his mind's eye during the weekend liberty. If he owned that car, he could see Nola more frequently, no longer relying on cadged rides, hitchhiking or shank's mare to meet her. He'd have freedom to do things alone with her, perhaps even away from new best friend, Miranda, the smoldering brunette who'd taken the place of Dixie Mae. Miranda wasn't dating anyone, he was told.

It was a rainy Sunday afternoon when Garson returned from the mainland, but the Chevy, its top pulled up, still beckoned lustrously, its Siren song still seductive. For the next several weeks, he calculated the car's cost and how he'd make payments from a paltry private's pay days. There was also the problem of the down payment the salesman mentioned. He discussed his dilemma with "Gar-Gar," the name some had given Henderson, a large, heavy-browed Marine from Tacoma. He offered to loan Garson the down payment, to be repaid over three months with a usurious interest rate. More, Gar-Gar would have use of the Chev whenever he traveled on liberty to his home.

When Garson returned to the Port Clinton car lot weeks later, he was relieved to see the gleaming Chevy still beckoning.

"Hey, good to see ya," Roister shoved his hand forward. "Name again?" Garson hadn't given it during the first encounter, but he responded now.

"Like to buy this car, but I can't afford the price you're askin'. And I'd have to make monthly payments."

"Well, let's see now. What if I say I can sell 'er to you for seven fifty? And I'll throw in the license. I'd need to get the boss's approval for that, mind."

"Tell you what." Garson surprised himself at his boldness. He explained that he had fifty dollars in his pocket now. He could afford to pay $25 a month for the next two years, and that would total $650." Roister gazed at Garson, scratching one stubbled cheek. He told Garson he needed to talk to the boss. While the salesman was away, Garson admired the Chevy anew; it reminded him of his Cousin Bob's 49 Merc convertible of similar color with rakish chrome, fender-mounted trumpet horns.

"Boss says it's a deal, if you sign for 26 payments instead of 24," Roister announced upon his return. Garson quickly calculated the total cost would be $700, a bit more with the interest added in. He momentarily worried that making such payments would leave him with but a few dollars to spend each month – on Nola and other things. Impetuously, he shook hands and signed the contract.

Within an hour, he pulled away from the lot, blue exhaust spewing in the Chevy's wake and the reek of oil redolent as he mis-clutched between second and third gear.

The lemony Chevy became a blessing and a curse. The former began when he drove into Nola's parents' driveway. Despite the gray dampness of the day, he'd taken down the top. She burst from the front door and bounded across the lawn. "You got a car!" she squealed, lips stretched in a broad smile. She quickly took "her" seat. Within days, they posed for photos – Garson and Nola sitting atop the front seat, arms folded. She insisted on another pose, with Miranda. Garson was discomfited.

After only a few dates with Nola, Miranda often in tow, the curse manifested itself. Garson, a worrier by disposition, was sleepless for many nights with concern over car payments and satisfying Gar-Gar's loan. He mulled over his precarious financial situation, recalculating and recalibrating bimonthly paydays in the darkness of pre-dawns. He owed Gar-Gar sixty-five dollars now because of interest on the loan. The $28 monthly car payments would leave him with only a few dollars each month. With virtual pennies for gas, he could socialize with Nola only sparingly now. Troubled thoughts whirled wildly coupled with scenes of her dating some burly football player who owned a car.

Within six months, the pressure of loan payments and failure to pay Gar-Gar more than half of what he owed was suffocating. In his bunk at night, while on guard duty, even when he and Nola dated, the responsibility for the caprice of the Chevy overwhelmed him. After an uncomfortable negotiation, Garson agreed to sign over the car to Gar-Gar in exchange for relief from the debt. He received nothing in return save absolution from worry – and a frayed relationship with Nola. He often paged through his photo album, gazing at numerous images of Nola in her cheerleader togs or posing in swimsuits that hugged her curvaceous figure. His loss, he lamented, was some civilian's gain.

One day over the winter, scuttlebutt circulated that Corporal Judson had shipped over for another six years of Marine service. Garson smiled that his nemesis would soon be transferred away. A week before his departure, Judson confronted Garson in an anemic attempt at rapprochement, he surmised.

"Hey, Warhead, gimme your sister's address now. Maybe I'll write 'er. Got a 30-day leave comin'. I'll look 'er up when I get back home. I'll tell 'er me and you're great buddies." What temerity, Garson thought, shuddering at the possibility of Judson wooing Lana. "I'm just sayin', wouldn't it be somethin' if I was your brother-in-law?" Garson responded to the galling prospect with a repulsive chortle.

"She's got a boyfriend, *cor-po-ral!*" In the weeks that followed, he sometimes awakened in darkness, promising himself that when he'd be discharged and returned home, he'd find the repugnant Judson in Milwaukee and kick the fuckin' shit out of him. But when he remembered these matters in the lateness of life, and determined to write about them, he hoped Judson might read his words and understand them as verbal vengeance. Garson took no notice when the acned menace finally departed Marine Barracks. He recalled no one lamenting

Emblematic of Marine Barracks' changing character was that more Marines now transferring in wore only a single decoration on their uniforms, the National Defense Service ribbon, pejoratively dismissed as the "Fire Watch Ribbon," signifying only that they served in the military.

Seldom heard in Marine Barracks Whidbey now were tales of combat, of the Inchon landing and the breakout from the Chosin Reservoir, or other glories of the Korean conflict. The truce brokered before Garson enlisted still held. Garson fretted that he and his "fresh fish" buddies were becoming soft, peacetime pogues. He worried that he and his unseasoned buddies weren't up to the daunting task of defending the nation against Soviet and Chinese enemies. Most conversation and exchanges seemed to focus on youthful hijinks and escapades, shared experiences of families and girls back home, and fresh, local affairs of the heart.

While Marine Barracks remained predominantly white, a scattering of black and brown and mixed faces were added to the photo panel of Marine Barracks personnel posted outside of the company commander's office.

"Why you 'allas' talkin' 'bout chow, man?" was Ortega's favored reaction when barracks' discussions centered on girlfriends, as most invariably did. He was among the newer Marines recently transferred in to replace draftees and veterans, short timers like Coleman and O'Toole.

Ortega was a slender sliver, the thin stalk of his neck containing an active Adam's apple that bobbed when he swallowed and laughed. The back of his pineapple head was flat, lacking cranial convexity; buddies chortled that the gap between his head and the sentry helmet was comically a yard wide. It was also readily apparent that Ortega's four front teeth were "replacements" — Marine Corps issue like Garson's rear lower denture. The Puerto Rican's teeth, Chiclette-like, gleamed whiter than the natural ones, and silver grounding clamps flashed when he smiled. He had a habit of popping the appliance loose with his tongue and holding it saucily between his lips. Most prominent was Ortega's aquiline nose that created a classic hooked profile.

"So, Hoss, we're P.R.'s, man, Puerto Ricans." He called everyone "Hoss," and many words and expressions sounded purposefully exaggerated.

"Don' bother me now, Hoss. Gotta 'chine' my 'choos'," he often proclaimed. Garson was convinced the stereotypical movie accent was an affectation. Always affable, Ortega usually seemed to be holding something back, his true self hidden behind linguistic posing and posturings of the Mexican movie actor Cantinflas.

"Now, where you from then, Hoss?" When Garson specified Milwaukee, Ortega's bulging black eyes bored in.

"Mili-wau-key?" he stammered to Garson's guffaw. Garson then realized that he and other Badger Staters mispronounced their own city's name, giving English words a Germanic cast.

"*Mill*-waukee," Garson stressed. "Near Chicago."

"Ahh, Chicago. Ceety of big shoulders," Ortego brightened. It was then obvious that Ortega was more knowledgeable than his masking verbal affectation. "So, Mili-wau-key makes Schlitz beer. Right, Hoss? We Caribes, P.R.'s, very much like Schlitz." Garson characterized his hometown, exaggerating that it was a cold place on a cold Great Lake.

"So, Hoss, tell me more 'bout your 'ceety,'" rejoindered.

"We got probably two seasons: Winters with snow and ice, and a few months of summer." Ortega said he'd been amused when Wisconsin Marines he knew mentioned "bubblers" instead of drinking fountains, sodas instead of pop, and other curious words. He laughed that Wisconsin guys like Garson said "dees," "dose" and "dat" instead of "these," "those" and "that."

Milwaukee couldn't match the verdant, crystalline beauty of Seattle and the Puget Sound, of course, but Garson's hometown did have sparkling Lake Michigan and a curving bay that some claimed was reminiscent of Florence, Italy. The house of his birth and upbringing, a common bungalow, was situated several miles west of the fine blue lake, and as a kid he'd marveled at the ranks of palatial estates that perched above the shoreline – Victorian manses with cupolas, corner towers, oriel windows, broad porches and ornate entryways, all done up with terracotta accents and adornments, the manses of corporate barons and politicos.

To Ortega and others who were patient, Garson described his

city's gridded streets west of the Milwaukee River, the ordinary neighborhoods he'd explored when movie going took him to scores of city theaters or downtown to the grand movie palaces displaying strikingly-ornamented exteriors, opulent marble and brocade interiors and multiple balconies. During Garson's youth, Milwaukee boasted many score "showhouses," as locals called them, where playbills included double features and much more.

"Cold you said, Hoss?" Ortega interrupted. Most Marines from sunnier climes were particularly interested in that aspect. Garson did his best to describe the frozen blasts that swept down on his town from Canada and the Arctic, keeping the city in an unremitting icy embrace from Thanksgiving almost to Memorial Day.

"Only once did Milwaukee give up — the blizzard of '47 when I was ten." Garson enjoyed telling the tale, embellishing details for astonished warm weather buddies. The late January tempest dropped many feet of snow, and blizzard winds piled it into mountainous drifts, many ten feet or higher. "My dad took the streetcar home but it got stuck, and he slept on it all night. Walked home the next morning. The only time Milwaukee surrendered." A month passed before everything returned to normal. "We can usually handle winters, and we keep moving no matter what," he boasted proudly.

"We're Americans, Hoss, citizens," Ortega averred. His home city was Mayaguez, but Garson had no notion where that was. "You took us over after that war – the war with Spain." Garson was uncomfortable with the inference of historical guilt. The spindly Marine added that he hoped his island would gain independence. "We belong with Cuba and Caribbean islands, not the States," he said, eyes intent.

"One of a thousand facts hardly worth knowing, Hoss." Ortega concluded that conversation. Garson was never certain whether his buddy still played him for a gullible naif.

"Why you wanna *chiquita* like that anyways?" queried another of the recently transferred Marines as he admired Garson's snapshots of Karen Sisko, the pretty Montebello girl with whom he continued correspondence.

"Man, you should just get yourself some California *rubia*, a blonde" the young Marine sneered. Like Ortega, Moldanado's complexion reminded Garson of swarthy screen actors; and while he was reticent to suggest it, Garson thought the new buddy would be a perfect movie villain. But Moldy, as he was called, was a Mexican Angelino.

Moldy's heavily-lidded eyes were invariably set at "half mast," creating a first impression of condescension and malevolence. More, his face was marked with raised scar tissue that angled over an inch below his right cheekbone. And the intersection of his left thumb and forefinger bore a handmade tattoo that some called a sign of *pachucos*. A few called him "Bat" because of the flare and sharply pointed ears.

Despite their arm's length relationship, Garson was troubled by Moldy's continual wheedling for Karen's address. For months, Garson resisted importunings, feeling protective of the girl who'd introduced him to smoldering kisses and irresistible fantasies; conjured troubling visions of his buddy dating Karen, just as he had when Judson prodded about Lana. Garson saw Moldy romancing Karen in some ham-handed way. Garson sometimes repressed guilt because he continued steady correspondence with Karen while dating Nola. He felt his fidelity was suspect.

In every command in which Garson served was one buddy referred to as "Baby Marine." This role had been filled in Boot Camp by him and cherubic Krupa. Nearing the halfway point in his enlistment, Garson had taken on a noticeable patina of maturation. He now needed to shave every three or four days instead of a week.

At Marine Barracks, NAS Whidbey smooth-cheeked Ramirez was

considered the company's most juvenile member. Less than a year past his seventeenth birthday (although some surmised he hadn't yet reached proper enlistment age) he stood only a few inches above minimum Corps-required height. His cropped dark hairline descended nearly to his brows, and he was given to brushing a hand over the short locks, searching, it seemed, for its former leonine fullness. His squinty eyes were rheumy, as though he should have been issued glasses. One of the most insular and impressionable Marines Garson had ever encountered, he often became a foil for a few of the supposedly worldly set. But he bore jests and jibes with patience and good humor, and was a steady, dependable Marine.

When Garson saw the James Dean film "Rebel Without a Cause," he immediately thought of Ramirez whose fresh face and bovine eyes were reminiscent of Sal Mineo. Ramirez revealed that his family lived in San Pedro, and that family fished for a living. An older brother had been killed on Iwo Jima.

"I joined because 'a him." Dark eyes clouded beneath brushy brows when he spoke of his sibling. He rarely dwelled on that loss, however.

"*Mamasita'd* like ta' start a *pequeña* taco shack," Ramirez said. "Says she kin do better than those Anglo outfits like Taco Bell that're opening up all over now. They ain' real tacos anyways. Maybe some'a you'd like ta' come an' try her *lunche* when she opens." Garson's photo album contained several images of the tiny Marine.

Garson's movie-going frequency had diminished dramatically, of course, Marine duty not permitting anywhere approaching the thousands of movies he'd seen in his youth. Oak Harbor offered only the one, a utilitarian venue open only four evenings plus Saturday and Sunday matinees. Even weekend liberties to Seattle afforded limited time to view more than a handful of films.

For Garson, movies had begun to lose the luster of his former life, perhaps because he'd viewed them only fitfully since enlisting.

He was certain that he'd already viewed the best films anyway — the great John Ford and Howard Hawks Westerns, the murky and unsettling film noir works of directors Siodmak, Dmytryk, Ray, Huston, Hathaway and others with Mitchum, Lancaster, Ida Lupino, Yvonne De Carlo and Gloria Graham portraying flawed and doomed protagonists. The great cinematic adventures of Mowgli, Robin Hood, Walter of Gurnee and Scaramouche would never be eclipsed in his mind. Even movie musicals that had thrilled him in boyhood now lacked the earlier artistry of Astaire and Rogers, Gene Kelly and Eleanor Powell. There was too much singing and folderol now, not enough splendid dancing.

He'd grown impatient with the new technical trickery of 3-D, Cinemascope and VistaVision that had overwhelmed impressionable story-telling and credible screen characters. His Boot Camp mentor, Ridley, the California college boy, would agree, he surmised.

"Getting lush," was the legend Garson printed under a series of album photos taken at an impromptu beach outing by a gathering of off-duty enlisted men who celebrated the Marine Corp's November birthday. None had cash for liberty because payday was still five days away. They assembled on a typical gray, raw late afternoon on a narrow apron of sand south of Ault Field's old concrete landing ramps, amid driftwood tangles and straggly beach grass. One of-age Marine had purchased a case of Schlitz beer. Cans popped and frothed as a lone rusty church key passed hand to hand. When the late autumn light began to fade, Garson and others piled up some shoreline driftwood, preparing a bonfire.

"Hail, Mother Marine Corps," they shouted as flames swirled and sparks spiraled, borne by on-shore breezes.

"How many years now?"

"One-eighty?"

"No, no, man, one-hundred-seventy-nine," a respondent slurred.

"Semper fuckin' Fi!" the assembly saluted with brews held high.

As was her wont in the trying days following the foreclosure on the family home, Garson's mother wrote sparingly, emotions nearly visible in her sad script. His father's confection business continued to fail. After they had been forced from Garson's childhood home, his parents relocated into cramped living space on a farmhouse nearly an hour drive north of Milwaukee. She maintained her dish washing job at Shorty's Restaurant, its meager salary necessary to pay bills. Sometimes, she bade her husband to drive past the pretty bungalow they once owned without mortgage that had provided years of comfort for the family.

More galling, when out-of-town business prevented Garson's father from returning to the city, she was forced to hire virtual strangers to transport her to and from work. She took pitiful solace only that she'd saved a prized household possession, a ceramic sunburst wall clock that had for years hung in her living room.

"It was the last thing I took from our house when we left," she shakily wrote in one letter. "I carried it on my lap all the way here." Garson remembered the gaudy timepiece, almost feeling the bitterness that would remain between his parents for the remainder of their lives.

In the final letter he'd received, his mother had promised she'd reveal a surprise when he returned home for an impending 30-day leave.

Chapter 3

INTERREGNUM

Briefly Back Home

Garson gazed into Lana's wide eyes – cerulean, as he'd imagined since being away in the Marines — but changeable to cobalt, cornflower, aqueous blue or other shades depending on her mood and humor, depending on the angle from which he viewed her. Save for the photos she'd mailed to NAS Whidbey, he'd not seen her in two years. Seventeen now, and a senior at Custer High, Lana had added comely curves to those evident in teasing snapshots she'd mailed him at MCRD. When Garson had departed, she still insisted on calling him "Li'l Brother," regarding him as a sibling instead of a suitor, maintaining the arm's-length relationship he long detested. Why was her legion of suitors more desirable than he?

If he'd carefully searched his motivations for enlisting two years past, he may have discerned that impressing Lana was among them.

Garson had stepped down from the Milwaukee Railroad's Olympian Hiawatha streamliner at the downtown depot a week before that evening with Lana. The two thousand-mile train journey from Seattle had commanded nearly a month's pay even though he rode coach. He carried only a small AWOL grip bag with a pair of khaki trousers, toiletries and changes in skivvies. He'd eschewed his uniform because its sleeve was mortifyingly devoid of chevrons after his demotion. He'd blanched at the first look at the diner car's menu, its prices daunting. During the three days aboard, he'd eaten sparingly, scrambled eggs and sandwiches each day, and left only a few coins for tips. He'd been awed in the observation car that revealed breathtaking Cascade vistas and, later, precipitous Rocky Mountain prospects and historic locales associated with Lewis and

Clark discoveries and the Custer fight. The journey west to San Diego two years past had been less scenically spectacular.

When he arrived, his parents, expectantly, had been overjoyed even though neither had fully accepted his decision to quit school and enlist. On the day of his arrival, his round, diminutive mother had been permitted to depart her dishwashing job at Shorty's restaurant early; she'd cooked a pot roast dinner with mashed potatoes.

The house, in which Garson had been raised, of course, had been lost in foreclosure while he was away. Ma and Dad had worked tirelessly during the World War and after to retire the mortgage and squirrel away a few thousand dollars in U. S. savings bonds. But anger was written on her fleshy face and intruded upon conversations: She wouldn't stop blaming Dad and his business ineptitude for their current precarious financial plight. She'd rented a commodious lower flat, larger than the former bungalow, in the same North Milwaukee neighborhood for his return — three bedrooms instead of two with a cavernous kitchen, dining room and a bright, sunroom that welcomed mellow morning sun.

She tucked the narrow bed of his youth with cotton flannel sheets; the bedding's stale odor, from storage somewhere, he surmised, didn't deter him from luxuriating in its warm embrace; he tunneled beneath the bedding against Milwaukee's autumn evening chill. He hadn't slept in a normal bed in two years, and wasn't discomfited by the absence of the reveille bugle call. He arose at eight, much later than he was accustomed. The house was empty as his parents had already departed for work.

To his mother's delight, Garson displayed the little plastic Christ Child statuette that she'd pressed upon him at the train depot when he'd departed for MCRD. She was somewhat chagrinned that one of its hands had broken off, and its colors faded.

"Brought me luck though, Ma, er, Mom. At the MCRD and

Whidbey Island rifle ranges. Carried it with me almost everywhere." He felt a pang of guilt for that lie. "But I'll leave it home with you now 'cause I want to make sure it doesn't get lost down the road." His mother still fussed over being called "Ma."

During the month home, Garson and his father drew a bit closer in amicable conversations and humorous memories. He asked about Garson's experiences in the Marines, about California and the Pacific Northwest. A little pride arose from his father's interest. Dad had traveled no farther than Chicago in his entire life. Once or twice during the month home he accompanied his father who still delivered popcorn to a few remaining local customers. He particularly recalled the Negro-owned bar they visited — Toran's Tropical Hut, near the old Bronzeville neighborhood; its name was betokened by the décor – palm fronds, coconuts and framed images of Caribbean beaches and cabanas and bikinied beauties.

After the World War, Black folks had emigrated by the tens of thousands, fleeing festering Jim Crow violence, segregation and discrimination in the South; no matter that they were greeted by only somewhat less overt circumstances in northern cities. Many had been drawn to Milwaukee, known as the "Machine Shop of the World," where heavy industry now employed more workers than the city's celebrated breweries. Negro neighborhoods expanded west and north into former German wards, where most housing dated from the turn of the century or earlier. Owners, often absentee landlords who'd fled farther west or into contiguous suburbs, rented the old properties to Negroes and poor white residents. Properties were sometimes left to deteriorate. Not many years after Garson's permanent return to his hometown, purulent problems of housing and education segregation exploded in protest and violence.

Garson's father exhibited a gregarious demeanor at Toran's. He'd always had a ready laugh. Garson took note of the handful of gray-haired retired habitués, second and third shifters who fortified themselves with a quaff or two before and after work in odiferous Menomonee Valley foundries. It wasn't unknown for his father to play a good natured game of snooker with such denizens.

"You sell a bag or two of popcorn, then buy a round of drinks, throwing away your profits.' Garson remembered his mother's criticism. "That's no way to run a business." His father's perspective seemed to be longer term, Garson came to appreciate, as he tried to build good relations and loyalty with customers. The day of their delivery the barkeep purchased three bags of the confection for the countertop dispenser – a dollar and a quarter for each two-and-a-half-peck bag.

Within a day or two of his arrival home, Garson strolled to the old block, its houses, alleys and driveways as familiar as the lines in his palm. In youth, he recalled, he'd determined to create a map of neighborhood, pacing off distances like Lewis and Clark; but he'd never found a sheet of the paper large enough to accommodate all of the geographic details.

While reacquainting himself with 41st Street, Garson slowed his step as he approached the former family bungalow. It seemed small two years after he'd departed, even a bit forlorn despite a recent coat of paint to the trim. His mother's bordering hastas and other perennials had also been revivified. He was tempted to enter the rear yard to determine if her cherished rhubarb plants had been similarly rejuvenated. That had triggered a piquant recollection of her delightful pies whose aroma had often permeated the entire house; an attendant vision came alive, of her rolling out leftover dough, sprinkling it with sugar and cinnamon and baking it into Garson's favorite delicacy.

More memories briefly welled up as he walked, of cousin Kenny and his parents, Aunt Lucille and Uncle John, Garson's godfather and favorite, who visited to celebrate Garson's first communion. They'd posed on the tiny front porch, and Kenny's golden wavy hair cascaded to his shoulders. Garson had never understood why his aunt permitted the hair to remain uncut until be started school. There was unrelated memory as he passed the old house that caused Garson to grin, of his mother's amusing ceramic goose she'd named Gertie that stood regally on the porch in every winter storm mantled in a snowy gown and tiara of rime.

Who now occupied the back bedroom – *his bedroom* — Garson wondered, retaining proprietary interest. Had his mother's off-white walls been papered over in some flossy pattern, had his broken closet door been repaired, had his window blinds been replaced with curtains or drapes, and the floor carpeted? The abode's spirit tugged at him. He recalled the comfort of the Soo Railroad freight line that nightly rumbled through the neighborhood, its mournful horn assuring him all was well. Another memory beckoned, of soothing summer symphonies struck up by insects and amphibians in the swamp below the raised train embankment.

In her remaining days, his mother never revisited the house again, nor would she forgive her husband for "stealing" it from her.

Toby, Garson's youthful pal, still lived across street, having never left home. While amiable, Garson was disappointed in his former pal: He was one of those who'd not joined the military. And the nurse Viv, who'd probably saved his life at age five or six, stitching shut the bloody gash in Garson's scalp at her kitchen table, still resided in a corner house.

In time during those weeks on leave, Garson encountered more changes to his former north side neighborhood. The dairy farm a mile west where his parents had purchased milk and eggs was now a graded open field, preparations being made for municipal public housing like Park Lawn. Beyond that, other nascent subdivisions were arising, formerly gridded streets and alleys in older sections giving way to curving thoroughfares, low ranch houses with driveways and wide lots that opened more space between neighbors.

"You hang out on Villard?" had been an oft-posed query by adolescents from other city neighborhoods. "You part a' that gang over there? Ain' it dangerous?" During the war, the avenue had been the locus of a band of ruffians who'd engaged in public drunkenness, thievery, robbery, assaults and miscellaneous mayhem. But when Garson was an adolescent, the petty criminals had been dealt with by police and courts. But the iniquitous repute lingered, lending caché to later habitués who frequented "The Burg," as commercial strip became known – after the German word *burgher*, meaning citizen. Garson and his contemporaries hadn't engaged in much more than prankish behavior. "Pacified" after the war, Villard had become a focal point for gathering, socializing and cruising, in cars and afoot, creating movie screen scenes portrayed by George Lucas for a later generation.

When Garson temporarily returned in the autumn of 1955, Villard's storefronts and shops had changed little, Garson mused as he ambled along the busy thoroughfare: Wilbert's Bakery, famous for its cream-filled coffee cake, remained popular and stable. Passing Pittleman's Market next door, he smiled with the memory of pilfering a case of Schlitz shortys, 24 seven-ounce bottles, from a sidewalk display, and sprinting down the gangway, into the alley and away to Smith Park where he for the first time tasted beer with pals. It wasn't to his liking and never would be.

Across the street, Winkie's Five-and-Dime, with its creaking, warped wooden floors was still a fixture, as was August Abe Funeral Home (from which in three decades Garson buried his parents), Kozol's Men's Shop, Lecher's Bowling Lanes, Militzer's Malt Shoppe and the Slovenian sausage store remained in business. One block east stood cramped Dean's Sports Shop and farther, diminutive Isaac Sager's widely popular Shorty's Restaurant where Garson's mother washed dishes; she'd finagled a busboy job for him there. At the intersection of Villard and Teutonia Avenue the garish neon of Towne Pride Custard stand still glowed; Lana still carhopped there summers, wearing roller skates and a fetching short pleated skirt that attracted too many approving male eyes to suit Garson. To the north of the main intersection with North 35th Street stood the dowdy A&P supermarket, his mother's preferred food store, and the storefront public library where earlier in life he'd poured over books about American Indians and pirates, the latter illustrated, he still recalled, by Howard Pyle. Farther north almost at Silver Spring Drive was Franny's house.

Perhaps it'd been one summer night, unlike now, when trees were fully leafed, mottling dim light along the Smith Park pathway, that Franny Ocowicz – or had it been Leora, Leora Hobowitz (as a writer of advanced years, his grasp of such details had grown less reliable). Garson had surprised himself by embracing her. But he'd been too timid to kiss. He and Leora had "dated" only once thereafter: They'd ridden the street car downtown to the Riverside or Warner Theatre, two of the several palatial motion picture houses downtown. Afraid of removing his right arm from her shoulder during the double feature, his limb, numbed with needles; it had grown useless when they arose to depart. He'd reflected that her tiny hands were uncommonly rough, their tips spoon like. Why he'd found this disconcerting he was uncertain, but it may have been the reason their breakup hadn't bothered him overmuch.

For Garson, Villard Avenue's crown jewel, albeit a gem of lesser prize, remained the Ritz Theater where he'd spent thousands of hours watching moving pictures, mostly unaccompanied because he detested distraction. This has been his temple of art, culture and education — after his parents, selected relatives and a few pals, his source of his character formation. The old marquee where he'd often observed men on tall ladders mounting cast iron letters for the next day's features had been replaced by a utilitarian vertical sign proclaiming a new, common identity — the Villa, after the street name. As in youth, he now scrutinized exterior movie posters for current and future programs, ruminating how, on fall Saturday afternoons like this, he'd purchased tickets in bright sunshine, but became depressed after sitting through two features, coming attractions and selected shorts, that daylight had ended.

Garson's mother had introduced him to the "pictures" at an impressionable age during the World War, at Tuesday "Dish Nights;" each admission also garnered a piece of tableware, a different pattern each year. Domestic dramas, "weepies" as some called them, had been the bill of fare — romantic fillips starring Sonja Heine or Deanna Durbin, screwball comedies with Jimmy Stewart, Spencer Tracy, Cary Grant paired with Katherine Hepburn, Jean Arthur, Roseland Russell; creations of Frank Capra, George Cukor, Preston Sturges, Howard Hawks and Billy Wilder. But his mother had been turned away from darkening post war dramas, stark creations of Howard Hawks, John Huston, Edward Dmytryck, Jules Dassin, *film noir* it came to be called, riven with skepticism and ambivalence.

"So, your mom tells me you got a girlfriend now," Lana mused. They sat in her unheated sunporch, the October temperature had precipitously submerged with the setting sun. Garson recalled a similar time from the past, when he'd unintentionally interrupted Lana and one of her parade of paramours, the muscular Custer High wrestler named Kawolski, from what Garson regarded as an overly-fevered evening interlude. Lana had later thanked him for the intrusion.

Lana had always been as Austen's Emma Woodhouse, ever prepared to play matchmaker for boys like Garson who lacked the courage to carry their own water. Indeed, she'd mated Garson with his first girlfriend, Franny. Yes, it had been Franny, his recollection was certain now. The girls, he and Toby had for a time been a foursome for Friday night Custer football games, school sock hops and nights at the Ritz. Toby's familiar "gray ghost," the ponderous 15-year-old Buick four-door known for its primed livery, had also carried them to what Garson regarded as inchoate romantic interludes at "Neckers' Point" on the Lake Michigan shoreline. This had been a favorite haunt of liberty sailors from the Great Lakes training base. Garson was invariably envious of Lana and Toby's front street rustlings. In contrast, Franny had been demur and resistant, less than eager for back seat strivings.

There was another years-old incident that elbowed its way forward in Garson's recollection while on leave, a clandestine one that had fueled imaginings about Lana: One late night after sitting through a Ritz double feature alone, he'd walked home through yellow pools of street lighting. When he'd passed the alley behind Lana's house, he noticed light streaming from her bedroom window, and furtively crossed into her back yard. Careful not to approach too closely, his legs jellied, for framed as in a movie screen was Lana, wearing only white brassiere and panties. She danced and undulated before a full-length mirror, like a seductive serpent, like Hedy Lamarr's Delilah. Nearly breathless with pulse throbbing in his ears, Garson was entranced for minutes, unable to free himself from the peeping-tom vision. Then he'd been startled by Lana's mother's voice, and the bedroom light was doused.

Of course, Garson had laid awake that night and others that followed, replaying Lana's performance, wishing he'd been there in the room with her, expressing his ardor, coaxing her passion to life. He'd desired more than mere brotherly affection, almost as now.

"Yeah," Garson had replied emphatically to Lana's question about a girlfriend, hoping to stir envy in her. "Betsy. Knew her from Messmer. We were in the same homeroom. Let me copy her homework." Betsy lived on the west side of Milwaukee, had graduated from St. Sebastian grade school to Messmer, the Catholic high school. He'd been virtually hypnotized by her luminous smile of perfect teeth (his were dull from lack of consistent care), bottomless black eyes, tight black hair that ended at the nape of her neck, and pulchritudinous shape. She'd been called "Tiny" for her diminutive height. While, to Garson, her coloration seemed Italian, her family name was German. But more, Garson had been taken with her unflagging sociable manner and academic achievements. They'd never dated while in school, Garson too intimidated in fear of rejection from so perfect a girl; he'd also lacked any but bus and streetcar transportation. Yet, she'd written what he took to be an endearing comment in his junior yearbook.

"So, what's she like?" Lana's interest was obviously piqued. Garson did his best to describe Betsy. He related that he'd begged an old classmate to obtain her address before he'd departed

Milwaukee, and had written her a letter while at Camp Pendleton. To his delight, she'd responded, and a correspondence had been initiated – not a robust one on her part; but she answered some of his missives. To his surprise while at NAS Whidbey, she'd mailed him a colorized eight-by-ten graduation portrait in a leatherette frame that he'd prominently propped in his wall locker, garnering admiring comments from Marine Barracks buddies. His intentions toward Betsy had intensified into yearnings and romantic designs.

"Hopes to go to Milwaukee Downer College," Garson informed Lana. "Plans to be a school teacher."

"So it's serious, then?" Lana queried. She was adept at such wheedling, Garson recalled. He couldn't be certain, but he thought that he discerned a shift in the coloration of her eyes, as though Lana might be reconsidering their oft-proclaimed sibling relationship. He didn't doubt, even though he hadn't admitted it, that she may have sensed that he was "experienced" now, having been deflowered by the comely Tijuana tart.

Yes, Betsy. Over months of correspondence with her, Garson had sometimes considered their relationship. Was she a mere pen pal, a fixation of the printed page — or more? Some of his Milwaukee pals and acquaintances who Lana had mentioned in her missives were in committed relationships now, a few even engaged, one or two nearing marriage. He'd mentioned Betsy to his mother, constructing an image that would secure her approval. The critical issue was religion: Betsy was Catholic. No matter how frequently Lana's mother, the widow, had championed Lana and Garson as a couple, Garson's mother had demurred because of the ludicrous impediment: She was Protestant, a Grand Canyon chasm for his mother.

For a frisky Marine of 19, Garson thought he was typical. But, while girls and matters of the heart were predominant among concerns of the day, there were other topics close to hand. Even before he'd departed Whidbey, he seen photos and reports of Ford's striking new sports car called the Thunderbird, a 1955 two seater in sea blue with removable hard top and side glass portholes, rear fenders topped with fins, dual exhaust pipes poked from the rear bumper were seductive. Broad, bleach-white sidewalls and a shrouded spare tire were perfect accents. It beckoned even more than the lemon yellow '47 Chevy he'd briefly owned at NAS Whidbey. When a salesman approached Garson when he visited the Ford dealer on Capitol Drive, announcing the car's price, Garson blanched. But he determined to put money aside each payday for a down payment over the final years of his enlistment.

"Those L.A. highways," Toby pronounced in one of their conversations; "Milwaukee's gonna build freeways like that soon enough. Gonna be a big time city one day," he predicted smugly. Bold plans and prospective images of such entangling spaghetti highways had been depicted in local newspapers, and Garson projected a vision of himself in a sparkling new Thunderbird, tooling along with its top down.

"Oh, I doubt, it," remarked Garson, forcing skeptical superiority in his conversations. Los Angeles, even Seattle, seemed much more sophisticated and liberal than his dowdy hometown. Their youthful friendship had sometimes been troubled, Garson now recalled, particularly when, after acquiring the mobility of a car, Toby found daring new pals like Chet, the hard-eyed confidant who'd considered Garson a "little punk." Chet had accompanied Toby one summer on their great Route 66 adventure to California, returning with what Garson had considered wildly fanciful yarns. He'd been there and knew better. Chet was another of those laggards who'd failed to enlist.

"Your dad still turn his car engine off and coast half a block home? To save some gas?" Garson chortled when he and his childhood pal conversed. Garson's parents always mused at the miserly World War habit that was the talk of the block. A mailman, Toby's dad even now remained a ham radio enthusiast, communicating through a towering roof antenna and from a basement bailiwick that, in Garson's childhood, seemed secretive and dangerous with its arcane language, boggling array of amplifiers, speakers and dials.

Because he'd departed NAS Whidbey a week before biweekly payday and had paid a hefty sum for the train ticket, Garson arrived home with only minimal cash in hand. He was reluctant to ask his parents for money, aware of the precarious state of their finances. Isaac "Shorty" Sager, the local restauranteur paid minimal wages, and Garson's father's snack business had deteriorated, as he now delivered to only a handful of customers in the wreck of a battered panel truck.

"Hey, wanna make a few bucks?" Toby asked one day. His boyhood pal was in business for himself now – construction, he boasted. He was erecting a concrete retaining wall for a parking lot near the Milwaukee River, he said, and offered Garson five bucks a day for help. The pals worked for several days or perhaps a week, shoveling and scraping away the remnants of an old foundation. Garson thought Toby was careful with measurements, but finally stunned that the concrete block wall they constructed seemed to meander instead of running true, its top row undulating. He felt guilty accepting Toby's payment. After he returned to NAS Whidbey, one of Lana's letters mentioned that the new retaining wall was quickly demolished by Toby's disgusted employer. Not long after, his old pal would follow his brother-in-law to Alaska, starting a company building man holes in a muddy town called Homer.

Preston and Rusty, with whom Garson had enlisted, were still stationed with Marine Air wings on both coasts. Garson was dejected that they had only one more year in service while he had two. Many others with whom he'd socialized in the past had enlisted in the army or air force after graduation. Several girls were exclusively involved with servicemen. Lana was now a senior at the new Custer, the sprawling single story high school, now called a "campus," on Sherman Boulevard. The cramped former neighborhood building now served as a junior high called Edison.

Missing on the block, of course, was the former ramshackle dwelling of the neighborhood tatterdemalion, the ragged, odiferous *eminence Gris* known to kids as "Deaffy." Only Lana had ever claimed she'd spoken. Now, where her yard had formerly been heaped with a rusty, decrepit assortment of junk and scavenged debris, stood a neat American Cape Cod with a manicured lawn and window flower boxes. During his childhood, Garson's and Lana's mothers and other empathic neighbors had given cast-off clothing to the silent recluse. But ultimately, arrear municipal taxes and a court declaration of incompetence had resulted in Deaffy's summary removal to an institution, and demolition of her woeful shack.

In their youth, Toby, long the font of intelligence unknown to others, had speculated that the addled old woman must have squirreled away satchels of cash, maybe gold or gems; he'd been proven wrong, however. Another neighborhood rumor had it that the recluse had years before borne an out-of-wedlock child, its fetus stuffed in a jar of formaldehyde; but during the demolition, little more than a tiny bisque doll in a quart mason jar had been discovered.

"She talked, you know," Lana proclaimed during another conversation. "Deaffy, I mean." Garson shook his head, swearing he or his pals had never heard a single utterance from the reclusive refuse collector, even as she'd been teased and harassed by kids. To Garson, she'd been a fearful childhood presence but never exhibited any more than silent stares at him. He'd sometimes assumed guilt for his pals' merciless harassment. He'd overheard the rumors that she'd been married to a perfidious Great Lakes ship's captain who'd abandoned her for a hussy in some other port; left in pregnancy, she'd delivered a child without assistance, a stillbirth. Neighbor gadflies had endlessly speculated about the aftermath.

Garson's memory brought forth childhood encounters and dreams Deaffy's ragged, shrouded, shambling countenance, face leathery and deeply lined, odiferous and mute, hooded eyes noticing little more than the discarded treasures she'd collected in a battered

Radio Flyer wagon.

"No, no, Deaffy talked," Lana insisted. "I know." She described an incident in vibrant, vivid terms when, as a small girl, she'd reluctantly walked the length of the alley to Deaffy's shack to deliver leftovers to the crone. Like Garson's mother, Lana's and others, even those who called her gypsy or witch, sometimes gave her leftover food.

"One time I took a piece of Mom's cake. I was scared just like you. Deaffy was in her yard when I came, and I handed her the cake on a paper plate. She just stared at me for a minute, then took it. 'Thank you,' she said, clear as a bell." Despite the supposed evidence, Garson never credited Lana's story.

Also while on leave that fall, Garson had a pleasant reunion with Mellish, his boon companion of youth and beau ideal raconteur. The police sergeant's son had been recently discharged from the air force after only two years because of some physical impediment, even though his enlistment had been a criminal court mandate. Now, Mellish worked at the sprawling Allis-Chalmers manufactory on the southwest side. He still planned to apprentice in the tool and die trade.

They reminisced about "old times," at once recalling summer Sheepshead games at Silver Spring Park, Custer High Friday night football games and sock hops, cruising The Burg.

"Remember Frontier Days in Butler?" Garson blurted. Butler was an obscure village west of the city, little more than a railroad marshalling yard with a pitiful assembly of saloons and store fronts. Local boosters planned to make more of their pretentious community than was warranted, and initiated late summer celebrations. "Where Milwaukee Ends and the West Begins," they touted; but the event became little more than a raucous and rowdy carnival with tent shows, amusements and rides where virtually anyone, save for baby faces like Garson, could quaff beer. Unpublicized attractions had included liaisons with worldly-eyed older girls.

"Remember Kawolski – wasn't that Lana's muscle-headed boyfriend?" Mellish laughed. "Wore a black ten gallon hat like some phony Texas *hombre*?" Garson recognized a bit of envy.

"Hey, think I still got a picture of us – you, me, Toby, Freddie, one or two others at Butler in '53 just before we enlisted," Garson put in. That image still resided in his pre-Corps album.

Mellish introduced Garson to Connie, a Custer High student, a year behind Lana; Garson had never met his pal's new sweetheart. Many decades after, Mellish admitted that his reputation as a rakehell has been undeserved.

"Connie puts me in my place," he proclaimed. "She's a classy dresser. Smart, too." Indeed, Connie was distinctive the night they double-dated, wearing a coordinated ensemble jacket, skirt with peplum and a creamy blouse. Upon meeting her, Garson felt intimidated, under-dressed in his Marine khaki trousers, shirt and sweater vest. Connie, somewhat reserved, looked older than her years. After picking up Betsy and Garson, Mellish drove north into the adjacent county whose local ordinance permitted 18-year-olds in "beer only bars." Mellish was quite familiar with the popular House of Blue Lights.

"Yeah, we come here because they never carded us. They also got an old upright piano back there that I plunk on" he said, motioning toward a back room. The couples sat at a formica table, and Mellish carried in two brimming pitchers of beer and plastic cups. Soon, he perched at a battered upright piano, his long, large-knuckled fingers stroking chipped keys. Mellish pridefully said he played by ear, and could read only a little music.

"Yeah, I play what they call stride piano like Art Tatum and old Fats Waller and some of them old cats." With an active left hand, he belted out credible ragtime tunes as well as honky-tonk and boogie woogie numbers, even overcoming the instrument's un-tuned shortcomings. He was less secure playing down-tempo standards. The girls were attentive for only a tune or two before turning to each other and conversation.

Engrossed in Mellish's playing, Garson was once more envious of his pal. Mellish was a natural raconteur with an expansive catalog of humorous yarns, real and fancied, about him and his adventuresome brothers. Impressionable Garson was invariably enthralled. Now Mellish exhibited musical talent as well. That brought to mind Holy Redeemer grade school teachers who'd suggested piano lessons to Garson's mother because her son's fingers fairly flew across the edge of his desk during music classes.

"We believe your son should take lessons," a St. Francis nun, Sister Sepulveda had recommended. But because of his parents' work schedules and precarious financial situation, Garson's hopes had not been realized.

Connie and Betsy's conversation continued comfortably, almost like school chums, Connie asking about Betsy's studies at Milwaukee Downer College. Garson sat mute, admiring his girlfriend's articulation, demeanor and charm. While he was a bit put off that she smoked (no matter that he did, too), his chest swelled, studying her generous smile and full lips, wide deep eyes, lovely skin tone and small, trim figure. He liked the way she dressed – long, form-fitting skirt and soft angora sweater; he also found fetching the red silk scarf knotted tightly about her neck, an affectation of the time. Posing for snapshots, Mellish and Connie encouraged them to embrace and kiss. Later, impatient for sleep, Garson reviewed the evening with a knot of concern about Betsy's lack of abandon. Still, his feelings for her simmered.

Garson could not remember how many times they dated during the 30 days leave home. He ached to take her to the movies, particularly to the opulent Oriental Theater on the east side of town, the incredible motion picture temple where he'd seen "Gone With the

Wind" as a child – more awestruck by the extravagant interior with its parade of ebony Chinese dragons flanking a majestic stairway to the balconies. But that desire was never fulfilled.

A few times he hopped the streetcar to her house, an upstairs flat with common furnishings with which he was familiar. He shuffled through a stack of 45 rpm records, playing a few tunes on her simple turntable, thumbed through a small collection pocket books – romantic flummery mostly, but an impressive title or two. They conversed about future plans, Garson telling Betsy he gotten his GED in the Marines, and planned to apply for an equivalency diploma from Messmer High.

"Wanna study journalism at Marquette with the G. I. Bill. Be a reporter, a newspaperman, maybe write books, too." He thought he sensed an impressive response from her. She was intent on finishing her degree and teaching elementary school. Perhaps she was unenthusiastic about romantic commitment at this time, he worried. Betsy was forthright; Garson was not.

Subsequently, a fantasy crystalized in Garson's mind. Mellish had announced that he and Connie planned to marry, but failed to admit until decades after that the union would be one of necessity. Garson thought he'd known no better girl than Betsy: Her looks and intelligence, her manner and charm, her future career, the memory of her solicitous demeanor back in high school. She was probably the one, he concluded. In days, he announced his decision to his parents. His mother was particularly pleased.

"You should talk to my brother, Vin," Garson's father proposed. "He knows a lot of people on the East Side, and maybe can get you a deal on a ring." No matter that Vin was a lifetime bachelor whose lone "romance," if such it could be characterized, had ended in a whimper a decade before. So there Garson found himself: He was in fact in love, and would ask Betsy to marry. Vin, for decades employed as a saloon keeper, bistro *maître d'* and even a failed Prohibition era bootlegger, introduced Garson to a hard-eyed, edgy man who sold rings and jewelry out of his tiny East Side apartment. Garson viewed stones and settings, selecting two or three that were priced well beyond his military pay means. He reluctantly selected marquis-cut chip of a stone in a silver mounting; the gem was miniscule but his intention monumental. He could make a down payment, and promised to send home money every payday for the next year. Vin's attestation to his nephew's reliability certified the transaction.

Of course, he knew little more of Betsy than when they'd been Messmer classmates. They'd exchanged written endearments, certainly, and now had had a handful of double dates and few conversations about the future. They'd embraced and kissed at length, stirring, Garson hoped, promising marital passions. Mellish and Connie applauded at the House of Blue Lights, cheering the proposal. Yet, pregnant moments passed that night before Betsy responded to Garson's proposal, her dark eyes welling tears.

"Of course," Betsy finally replied after an audible swallow and an uncomfortable pause. "Yes." She seemed nervous, and hadn't said she loved him. Oblivious to such portents, Garson's head swam and heart soared. But months later when Garson analyzed those moments, he should have taken her hesitation as an ill omen. He'd placed her in an uncompromising position from which she had no escape, he mourned.

As he prepared for his return to the Pacific Northwest, autumnal daylight faded by mid-afternoon, ushering in crisp evenings; ground vegetation sparkled crystalline and hoary each morning. The entire deciduous verdure became painted in brilliant Klimt golds, Van Gogh yellows, Matisse reds, Rembrandt browns. Towering elm trees that had created verdant summery Gothic arches were now but desiccated skeletons, abandoned leaves cackling and scratching with the wind along streets and sidewalks. He could not know that when he returned two years hence, municipal workers, like Wisconsin lumbermen in the preceding century, would be felling stately elm trees infested with disease, returning Milwaukee streets to their once barren urban countenance.

On the final Milwaukee evening with Betsy, they again comfortably double dated with Mellish and Connie, eating burgers, fries and Cokes at Shorty's Restaurant then driving to Neckers' Point on the Lake Michigan shoreline, parking amid scores of cars intent on moonlight romance. He deflated when she announced she could not stay out too late because of a "heavy" college assignment, nor could she accompany him to the train depot next day. The evening ended too quickly, even prematurely, he thought, because she had school work to complete. They stood at the rear door of her parents' house while Mellish and Connie waited in the idling car.

"I'll write to you as often as I can," she whispered. Garson would later regard the promise as less than effusive. Still, he would pen hopeful, weekly missives in the months ahead, writing enough for the both of them, he thought. He loved her truly, madly, deeply.

"I'll miss you," Betsy murmured sweetly. It was late, their friends waited. She didn't want to disturb her parents. He was thrilled wrapping his arms around her, inhaling her subtle scent that intoxicated him. She was certainly his "main squeeze" now. While he felt little more than the bulky coat she wore against the evening chill, he murmured endearments and promises, hoping they'd seal her heart for him. They kissed several times, but he ached in vain for her lips to be more responsive, to open invitingly, if only a sliver. And she still had not said those precious words: "I love you." More portents for Garson to ponder.

Chapter 4

NAS WHIDBEY REDUX

"Brig Rats"

"Permission to cross the white line, *sir!*" the Brig Rat DuFresne shouted, throat rippling as he swallowed. The slender prisoner stood stock still at the broad stripe painted on the brig's deck, the floor.

NAS Whidbey's brig was situated on the second floor of a utilitarian building clad in gray slate that stood across the roadway from the base's Gate One. It also housed the on-duty Marines. The detention facility consisted of a dozen two-man, heavily-barred cells arrayed about a common open area. The deck was sheeted in large sections of tin that audibly registered every footfall. The white lines, the Corps's iteration of the "dead lines" of the Confederacy's Andersonville prison during the Civil War, were visible at the portal of every cell, entry to the prisoners' head, and other access points. Inmates were prohibited from stepping over any painted barrier without verbal permission from Marine guards.

Once an airman third, Brig Rat DuFresne, known as "Forger," had served as an administration clerk; he'd been charged with destruction of government property, having doctored his identification card's birth year to fraudulently gain access to bars; court martialed, he'd been reduced in rank to ordinary airman, fined two months' pay and incarcerated for 60 days.

NAS Whidbey brig usually housed ten or fewer of such miscreants. Hard core offenders with harsher sentences of over six months were shipped down the west coast to Mare Island Naval Shipyard near San Francisco, the big time prison.

Forger and other confined sailors wore blue utility bell bottoms and work shirts whose backs were emblazoned with large white "P's." Typically, at least one Whidbey Marine was confined, as well, usually adjudged guilty after a Captain's Mast procedure of such derelictions as short-term AWOL, insubordination or disobedience of a lawful order. (Garson, of course, was familiar with that Uniform Code of Military Justice procedure.) Not only was the Marine not identified with the onerous "P," he was never assigned a cellmate.

One of Garson's fellow Marines who'd been briefly incarcerated was "Pappy" Trost, whose severe widow's peak suggested a brushy head of hair despite the current military trim. Wisps of gray at his temples betrayed that he was older than most enlisted Marines. He'd served only ten days brig time for returning an hour late from a weekend liberty; scuttlebutt had it that Pappy had corralled a comely Seattle girl.

Garson was discomfited by recurrent visions the first few nights back from leave in November, tossing in his bunk with troubling premonitions of a wintery gravesite in the St. John's churchyard back home where his maternal grandparents had been buried. Ma, the youngest of the European-born siblings, had come of age in the dirt-road village northwest of Milwaukee after crossing the Atlantic with her family early in the century.

On those nights, Garson was awakened by torments that he'd never again see his mother. Back home, he'd noticed her hair was grayer than it had been when he'd departed for the Marines two years earlier, her face more deeply lined and care-worn, eyes deeper and hollower, her body more stooped from years of labor during and after the Depression. She was only 51. She hadn't put to rest her abject disappointment of her son quitting school to enlist.

In recurrent late night lament, an incident came to him that had occurred even before he was a teen, when, for a reason he could not summon, he'd reacted to something she'd said or something she'd denied him, not with a simple "Damn!" but with the despicable "Damn *you*!" Almost before he realized it, her hand flew up, landing a solid, stinging blow to his left cheek. He was shocked and stunned, even while suspecting she'd regretted the slap more than he did. Only his father had meted out such corporeal punishment, and then only once in his life. Mother and son stared wordlessly at one other for moment or two before Garson rushed away. Days had passed before the silence between them was broken.

Garson held tears in check those first nights back at NAS Whidbey, audibly in-taking breath through his nose, worried he hadn't spent enough time with her during those weeks home, more occupied in reunions with old neighborhood pals and in courting Betsy. On the third night, he castigated himself: Nearly a veteran Marine now, two years in and age 19, putatively prepared for combat and defense of the nation, still stifling sobs like a child.

Two days after his return, Garson was notified by Supply Sergeant Walters that a box awaited him. When Sergeant Coleman, Garson's buddy "G. D.," had been discharged in Garson's absence, the Chicagoan had packed several items in a box, designating them for his buddy. To Garson's gratitude, he'd found those coveted, glossy combat boots, a dark green wool dress shirt and the salty, starched Old Corps dungaree cap — items no longer issued by the Corps. There were also several lustrous brass ornaments that his buddy had polished to perfection. A penciled note read:

"Hey Warhead! When you get to Chi-Town, look me up. Maybe I'll be in L.A. though. Take good care of that pretty <u>Main Squeeze</u> of yours." Garson grinned. G. D. had meant Karen Sisko, of course; he was amused by that sobriquet: "Main Squeeze." "Don't let those chooches get you down. Good luck and Semper Fi," the note ended. "Your buddy, G. D. Coleman."

While Garson never saw the Negro Marine again, he remained clearly in memory for decades, one of the several buddies with whom he'd found true friendship; G. D.'s influence and mentoring nurtured seeds planted in childhood by his mother and movies, of college and a professional writing career. Garson would be forever grateful.

"Get the fuck outta the'ah, you dumb fuckin' deck ape!" growled the sergeant of the guard. Forger, technically not a sea-going "deck ape," waited at the cell doorway, eyes downcast, shoulders hunched. Garson never coupled the NCO's name and home state orally, but thought of the two as one in print. Gunter the German's thick neck, massive body, large head, and ferocious coal-black eyes were intimidating.

Gunter the German was ever wont to praise the glories of the Old Confederacy. He claimed a small town upbringing near Stone Mountain, Georgia. Over several conversations he'd boasted that his home was within sight of the revered bas-relief rock sculpture of Lee, Jackson and Jefferson Davis then being hewed from granite. Garson's interest was piqued because of an early but inchoate fascination with the Civil War.

"It's bein' carved into a giant rock dome," the sergeant described in his thick drawl. "Taller'n 500 feet from the ground up, I he'ah, wider'n two football fields when it's finished," Gunter the German touted. "A beautiful memorial to ow'ah great Reb ancestahs." When, years later, Garson found more facts about the landmark, he learned that it had been conceived early in the century as a symbol of the Jim Crow South, and emblematic of the Ku Klux Klan's rebirth and influence in 1920's. Forty years after it symbolized the old Confederacy's reaction to the Civil Rights era.

"We'all calls it 'The Wa'ah of Nawthrun Aggression' and 'The Wa'ah fo'ah Suthrun Rahts,'" Gunter the German always proclaimed. Still, the irascible sergeant seemed to get on with Negro Marines, especially those from the South.

In youth, Garson had been curiously attracted to movie images of gallant Rebel cavaliers and their lost quest for nationhood, not contemplating what historically would have resulted had the Confederacy prevailed. His unwashed fascination (he'd once painted a Rebel battle flag on a metal trash container) had been tested, however, by the troubling William Wellman movie "The Ox-Bow Incident," a cautionary tale of mob mentality and lynching of innocents. Leading hell-bent town vigilantes, vainglorious former Reb Major Tetly, portrayed by familiar character actor Frank Conroy, donned gold-braided Confederate uniform, boots, slouch hat and saber.

Gunter the German had arrived at Marine Barracks a few days after Garson departed for his leave; he was firmly ensconced when Garson returned.

In Garson's absence, Whidbey Marine Barracks had been relocated from its former locale to the seaplane base, and proximate to hangars, runways, and to the rocky Puget Sound shoreline. The two-story, gray U-shaped wooden World War era billet stood solitary, in an area devoid of trees or accenting greenery. To the satisfaction of Garson and other Marines, their new abode was separated from the thousands of naval personnel and their dependents. More, the exclusive Marine mess hall had been abandoned, and the guard company relegated to the navy chow hall among crowds of blue uniforms; thankfully, Garson and his buddies enjoyed a segregated seating area. Garson rapidly warmed to the navy fare.

"Gotta say this: Swabbie cooks're sure better than the Corps has," Garson opined. "Them big-bellied Jarheads'll take the best meats on God's green earth and turn 'em into shoe leather every time." Still, he particularly doted on the navy's version of military breakfast gruel, "Shit on a Shingle" – chipped beef on toast floating in viscous white sauce. The navy's version of the morning staple consisted of a similar glutinous gruel in which swam stringy pieces of beef. "Foreskins on a raft" was how Garson and others identified it.

NAS Whidbey prisoners were assigned to numerous daily duties about the base — policing roadways, walkways and open areas — "Dive Bombers" they were called, wielding broomsticks embedded with spikes to spear debris. They mowed grass, trimmed shrubs, cleaned and painted vacant billets, moved equipment and more.

A minority of Marine guards with whom Garson sometimes guiltily joined, took perverse pleasure in harrying and harassing swabbie prisoners. Gunter the German, to Garson's selective recollection, was among the foremost. These swabbie brig rats were lamentable fuck-ups, after all, unpitied, unworthy of common consideration. Some Marines were given to borderline sadistic behaviors toward their unfortunate charges, rousing inmates in the middle of the night, for example, and forcing them to stand at attention before the brig's white lines as they swayed in bleary-eyed weariness. Maltreatment was most often petty and nonsensical, sailors made to repeatedly sing every stanza "Marine Corps Hymn." Others who exhibited particular sensitivity were singled out for special abuse, made to sit cross-legged like children on the tin-sheeted deck while guards repeatedly tapped their foreheads with a baton. Other brig rats were ordered to confess to unseemly proclivities.

"So, didja ever see how them sheep's ears prick up when y'all's pokin' 'em?" Gunter the German might ask. When a prisoner said "no," the sergeant responded with "Sure, you do, boy. I kin see it in you'ah eyes." He spewed particular venom at Northern city sailors.

"Hey, the'ah, buckaroo," Garson recalled the glowering Georgian once commanded a prisoner read a girlfriend's letter aloud, "Betcha that big-titted gal' a yourn's gettin' poked by some good ol' boys back home with bigger dicks'n you'ahs, *right now*, while y'all's in here with *me*, don'cha know." Gunter the German reminded Garson of his old nemesis, Corporal Judson.

The weeding of Korea era veterans through discharges, re-enlistments and transfers continued. Marine Barracks youthful replacements were usually nondescript and unaccomplished and, like Garson, urban youths with limited prospects. There were also more men of color — Negroes, sons of Mexican immigrants and Puerto Ricans. Garson would look back from six decades perspective to conclude that his education into reality had dawned, of a changing, multi-hued American society different from the white middle America he'd known.

Spanish conversations increased, many exchanges now seasoned with common argot and expletives – *hombre, cojones, cholo, cavrón, coño, felació* even, of course, *puta, coito, chinga tu madre*. Garson sometimes lamented that he was unable to understand confidential conversations among newer buddies like Moldy, Ramirez, Ortega and others. More, Garson admired his new fair mindedness; after all he'd dated Sisko, the smoldering Montebello girl with whom he continued regular correspondence. He claimed to see beyond the ethnic social divide, regarding her as but a lovely *café con leche* girl with simmering black eyes and lustrous hair, plummy lips, and simmering smile.

Then, there was Nola. Before departing on the month leave home, he'd been invited to Nola's for his birthday fete. An image of him holding the gorgeous candle-studded cake baked by Nola's doting mother still graced his photo album. He long suspected the mother liked him, a son she'd never had, so far from home and family. Garson liked to regard that she harbored a hope of something more substantial than mere youthful fancy between her daughter and the young Marine.

But, now, since Marine Barracks, a mile or more distant from Oak Harbor was devoid of dependable transportation, Garson could no longer monitor classes at the high school or sustain steady contact with Nola; a once blooming friendship with the comely island blonde was slowly ebbing.

It may seem that Garson's Marine Corps years were naught save flirtations with girls, attraction to cars and other extracurricular diversion – much fatuous and ephemeral. Beyond that, most of his NAS Whidbey days were filled with the predictable and prosaic – guard duty, prisoner chasing, weapons' training, refresher instruction in combat tactics — an often dull and droning routine. Even hardened Marine veteran authors like Robert Leckie and Eugene Hedges would note that time between battles weighed heavily on them. Thus, it was that the uncommon, the differentiated, the accentuated remained clearest in memory.

Every Marine was obliged to annually re-qualify with the Corps's basic combat weapon, the .30 caliber M-1 Garand rifle. Garson had performed admirably, he thought, in Boot Camp, missing an Expert badge by only three points. But during his first year at NAS Whidbey, he'd slipped badly, qualifying for a mere Marksman medal; he'd dejectedly replaced the Maltese Cross medallion on his uniform with a basic bar, thinking it an appropriate complement to a sleeve devoid of stripes.

NAS Whidbey firing range was an unimpressive facility with fewer than 30 individual positions, a dramatic contrast to MCRD Boot Camp with multiple ranges, the largest of which accommodated perhaps a hundred shooters in a relay. The navy seemed not to require regular weapons qualifications for its personnel.

The M-1 issued at Whidbey was a battered old clunker, he thought, serviceable and dependable, but not a gilt-edged competition weapon. More, Whidbey Marines were only accorded two days of range preparation before the qualification match. As the year before, Garson struggled to find the correct "dope" for each distance – 200, 300 and 500 yards. And since the fine-edged body tone developed in Boot Camp had dulled in the year of relative physical slackness of the guard and security company; he lacked former strength and muscle tone to steady the nine pound rifle, especially in off-hand. After the 50-shot match, he was exhausted physically and psychologically. While he bested his pitiful performance of the year before, the score was insufficient to recapture the higher medal. More, his cheek was again bruised from rifle recoil that drove his right knuckle backward with each shot.

Still, the wreathed, Expert pistol medallion set him apart, and this resulted in selection to the Marine Barracks intermural pistol league team; he was the lone non-NCO so named. Expectantly, he banged out solid scores during the competition, but the Gyrene quartet was easily bested by a grizzled navy team of veteran petty officers. A photo in the base newspaper, *Prop Wash*, was small comfort.

Coincidentally, Garson successfully passed the promotion test, and regained his single stripe. The payroll officer now biweekly counted out nearly $50 in crisp bills for a PFC with more than two years of service, an increase of three dollars a month. Still, he was heartened to sew the chevron back on his uniforms, cursing that martinet, Judson, with each whip stitch. He coupled the promotion with successful completion of the GED exam and several correspondence courses in literature and history. His image beside a congratulating Captain Cathcart was also printed in the 12-page weekly. Halfway through his four-year enlistment, he felt he was making progress toward whatever career choice to be made in the final years.

Occasional articulate Marines were invariably called college boys, but most latter day enlistees were, like Garson, uniformed beyond headlines. Barracks reputations were earned through friendships and burnished by colorful yarn spinning. Garson suspected that many hometown escapades and adventures were, like his own, often constructed from whole cloth, or at least embellished and inflated. Garson himself often employed what was called "swank," hyperbole intended to impress. As at former duty stations, Garson sought out buddies who exchanged family experiences.

"We lived above a tavern," began the South Side Milwaukeean who was predictably called "Ski" for his Polish surname. He was another of those with whom Garson swapped stories. Garson was familiar with that neighborhood from other family tales, studded with distinctive "Polish Flats," narrow, shotgun houses cheaply constructed by first generation immigrants who later raised the dwellings, adding a lower living level for married sons or daughters.

Those neighborhoods were sometimes called "Babushka-towns."

"One day my Auntie Mary, one of the Golombowski (he pronounced the name "Ga-woom-bowski"), Ma's family, came to live with us." "Wasn't really my auntie, but a great aunt, I think. Came to town on a Greyhound from Black Earth out in western Wisconsin, carrying just a little beat up ol' satchel, almost cardboard. Widowed, you see, when her husband lost his arm in a farm accident and died within a month.

"Ski" had grown up in one of the city's ethnic south side conclaves. He'd followed a typical path through Catholic grade school and on to public South Division High. Unlike Garson, he'd graduated before enlisting; a path Garson now regretted he should have followed. As was the way of such matters, Garson doted on the Milwaukeean's colorful experiences.

Of medium build and height with modest facial features, grayish eyes, a strong jaw often bluish in a whiskered cast, Ski displayed rabbity front teeth and an overbite. Like Garson, he admitted excelling at little in life thus far; seeing few prospects, he'd joined the Corps the summer after graduation. Garson understood that his partiality to the Milwaukeean stemmed not only by their shared background but from family yarns that the south sider spun — much like Garson's boyhood pal, Mellish, who regularly regaled the Villard Avenue "gang" with tales of yeasty derring-do. Ski continued:

"'There's no place for me to go now,' Auntie Mary said.'" Garson was attentive to Ski's revelations. Her dead husband had been a failure as a farmer, losing money for years – another point of convergence between family histories because Garson's father struggled for solvency with his flagging confection business. Foreclosure loomed after Ski's uncle's death. With matted gray hair, lonely dreamy eyes and deep facial creases, Auntie Mary looked much older than her 65 years.

"'Can you take me in for just a little while,' she asked Ma, 'maybe for couple'a weeks, month at most – til I collect my wits an' figure out what I'll do?'" Ski said. "Ma for years always took in stray dogs and poor relations." Garson related to this. His mother, cut from similar immigrant cloth, had done the same thing during and after the war; without discussion or ceremony, shoe string relations who came to town for work or school had invariably dispossessed Garson of his back bedroom. He'd been shuffled onto a lumpy roll-away bed in the dining room. Ma had once taken in couple of strangers she'd met on a bus, army veterans discharged in 1946 from the military barracks near Garson's house. His mother always had poor resistance to sad stories of need. One of the buddies moved out, but the other, a burly, red-headed man nicknamed "Spot" for a face full of freckles and a hairy body, had married; he and his bride lived with Garson's family for about a year after that.

"'Sure,'" Ski continued his Auntie Mary story, "my Ma told her she could stay as long as she had to. 'We'll bunk the girls into one room, and you kin stay in Gloria's.' Auntie Mary was hard a hearing, I can tell you, 'cause she always called Gloria 'Girlie.' My sisters were put out, losing their own bedrooms. Turns out, Auntie Mary was with us for more'n 15 years. Actually, she died sometime in her 80s. Buried 'er in our family plot at St. Adelbert's."

Girls and putative romance also remained prime topics of consideration and discussion, and often, what passed for erudition and maturity in such matters sounded like this:

"Said she got a rag on," little Ramirez, the Sal Mineo Marine proclaimed. "Got a weekend libbo once, take her for burgers and a malted, a movie and I don't get a fuck from 'er." His outsized rheumy eyes seemed to water. Garson always doubted that the cherubic Angelino was capable of serious seduction. "She won't even jack me off. 'Smelly,' she says. 'Disgusting.' My dick, she means! *Puta!* She ain't the only toots in this here town – Seattle, I mean. They're plenty out there itchin' to see my seven-inch *schlong!*" Garson and others snorted at the young Marine's braggadocio.

"Why you allas takin' 'bout chow, Hoss?" hawk-beaked Ortega put in as expected whenever conversations meandered to girls or amorous adventures. Even while he served with Garson at NAS Whidbey for less than a year, Ortega left an impression that readily revivified after six decades.

Ortega was a slender sliver, the thin stalk of his neck containing an active Adam's apple that bobbed when he swallowed and laughed. The back of his small head was flat, lacking typical cranial curvature. It was readily apparent that his four front teeth were replacements — Marine Corps issue like Garson's rear lower denture. Chicklet-like, those prominent teeth gleamed whiter than Ortega's natural ones, and the silver grounding clamps flashed when he smiled. He had a habit of popping the appliance loose with his tongue and holding it between his lips. Most prominent was his aquiline nose that created a classic profile.

"Don' bother me, Hoss. Gotta 'chine' my 'choos' now," he often retorted when interrupted. Garson was convinced the stereotypical movie accent was an affectation like O. D. O'Donoghue's at Camp Pendleton. Usually friendly but not gregarious, Ortega seemed to be holding back, hiding something behind the linguistic posing and Cantinflas posturing. Garson never determined what.

"So, Moldy says you got yourself a little *cholita* down in east L.A., Hoss, a *mestiza*." Garson learned that meant a Mexican girl of Indian ancestry with high cheekbones, narrow eyes and dark skin. Moldanado, another prominent Puerto Rican, still remained at NAS Whidbey Marine Barracks. Garson's relationship with him had been somewhat testy because of Lana.

"Well, I write to a girl I met when I was at Pendleton. Don't know about all of that *cholita* or *metiza* stuff. She's pretty is all I know."

Despite his lone sexual "exploit;" Garson remained virtually virginal since. He and Nola had once, perhaps twice, he thought, breathlessly reached passion's precipice during a few nights at her house, his hands active on the living room sofa; only her caution about her parents sleeping a room away and her unbreakable resistance had prevented their "fall from grace." Garson's "blue balls" would not soon be relieved, he feared, and that ultimate itch would remain unscratched.

Late in the year, another young enlistee was transferred into NAS Whidbey Marine Barracks, a rotund, short-legged and seemingly unfit Marine who'd followed a well-worn trail from MCRD Boot Camp to Camp Pendleton to the Pacific Northwest. Vandy as all called him was conveniently from Spokane, and took every weekend liberty he could afford to his hometown by Greyhound. It was through the topic of movies that Garson was initially drawn to the portly Evergreen Stater. They shared their enjoyment of "Singin' in the Rain" that Garson had recently viewed several times at Seattle's second-run theaters. They also reveled in memory of vintage Busby Berkley extravaganzas, Astaire and Rogers dancing, Kelly's athletic Technicolor performances and other movie musicals seen in their youth.

Vandy's old great uncle was Alexander Vandegrift, he revealed, the famous Marine general and commander of the vaunted First Marines who'd famously swept ashore at Guadalcanal in the Solomon Islands early in the Pacific war and later took Bougainville. He'd earned the Medal of Honor and been designated Commandant of the Marine Corps after the war. The force of their relationship had all but "forced" Vandy to enlist.

"Graduated from Gonzaga Prep, the Jeb [Jesuit] school," Vandy boasted, much to Garson's discomfort as a drop out. "We were the 'Bull-Pups' while the university was the 'Bulldogs'," he added. The all-male Jesuit school and university on the north side of town were affiliated. "I was in the first graduating class in the new building," he added with pride. He planned to further his education at the university after his three-year enlistment, a cause of Garson's envy.

Vandy, tellingly, possessed a rich vocabulary, and was conversant with Latin, a subject with which Garson had struggled in grade school. But it never seemed that this new buddy was pretentious or threw his education in anyone's face; he seemed to pull verbal punches, rarely unlimbering his full erudite arsenal. And in private conversations, Garson heard words he'd heard spoken only on movie screens and from cloistered teachers at Holy Redeemer and Messmer High. Decades later when Garson thought of those days, he couldn't recall his new buddy using contractions when he spoke. For all of his unmanly manners and peculiarities, Vandy became a new confidant.

"Seems like a little 'Miss Nancy, if you ask me,'" Gunter the German sneered to Garson's discomfort. "Maybe a little bit swishy?" This reaction came after a discussion in which Vandy suggested that William Powell as Nick Charles in "The Thin Man" was crapulent.

"Now, Vandy, Ah don' know big words lahk y'all. But Ah think crapulent means fat, like you." That was a surprise observation from the NCO. Vandy winced at the castigation.

"Well, Sergeant, that is not correct." Vandy's eyebrows furrowed. "Actually, crapulent means given to drink. The word 'corpulent' means overweight...like me, if you insist." Another brief exchange established a basis for future antipathy.

"Question fer y'all," Vandy posed, limning Gunter the German's drawl. "When a tree falls in woods with nobody around, does it make a sound?"

"'Course it does," insisted Gunter the German.

"No, you are wrong, Sergeant. A sound not only supposes a source — somebody or something to initiate it. It also supposes a receptor, something or someone to hear it."

"That a trick question?" Gunter the German scowled as he walked away.

"I know what Vandy's gonna say: No ear, no sound, right?" Garson put in. He recalled that his respected Boot Camp buddy, the college boy, Ridley, had thrown out such rhetorical inquiries.

"It's called a conundrum." Vandy clarified.

"How 'bout this one, then," Garson injected: "A wet bird never flies at night!" Lowered eyebrows and stern expressions regarded him.

"Makes no fuckin' sense a'tall!" Gunter the German caviled.

Because of his obvious education and skills, Vandy was assigned as an administrative clerk typist, a daily "pogue" position without guard and security responsibilities. Many, envious, cast more aspersions on the portly PFC.

Taking a page from the brig rat "Forger," Garson asked Vandy to help doctor the identification card issued in Boot Camp. At 19, Garson still bore the fresh-faced, seldom shaved countenance of youth.

"We can peel the lamination off – it's already lose at the corner anyway, see here. Take it all off, and change the last number of my birth year to a '4.' I'd be 21 then. Get into bars and buy booze from bottle clubs." At first, the Spokane Marine was reluctant, but Garson's weeks of wheedling wore down his new buddy. On a typical weekend when Captain Cathcart, the top sergeant and headquarters staff were absent, the culprits clandestinely entered the office, worried the lamination free, erased "6," and carefully typed in the fraudulent digit. The lamination machine was heated to complete the task. Vandy even admired his handiwork.

"It is inadvisable for you to use this at The Canteen downtown, you know," Vandy cautioned. "They will know you are not old enough." Garson nodded. But the clandestine forgery did not tempt Vandy to doctor his own identification

"I am abstemious," the portly Marine affirmed.

The identity of the buddy with whom Garson "test drove" his fraudulent ID card was lost to memory; yet many details of that night remained clear. They pulled up at a Western flavored night spot near the Port Clinton ferry dock at the south shore of Whidbey Island. Garson was struck by the similarity of the facility to spacious venues he recalled back home rented for weddings of older cousins after the World War – cavernous and roughhewn interiors of knotty pine or pale oak, expansive bars like movie saloons, band risers and globes of light swirling the floor with dizzying, multi-colored sparkles. Known as a bottle club, patrons carried their own hard liquor inside, purchased at a "party store" that conveniently shared the parking lot; booze was "disguised" in paper sacks.

Seated at a wobbly table on the dance floor's periphery, a waitress in a long, Western skirt and high-heeled boots sidled up.

"What're you two havin'?" Tall, blonde, pretty even without a smile, her heavily lidded eyes and mascaraed lashes projected scant hospitality. She disinterestedly glanced at their IDs. When she strode away after accepting payment for a quart bottle of cola and paper cups, Garson growled.

"Fuck man! Two bucks for a jug a cola. Ain't even Coke!" It was rumored that the local sheriff nightly traipsed through the club, but seldom seemed to notice any under-age liquor consumption.

"Heard the club owner pays 'im off for his blindness," Garson's buddy opined. Given to alcohol only as a pose, the excitement of drinking openly in a saloon paled quickly that night. He watched girls dancing, only a handful with male partners. Garson was discomfited by the dreaded "shit-kicking" music from a quartet of thumping drums, whiny steel guitar, acoustic base and girl singer. As he poured another smidgen of rum into his cup, the tunes set Garson's teeth on edge.

He noted at a table across the floor a trio of girls in jeans and tight blouses; none was accompanied. Garson had observed two of them dancing together some minutes before. Between numbers, they'd cast glances about the hall, likely looking to attract male partners, he felt certain. Bolder than he knew himself to be, Garson arose, alcohol fueling his uncommon daring, and strode across the floor. As he neared the table, he focused on the prettiest of the trio, a slender, dark-haired girl with a round face and slightly puffy tissues above narrow eyes. Her friends were both chubby, he saw, one wore rimless spectacles that flashed from the swirling mirror ball. The girl he addressed was about Betsy's height, several inches shorter than he, but her straight hair fell far below her shoulders. With a smile, she accepted his invitation, offering her hand.

The song wasn't particularly suited to the dance Lana had taught him, the foot twisting Apple Jack that he'd performed at the senior prom with Nola. Dance partners never touched, all action limited to fleet footwork, pelvic gyrations and arm motions. Garson did his best, watching his own feet as he shuffled and swung to the beat. It seemed like years since he'd last been on a dance floor; half way through the jerky tune, his ankles began to protest, leg tendons and muscles burning. He said nothing, and failed to ask his partner's name; he concentrated only on his movements. During the final minutes, the girl's expression wore a disinterested expression; Garson had impressed her not at all. When the music subsided, he walked her back to her friends, thanked her with a small nod, and strode back to his buddy. He felt his face flush and hair follicles buzz, thinking it likely that the girls were tittering about his limited dance skills and lack of *savoirfaire*. He should have worn his uniform instead of civvies, he fussed to himself; it might have at least conveyed Marine manliness.

"Only one dance?" his unremembered buddy asked as Garson sipped the weak rum drink; it sounded like an admonition. Who was his buddy to cast aspersion; he hadn't asked any girl to dance. The evening ended prematurely as Garson's head spun and his stomach churned, as much from embarrassment as the alcohol. He fussed over the evening's shortcomings.

Days after, the memory of that inchoate night still stirred in him while on a midnight to four watch on Gate Two that led to the seaplane base. For two hours, there'd been sparse week night traffic of navy and civilian vehicles. He dutifully inspected each driver and passenger for proper documents – identification card and liberty pass, focusing the flashlight to compare mugshot to document. At the top of each hour, he was obliged to pencil into the log book. "Nothing to report." Always the same unimaginative words. The radio had been silent since he'd relieved "Ho-Now" Logan on the post.

He paced the half dozen steps back and forth inside the confined space, gazing for the thousandth time through the three-sided glass and rear door window. Fog and mist from the Strait of Juan de Fuca billowed, obscuring even a twinkle of light from runways, hangars and swabbie billets. Even the gate shack's heavy floodlights struggled to penetrate father than a few feet. To keep his mind from succumbing to sleep, he imagined Commies approaching, brandishing rifles and machine guns, attempting to breach NAS Whidbey's security perimeter. He slapped the pistol holster like a kid with a cowboy six-shooter.

He was jolted by a bob of white outside, floating like a wraith in the air beyond the outboard floodlight halo. Garson squinted, and in seconds the white materialized into a sailor hunched under a pea coat collar, his Dixie Cup cap slanted rakishly.

Late from a Cinderella Liberty, he'd probably gotten laid by some local toots, Garson surmised jealously. Without breaking stride or even glancing at Garson, the airman perfunctorily flashed something and strode on without pause, lurching and weaving. Garson presumed the sailor had waved his ID and liberty pass, but not long enough for Garson to inspect properly. He opened the gate shack's door and hailed, demanding to see proper identification.

"Showed it to ya'!" was the belligerent retort. Garson repeated the command as the sailor reached the periphery of light, his white cap once again being swallowed by the dank gloom.

"I said, you need to produce your identification," Garson shouted, his gorge rising quickly. But the sailor continued striding. At that, Garson withdrew the heavy .45 automatic from his holster, and jacked a round into the chamber. The deadly metallic sound was loud in the silent night air. The pistol was loaded, and "ready to rock" if necessary. He held the weapon at an upward angle, at high port, pointed only at the sky. The sailor halted immediately, turned briskly and marched back toward Garson. Without comment, the enlisted man deliberately withdrew his wallet, removed the documents and held them aloft unsteadily. Garson gazed intently for unnecessarily long moments, passing his gaze from mugshot to sailor's face and back again. He noted the airman third outranked him. Then, with a hard-eyed scowl, Garson waved the airdale through the gate with his free hand.

Back inside the guard shack, Garson prepared to unload the pistol, popping its magazine free from the handle recess. He feared accidentally discharging the piece. His hands trembled, and his jaw quivered; breath came in pants. He carefully pulled back the slide to eject the lone round from the chamber. The brass and lead bullet flew out and popped to the deck, onto the wooden egg-crate floor matting, rolling between the wooden slats onto the concrete floor. With difficulty, he retrieved the errant round and reinserted it into the magazine; he carefully slammed the slide shut and re-holstered the weapon. In immediate seconds afterward, he chortled as he watched his hands shake uncontrollably, like a drunk with delirium tremors. Against Marine directives, he failed to enter the incident into the log book, or even mention it to his relief, the sergeant of the guard or even to buddies. For uncounted nights, his unquiet mind would not still, fearing the sailor would report the incident, causing dire consequences. Gratefully, after weeks of anguish passed, nothing came of the confrontation. But even decades later, Garson relived the ominous confrontation, mindful that he'd come just that close to shooting someone – not a Soviet or Chinese Commie, but an American.

Gunter the German, as might be expected, was partial to "shit-kicking" music, and effusive about its popular performers of the day. He was often heard humming country-western tunes, and knew the lyrics of such singers as Wells and Cline, Williams, Huskey, Tubb, Frizzel, Acuff and Atkins, and even nasally Hollywood cowboy, Autry who Garson called Gene "Artery." He could not abide the dreary drivel of lost dogs and sweethearts, garnisheed wages, overdue rent and repossessed pickup trucks. Out of the sergeant's earshot, Garson gagged at the sound of "Here Stands the Glass" and similar anthems, finding favor only with gunfighter balladeer Marty Robbins, especially evocative "The Streets of Laredo" and "El Paso."

> Beat the drum slowly and play the fife lowly
> Play the Death March as you carry me along
> Take me to green valley, there lay the sod o'er me
> For I'm a young cowboy and I know I've done wrong.

Garson and others bristled when Gunter the German regularly demeaned the rigor of MCRD Boot Camp, calling its graduates "Hollywood Marines."

"Fuck, man, "Parris Island'll make MCRD look like Sunday school," he'd brag. It was said of him that he'd served as a prisoner chaser at some Japan brig — Yokosuka or Sasebo – before returning stateside. Scuttlebutt had it that he'd been transferred under a cloud of accusation about misconduct toward brig rats; no specifics were ever revealed, but detractors were certain that a Negro prisoner from Philadelphia had been involved.

One final detraction reinforcing Garson's antipathy toward the Georgian was a snide comment he made when observing the collection of paperback books in Garson's foot locker.

"Readin' gives y'all folks foolish notions ya' know. It's nonsense mostly, 'ceptin' maybe fer the 'Good Book,' a'course." Yet Garson never noticed the nettlesome NCO attending any church services. Nor did he bend his head over the Corps's bible, *The Guidebook for Marines*.

Pappy Trost, a short time Marine brig rat, wore a pair of service stripes above his uniform sleeve cuffs, indicating at least eight years in the Corps. The filigree of facial age lines inched from the corners of his eyes and mouth, and onto his cheeks bespoke of a mature man. Someone claimed Pappy was pushing 40. His mouth seemed constantly busy with pearly Marine choppers. Scuttlebutt had it that he'd served in the army during the World War and later signed with the Corps. While he wore more than a row of campaign ribbons, the fact that he was only a PFC indicated some shortcoming or misadventure. He'd not been demoted during his brig time, indicating his offense was minor. In Garson's memory Trost wasn't stationed at NAS Whidbey long. He was approachable and good-natured, and a good audience for jokes and humorousbantering.

To everyone's surprise, Pappy Trost appeared at Marine Barracks one Saturday afternoon resplendent in dress blues and white gloves and accompanied by a doll-like, waifish woman, who clutched his protective arm. Doll-like, she stood less five feet tall. Pappy visited to introduce his new wife, Zelda, pretty in a silk brocade dress underpinned in voluminous crinolines, high-heeled shoes and a matching pillbox hat later popularized by the widowed wife of a young president. She smiled uncomfortably amid fawning attention from the gaggle of off-duty Marines who hovered about the couple. She offered no more than a few words. From Seattle, she seemed of mixed parentage – Japanese and American, most thought – with distinctive cheekbones, penetratingly dark ovate eyes and sleek, black hair. Interestingly, a faded color Polaroid photo of Pappy and Zelda taken that day survived in Garson's album for decades.

"I was wise before I married," Pappy quipped. "Now I'm otherwise." His tiny wife pouted and poked a sharp elbow into his side. Pappy, visibly proud, and Zelda soon departed Marine Barracks to permanently take up abode in NAS Whidbey's dependent housing.

Late that final summer at NAS Whidbey, Garson joined several other liberty bound buddies on a three-day junket to British Columbia. They rode the ferry from Port Angeles, Washington to verdant Vancouver Island, the largest North American Pacific island. While he did not accompany the detail, Vandy had provided directions and suggestions for the excursion, saying the Pacific coast up there was spectacular. The liberty detail rented two classic wooden speedboats for a four-hour exploration along the estuary. To Garson's disappointment, they saw no whales, but spotted other marine life and numerous breathtaking coastal vistas. Over evening seafood and beers, there was this:

While some grumbled that the jaunt had cost too much and was sadly devoid of girls, Garson and one or two others took solace in having seen unique natural Pacific magnificence - - primeval, sylvan, dankly arboreal with rocky bays and inlets guarded by surf-lashed stony sentinels. We've seen the trees and the forest, Garson mused. It had been his first foray outside of the 48 states. He couldn't know that within not many more months, he'd travel far beyond these environs, into a frozen *terra incognita*.

Several months had passed since Garson had been "downwind" of a girl and on a date. But to his delight that night, he once more found himself in the backseat of a car, parked in a sequestered spot, this time overlooking Lake Washington east of Seattle instead of Lake Michigan back home. Goodman and his girlfriend, Char, scrunched down in front, rustling and murmuring. Garson inexpertly affected an air of suavity and maturity, hoping for a bit of febrile gamboling.

"Name's Eevie," the girl said thrusting her hand forward at him earlier in the evening. "Garson, right?" He'd been momentarily taken aback by the confidence of her voice and manner, no demur damsel here, meeting a salty Marine for the first time. He'd met her hand midway between firm and limp.

"Eevie? Goodman said it was Ivy," Garson had responded.

"Aww, what's he know? Name's short for Everdene. The Hardy novel, you know?" The arranged double date that night had resulted after meeting a new NAS Whidbey buddy, a well-toned six-footer named Goodman, devilishly handsome and well-spoken, another college boy planning to complete his degree after discharge. He'd served in the Marine reserves, and shipped over to two years of active duty – a not unusual decision for students during the Korean era: They served Stateside, assigned to duty stations while Marine divisions patrolled the Far East and Mediterrean.

"Hey!" had been Garson's glib response when he first heard given Goodman's, Avery. "We should call you 'A Very Good Man,' you know, Avery Good-Man." By his expression and reaction, it was obvious the taller Marine had heard similar half-assed comments before. But because he was affable and mannerly, he'd seemed to overlook the *faux pas*. A bond was rapidly forged between them.

When Garson at distant remove wrote of these days, he realized he'd need to flesh out characters from amorphous, whispery memory. Only the ragged photo album from those Whidbey Island days served as a guide. This much was clear: He'd developed only a few memorable relationships with fellow Marines over three years, generally because of the brevity of service together, or because of tenuous affinity or commonality. Goodman stood out, like Ridley, the Boot Camp college boy, and G. D. Coleman, with whom Garson found affinity and guidance — Marines with education, expertise and articulation – attributes he sorely lacked and envied.

Goodman wore his dull blonde hair longer than regulation white side wall trim. He hadn't long to serve, and Marine Barracks permitted some slackness for such short timers. Garson was envious of his buddy's considerable civvie wardrobe, especially the A2 leather jacket and Wellington Boots that seemed to be out of his reach. Goodman served on the same aft watch as Garson, and he took semi-monthly weekend liberties to his home in Bellevue across Lake Washington from Seattle. Since Garson's relation with Nola had grown tenuous, he'd returned to solo big city liberties, sometimes cadging rides to town. Goodman usually drove the northern route, crossing the Deception Pass Bridge to the mainland (they'd several times parked at the wayside, taking in the breathtaking view), then south down Highway 99 to central Seattle. But on one fateful journey, Goodman headed south from Oak Harbor, down the meandering highway along the sylvan island's spine toward the Mukilteo ferry dock.

"You like Seattle, right?," Goodman queried rhetorically. "Maybe Char can dig up, er, fix you up with a date sometime. We could get some chow, see a movie or something." Garson had seen the photo of Goodman's girlfriend perched prominently in his buddy's wall locker, like Betsy's, a colorized graduation studio portrait. Close inspection revealed dark eyes and shoulder length hair, pinched facial features, and, tellingly, prominent breasts jutting beneath the dark school gown.

"Wow, she's sure a looker!" Garson gushed, even though he found Char not particularly alluring in the photo or when he met her. Her cheek bones jutted too sharply, he thought, her overly wide mouth and scarlet lips bringing to mind Anne Blythe, even suggesting Katherine Hepburn, neither of whom he'd found appealing on the movie screen as a youth.

Garson and Goodman conversed incessantly while heading south down the island's narrow main road until a few miles past the unincorporated gas-station-auto-repair-general-store-saloon town of Coupeville, they were slowed by a trailer truck laden with a heavily-chained pyramid of massive logs. Garson concentrated at the myriad growth rings of the severed lumber, surmising that the trees must have been a hundred years old or more when hewn. Goodman tromped on the accelerator and pulled into the left lane to pass. At that instant, the lumber rig's brake lights flashed.

"Fuck, man!" Goodman blurted. Garson snapped his gaze to the left as his buddy drove alongside the semi-trailer. Ahead of the swaying truck puttered a battered sedan, unseen when Goodman began his passing maneuver. The four-door was now turning left from the roadway toward an unpaved driveway. Collision was imminent. Garson jammed his feet to the firewall and braced his arms on the dashboard. He shut his eyes.

Goodman plunged both feet onto the brake pedal, ignoring the clutch, and wrenched the steering wheel. Ensuing moments seemed like centuries as the pickup fishtailed on the blacktop, striking the car on its left rear quarter, sending it caroming into a shallow culvert, dust and dirt showering conjoined vehicles. Garson recalled not one sound, not a howling brake, screeching tires on pavement, not crunch and grind of metal. He hadn't even noticed that the pickup's tiny corner window behind his head had popped out.

Garson sucked in and expelled breath, pulse twitching in his neck and arms, eyes watery, legs rubbery and boneless. He'd never before been in an accident, and didn't know how to react. The pickup's engine lurched and died with a jolt.

Goodman leaped from the cab, and sprinted to the car, tilted in the roadside depression. He jerked open the door, leaned in and spoke to driver and passenger, a gray-haired, elderly couple, Garson now observed. Simultaneously, the rear door of the house down the driveway flung open and a woman in striped dress and apron bolted toward the vehicles. The lumber truck driver had sprinted back perhaps 30 yards from his rig, pulled over on the road's shoulder to offer assistance. The trio gingerly helped the car passengers into the house.

Shock subsiding, Garson stepped from the pickup to survey the damage. Passing cars slowed and occupants gaped at the scene. The panel behind the old sedan's left rear wheel well was crumpled, scraped and smeared with pickup paint. Goodman's sturdy Ford, actually his father's vehicle, had sustained a caved right bumper and watermelon dent under the headlight. Both vehicles were drivable. In time, the Whidbey sheriff arrived to jot down depositions from principals, including the lumber truck driver who, with Garson, confirmed that Goodman had not exceeded the 45-mile-per-hour speed limit, and had, indeed, attempted to pass in a proper zone. The shaken old man admitted he hadn't lowered his window and extended an arm for a left turn. No injury save for elevated pulses and palpitations were detected. Goodman escaped any official sanction. The almost calamitous incident seemed, like the first letters of their names on a roster, to draw Goodman and Garson closer.

"We call it Neckers' Point," Garson had once told Goodman about the parking lot back home overlooking Lake Michigan, a favorite haunt for Milwaukee youth and liberty sailors from the Great Lakes Training Center, in town seeking putatively nubile Polish girls. Sailors it was reputed were universally bent on the famed "submarine races," as they came to be known. Milwaukee deputies patrolled the romantic lakefront hotspot, warning car occupants with flashlights that shoulders must be visible above window lines. Garson and his first girlfriend, Franny, were far less adventurous in the rear seat of Toby's four door "gangster" Buick than his pal and

Lana were in front.

"Char says her friend just broke up with a guy," Goodman had averred. "Name's Ivy. She and Char knew each other back in high school." It later became clear that the former classmates hadn't had recent contact, for they expended considerable conversation "catching up."

Ever since Goodman had informed him of the double date, Garson carefully crafted a mental image of the girl, a virtual Hedy Lamar or Merle Oberon in his mind's eye — dark, smoldering, alluring, and, in Marine parlance, "ready to jump." But he'd been deflated at first meeting. She was tall, perhaps a half inch more than Garson, who attempted to stretch himself when they stood close, to match her height; angular with narrow eyes like his, quizzical brows, downturned mouth, an indelicate nose and a short helmet of pitch black hair like Keely Smith, Louis Prima's musical foil. "Any port in a storm," was the watchword said of girls with ordinary looks.

After an enjoyable early evening meal, Goodman took a ramble about several downtown Seattle streets and intersections, pointing out commercial landmarks, movie houses and more. Garson was startled by one site, a garish drive-in called The Chicken Shack with its large leering black sambo exterior. Goodman was apparently anxious to show off his new two-tone Chevy coupe, its distinctive odor of newness evident. He proudly boasted he'd saved judiciously while on active duty for the down payment. Later, after a winding drive up to a prominence, he parked at Hunt's Point, a spot, like Milwaukee's Necker's Point, famed for heavy breathing and lustful promise. The Chevy faced west over the Lake Washington, reflections of Seattle's city lights rippling on the water's surface, for any who cared to notice. Not yet particularly self-aware, Garson was unable to put his finger on the reason for ill-ease, but it may have been that he didn't know what Eevie expected of him.

"Eevie, huh?" Garson grunted after Goodman turned off the engine, and he and Char all but disappeared behind the front seat.

"Yeah, Eevie. Like I said," impatience obvious, "heroine of the Hardy novel. *Far from the Madding Crowd*, you know. My mom must have read it dozens of times. Know it?" He didn't.

"Oh, yeah!" he blurted. "Read some of it in high school. Guy's name's, Oak or something like that?'" He knew only that much; perhaps Betsy had told him. He'd been no more than a casual student, but recalled the cloistered teachers at Holy Redeemer and Messmer High encouraging an inchoate interest in reading, no matter that he'd now left behind classics like *Silas Marner*, *The House of Seven Gables*, *Julius Caesar* and Fletcher Pratt's engaging Civil War history, *Ordeal by Fire,* and others in favor of cheap paperbacks — Erskine Caldwell's notorious *God's Little Acre* and *Tobacco Road,* the science fiction of Robert Heinlein, Isaac Asimov, Ray Bradbury, A.E. Van Vogt, and hard-boiled detective novels of Dashiell Hammett, Raymond Chandler, even notorious oeuvre of Mickey Spillane, all packaged in prurient and fleshy paperback covers. Several of these pocket books were ensconced in the bottom of his foot locker.

While amiable over dinner, Eevie had exhibited no simpering deference to Garson's military status, almost exclusively conversing with Char while he and Goodman ate quietly. Now, in the dark rear seat, this forward, self-assured girl kept him largely at bay. Conversation lagged while incessant rustlings and tittering from the front seat indicated Goodman and Char were much engaged.

"Plan to go to college after I get out of the Corps," Garson at one point averred, trying to thaw the iciness, "maybe at Marquette back home, study journalism, become a member of the Fourth Estate, as the say – a reporter, newspaperman, maybe a book writer." It was his well-rehearsed prospect. "I write a column for the base newspaper now. You know, kinda training myself." Not mentioned was his limited authorial proficiency, and not admitted was that he hadn't even finished high school. He was running short of things to tell her, and lacked conversational adeptness to draw her out. Another silence ensued interrupted only by front seat stirrings.

Garson's thoughts reeled. What tactic might he employ that would melt Eevie's glacial resistance, to gain her sympathy?

Steeling himself, Garson leaned toward Eevie, placed his hand on her knee, and touched his lips to hers. He expected some responsive spark, an oscular rejoinder, as Vandy might have it, perhaps not like those he'd received from Karen, the Montebello girl, or from Nola, but at least some scintilla of interest. But, no: Eevie maintained tightly drawn lips, hers as thin as his. Why, as they bused, did he recall the light lipstick smudge on her glass that had disconcerted him at dinner? He couldn't say. Perhaps a different tack was needed.

"So, what about you?" Garson asked at wit's end. Eevie offered that she worked in men's furnishings at recently-expanded Frederick & Nelson's downtown department store, but hoped to continue night classes at Northwest College, business perhaps, retailing, but she wasn't sure. No more was forthcoming. She was obviously uninterested in exploring possible affinities between them. Silence once again descended into the back seat. Perhaps it was Garson's smoky breath, something he'd eaten, his face, his manner. Still, he pressed on.

"My buddy (he nodded to the front seat) told me about Lake Washington races. Boats with surplus World War airplane engines. Hydroplanes, he said, rooster tails of water sprouting behind." A cloddy attempt at innuendo. Eevie, mute, peered out the side window, her chin supported by the heel of her hand, one foot keeping time to some unheard beat. Garson mulled a different tack to win favor. He drew a deep breath and blurted:

"Gonna save myself 'til I marry" — a verbal phosphorous shell into the backseat gloom that couldn't be reloaded. He immediately regretted the asinine admission. Bile welled in his stomach. Here he was, heir to the vaunted heroes of Chapultepec, Belleau Wood, Iwo Jima and all that, unable to "slow walk and break her down," as his Negro buddies were fond of saying. He'd even lied about his innocence as though the Tijuana whore hadn't busted his cherry two years before. What must she think of him? What would she tell Char? Long minutes of silence followed, and Garson was at a loss.

An extraneous thought intruded: He recalled that one Villard Avenue wag of his youth claimed kissing involved 150 muscles – facial and other. Apparently, he'd not use any of them this night. That mental thread led to another – smoldering Karen must have exercised every one of those osculating muscles during their piquant Los Angeles movie date two years before.

It was coincidental that during his written recreation of the date with Eevie, Garson happened upon an observation by Irish author John Banville that aptly summed up his squirming discomfort. In the novel *Ghosts*, the writer caviled:

It always seemed to me a disgrace that the embarrassments of early life should continue to smart throughout adulthood with undiminished intensity. Is it not enough that our youthful blunders make us cringe at the time, but must stay with us beyond the cure, burn marks ready to flare up painfully at a mere touch? No: an indiscretion from earliest adolescence will still bring a blush to the cheek of the nonagenarian on his deathbed.

In not many months after the Seattle liberty, Goodman was discharged and departed Marine Barracks; to Garson's relief, Goodman didn't mention Eevie's impression, if any, of the modest evening.

After more than a year and a half stationed at NAS Whidbey, Garson was regarded as a Marine Barracks veteran. He'd lived only one place longer – home – and had grown comfortable in the maritime clime, not missing Milwaukee's long fierce frigid season. Contrastingly, he'd grown comfortable in the Pacific Northwest's mountainous coastal vistas these past two years – the magnificent Cascades to the east and south of Puget Sound, with towering, snow-topped Mount Rainier visible on clear days, and to the west, the dank arboreal forests of the Olympic Peninsula. Only occasionally did he feel hemmed in by the cloud-crowned prominences, morning light arriving tardily, and afternoons prematurely shadowy.

"Can't believe how these Washington people don't know how to drive in a little snow," Garson crabbed on more than one occasion. "They panic with a dusting, slipping and sliding all over the place." A few vehicles nearly grazed Marine gate sentries.

Southeastern Wisconsin, in contrast, was fairly flat with only a few gentle landform rises. Save for the times farthest from the Equinoxes, daylight back home was long. Garson missed southern Wisconsin's clear delineation of seasons, the blooming days of May and early June, summer's shady cathedral of elms; the crisp evenings of September and October, autumn's fallen leaves comprising a quilt of red, yellow and umber.

"Ever heard of 'Galloping Gertie?'" Vandy asked during a slack evening. He exhibited a font of knowledge and lore about his state. "Suspension bridge across The Narrows between Tacoma and Kitsap, the peninsula. That is south of here a ways. It was supposed to be the third longest suspension bridge in the world, only somewhat shorter that Golden Gate." The dramatic span took two years to construct.

"But even before it was finished, engineers noticed that high winds caused the deck to sway, gyrating like some shimmy dancer. That's how it got its nickname, 'Galloping Gertie.'" Garson was fascinated. "They tried to fix it, but no luck. After it opened before the war, in 1940, I think, it was like a carnival ride, some drivers said, until it actually collapsed one morning." He said there were dramatic movie scenes of the disaster.

"Do you know about this new state out here? Called Jefferson?" Garson asked. During his Greyhound ride to Whidbey from Camp Pendleton, he recalled seeing roadside signs in northern California and southern Oregon proclaiming such a state. Goodman had not heard of it. As expected, Vandy expounded about the so-called "state."

"Oh, that was a collection of eccentrics with hunting rifles who, just prior to the attack on Pearl Harbor, stopped traffic on Route 99 near Yreka. Said they had formed a patriotic rebellion bent on seceding parts of California and Oregon to form the forty-ninth state. Called it Jefferson. My Jeb history teacher laughed about it. 'Just a handful of anti-government cranks,' he said." More than a half century later, Garson mused that the heirs to that "dizzy discontentment," as Vandy had called it, were still abroad in the land.

"Whatcha got there, Vandy?" Garson asked sometime after the new year as he passed the Marine Barracks bulletin board.

"Transfer postings," the stout clerk typist returned, thumb tacking the sheets. "One here for Adak, of course, that one is always here, but we never get any takers. Interested?" Garson violently shook his head. "Here's Okinawa, and a Med cruise." Garson's eyes widened.

"Man, gonna put in for the Med. Been here on this island close to two years. Must have seniority among privates and PFCs by now." Since the days when he'd first served at NAS Whidbey with World War and Korean combat vets, Garson had yearned for the duty stations that they'd seductively described – the Mediterranean or the Far East. He'd constructed a hierarchy of preferred assignments, foremost among them the "Divvie," the Fleet Marine Force. It had been organized in 1950 to forestall efforts by President Truman and others who'd threatened the Corps's very existence. The FMF was designed as a flexible fighting force for rapid response to potential crises, especially in Cold War Europe. The unit was composed of a thousand Marines, augmented with vehicles, aircraft and supplies that plied Mediterranean waters for six months at a time; Marines made mock landings on many European shores. This was the *beau ideal* of post-Korean War assignments.

Garson had long dreamed of becoming a combat Marine, to test himself, if not in war, in simulated fighting situations, to toughen his body and mind for the rigors of conflict. That was the reason he'd enlisted in the first place. But, truth be told, he yearned to discover exotic liberty ports – Marseilles and Paris, Barcelona and Naples, and more. Scuttlebutt about weekends ashore had been planted in his brain since he'd first arrived at NAS Whidbey.

"Why not put in for embassy duty," Vandy suggested. "You are punctilious and well turned out. You would look great in dress blues, tennis shoes and a light coat of oil," he smirked. Such was the paragon of Marine Corps assignments — guard and security at United States embassies around the world — proud, visible representatives of the nation, not to mention the availability of attractive liberties in the world's great capitols. But Garson was reluctant because candidates studied and trained at Marine Corps headquarters in the nation's capital. Candidates needed to be virtually peerless. Having no more than a GED and with a record marred by the Captain's Mast, he demurred. He was also reluctant to ship over for additional years to qualify.

Then there was Sea School duty. Indeed, Garson had been attracted to that service since briefly serving in MCRD's Casual Company after graduating from Boot Camp while awaiting orders. He and others shared the well-set and supplied mess hall with natty Sea School students being trained to serve shipboard, providing security and manning the brigs on carriers, battleships and other large vessels.

Of course, Far East duty stations were another of his preferred postings – Japan, Okinawa, even Seoul. He'd accepted that the Polynesian O'Toole had burnished off-duty experiences in Tokyo and elsewhere with claims of nubile, pliable *mama-sans* readily given to satisfying any lusty Marine's desires; even Coleman's more reasonable recollections about such extracurricular matters had generated Garson's fevered visions. Antithetical to all of these possibilities was the dreaded Aleutian Island outpost.

"But, hey, you know what they say: A woman behind every tree on Adak," Vandy guffawed. "Ain' any trees though!" Indeed, the negatives about the Bering Sea duty station were monumental. No girls, no liberty, not even animal life. Garson shuddered at the thought of a year out there, halfway out in the Pacific, closer to Russia than home. He recalled a Marine instructor's description of what was called the "Thousand Mile War," when Japan attempted to invade the Aleutians in 1942, capturing a few thinly held islands until the army air corps pushed back. How cold must it be, he wondered, how bleak and desolate? When no volunteers stepped forward – which had always happened during Garson's Whidbey years – Marines were plucked to fill the draft based upon seniority. As Garson's time passed, the Damoclean Sword of seniority sagged lower.

Garson's aft watch had just returned to Marine Barracks after its 24-hour duty when Vandy encountered him.

"Gunny wants to see you, chop-chop." The hair at the nape of Garson's neck bristled in premonition. Long-faced and slender, the chest of Gunnery Sergeant Stevenson jacket displayed rows of service ribbons from recent wars as well as the Purple Heart with a star denoting two battle wounds. Despite his rank, he was personable, even to Garson after the Captain's Mast.

"Got some news for you, PFC. You're being transferred." He paused. "To Adak." Garson's heart plummeted, breath clutched in his lungs and he fought back anger; his face and ears colored. It was a crushing blow to his ego, to his Marine career, to his sense of worth; it confirmed that he was but a marginal Marine, undistinguished, not fit for the Corps's combat assignments, destined only to serve in backwater commands with other dregs. No matter that Gunny Stevenson attempted to soften the bitter news by putting it in a better perspective, Garson considered himself even less than cannon fodder.

Before he began packing his seabag, he took another solo liberty to Seattle sitting through the controversial movie that had stirred his emotions — "The Man with the Golden Arm," Otto Preminger's visceral depiction of drug use. Garson had read sensationalized reports about "dopers" among jazz musicians – Charlie Parker, Billie Holiday and others. He recognized the movie's familiar studio backlot setting of a grubby, claustrophobic cityscape. But he was convinced by Sinatra's wrenching portrayal of Frankie Machine and Kim Novak's sympathetic portrayal of Molly. The propulsive score featured Shelly Manne drum solos and Shorty Rogers's trumpet.

The Oak Harbor theater refused to screen the movie because the studio had released it without Hollywood's seal of approval; he suspected the Ritz back home had done likewise. Garson watched two showings in Seattle that weekend. All of this seemed to reinforce public opprobrium of boyhood Garson's Hollywood heroes Robert Mitchum, who'd dabbled in marijuana, and Errol Flynn's dalliance with a girl of Lana's age. Such events had disturbed Garson's screen-induced visions of the world.

Near the end of Garson's NAS Whidbey tour, troubling scuttlebutt filtered into Marine Barracks. Something ominous had occurred at the Parris Island recruit training base in South Carolina. As days passed, details accreted and circulated. Word had it that some recruits had been killed in a training exercise. A DI faced possible court martial.

"Corp's always been under a microscope," Gunter the German pronounced, "since Truman tried ta' kill our beloved 'Muthah' Marine Corps a few years back." He and others could still recite an old self-serving doggerel:

First to fight the Army's battles, and to win the Navy's fights,

And still our old friend, Harry, tries to bruise up all our rights.

We have honor, we have Glory, we're the finest ever seen,

But still our propaganda is the second rate machine.

Indeed, Garson, like all Marines, had been regularly inculcated about the jealousy by the army and navy over the Corps's matchless reputation among civilians. The Mexican War, Belleau Wood, Tarawa, Iwo Jima, the Chosin Reservoir and other battles were legendary. John Wayne, as had Wallace Beery before him, personified the public's peerless vision.

"In the army," one dogface writer had satirized, "a squad consists of thirteen men. In the Marine Corps, it consists of twelve men and a press agent." The war for the Corps's vaunted reputation had continued apace after Korea. Garson and his buddies bristled about another digging ditty:

The Marines, the Marines, those blasted Gyrenes

Those sea-going bellhops, those brass-button queens

Oh! They pat their own backs, write stories in reams,

All in praise of themselves – the U. S. Marines.

"Here is the scoop," Vandy said in an unsettled voice. After his daily clerk typist duties ended, he was surrounded by a knot of Marines. "A Parris Island DI, staff sergeant named McKeon, got drunk and ordered his platoon on a disciplinary night march into a swampy place called Ribbon Creek. Six, some who could not swim, drowned. They will court martial McKeon."

"Jesus H. fuckin' Christ!" fulminated Gunter the German. "This heah's fuckin' bullshit! Sorry 'bout them dead skinheads, but Boot Camp's Boot Camp. Gotta be ready foah a shootin' wah. But betcha the Corps's gonna go soft after this." The sergeant was prescient: Ramifications would transform Marine recruit training in the years ahead, ultimately altering the elemental ways of the Old Corps.

In all of this, Garson brought to mind the physical confrontations he'd experienced at the hands of his own Boot Camp drill instructor, Staff Sergeant Maddox, and rough treatment meted out by Corporal Reid, the MCRD junior DI and fearsome bandy rooster. While, it may have been borderline maltreatment, he'd come to regard it as necessary corrective to his soft and undisciplined civilian ways, transforming him in three months from slack and simpering civilian into man and Marine. He would be ever grateful to the former, the paragon of Marines in his eye. More would come of the Parris Island incident after his transfer from NAS Whidbey.

"Hey, Garss," Moldy beckoned. "Hear ya're gettin' shipped out to Adak." His slitted eyes, crooked smirk and sinister facial scars seemed accusatory. Yes, Garson agreed silently, those ears were bat-like. "You still writin' to that *chiquita* in Spanish L.A., man?" Garson nodded. "Well, *homme*, whyn't ya just gimme her address like I asked?" Garson had never considered Moldy a buddy, having kept the Angelino at arm's length these many months. "No Anglo like you needs more'n one *novia*." He swiped a hand over his pitch black hair. "'Sides, they say you got some *rubia* in Oak Harbor anyways, man." Garson hadn't mentioned that he and Nola's relationship was suffering from neglect. Of course, he was torn, protective of Karen, and regarding Moldy as merely a Marine on the make; he feared what the swarthy seducer might do with her. But resistance finally failed, and Garson, riven with guilt and disloyalty, watched his buddy jotting down the Montebello address. Moldy didn't even say thanks, only grinning triumphantly.

Lana wrote in her usual comingling of careful cursive and printing. She'd increased the frequency of her letters since he'd returned from leave months before; she now sent a double-sided page or more every other week, and Garson dutifully responded. But, it must be, he thought, that she had a current paucity of supplicants to display such solicitousness toward him. He could remember many names in that parade of paramours – Toby, Kawolski, even Mellish, the somewhat mysterious older guy who drove the sparking new Ford convertible, and unknown others. When, in the fullness of decades, he reviewed the words he'd written about his putative "sister," he chuckled that Lana had worked her way through numerous suitors and three husbands, in the end having no regrets. "I didn't' marry very well," she'd often boast, "but I often divorced *very* well."

"Saw your mom at Shorty's the other day," Lana wrote. "She looked very tired." Lana's letters chirped about senior year activities at Custer High, especially her dance recitals. Garson still regularly looked at the photos she'd sent to him at MCRD, of her striking provocative Cyd Charisse poses in leotards and net stockings. More, his recollection of the clandestine view of her seductive bedroom dance when they were teens remained vividly titillating.

He also wrote to Betsy, of course, dutifully filling Marine Corps stationery with chatty details and endearments, yearnings and importunings, expectations of their marriage and a wonderful future together.

In the week before departure, Garson purchased a hard-sided piece of luggage, and fitted his meager collection of civvies inside. He jammed summer uniform khakis and worsteds into the bottom of his seabag. Seasons on Adak, according to wags, didn't change: It was always foul weather, with, in addition to other Marines, only swabbie airdales, rats and ptarmigans available as companions.

Chapter 5

NAS Adak Island

"Playground of the Bering Sea"

In the depth of that night Garson's bunk was jolted, startling him awake from a dark dreamless sleep. Beneath him, his rack's metal legs screeched across the tile deck, skittering catawampus, carrying him to the middle of his cubicle. Befuddled at first, he soon realized it was some Marine much in his cups late returning from the "slop chute," bent upon rousing buddies.

"Fuckin' dipshit," Garson called out, bleary eyed. He lifted his torso, supporting himself on his forearms, peering toward the foot of his rack to identify the culprit. Garson saw no one.

"Gonna kick your fuckin' ass!" Shaky Blake shouted from the adjacent cubicle. Still unseen, the harassing culprit had apparently moved down the squad bay.

Garson's head was jerked to the windows where an ominous visual display assaulted from outside — lurid flashes of dazzling whites, bloody reds, sickly yellows, freezing blues – that ripped the blackness apart. A thunderous crack and rumble rolled in from the surrounding highlands as Garson's bunk shuddered anew.

Marine Barracks itself gyrated, swayed and shimmied. Steel helmets and marching packs crashed to the deck from atop wall lockers. Ceiling light globes rattled, threatening to fall and shatter. The very earth, the most existential aspect of Garson's life convulsed and contorted. Pounding feet and terrorized shouts and screams amplified the unnerving cacophony. It must be the end of the world. He was paralyzed.

Somehow in the tumult and without realizing it Garson had found his rosary, the talisman pressed into his hands before he'd departed for Boot Camp by his pious Aunt Ida who frequented Wisconsin sites of Virgin visitations. But instead of reciting "Hail, Marys," Garson brought to his febrile mind the Negro aphorisms of Corporal Falson. "Ain' scared a' dyin' 'er returnin' ta my Heavenly Father," he'd intoned. "But I ain't homesick yet." The Florida NCO typically deflected suppositions of his piety. "No, no, man, I'm standin' in the need a' grace myself."

"It's a quake! A goddamed quake!" Scenes from the movie "In Old San Francisco" popped into Garson's mind: Buildings swaying, walls cracking and tumbling, pulverized into dust, bodies crushed. Fires flared. Another image quickly followed: Adak Island, he'd been told early after arrival, was precariously perched on three unstable undersea peaks, a three-legged Aleutian stool that could be toppled by some volcanic paroxysm such as this. He wished for the little Christ Child statuette he'd left home during last fall's leave; it had brought him fortune in the past. But earth's concussive convulsions continued, endlessly it seemed, hours certainly, tens of minutes surely. No metaphor, analogy or simile was adequate to verbally measure the experience. But all of that was yet to come.

Every Marine Garson encountered who'd served on forsaken Adak Island recounted a nearly identical recollection of his introduction to the volcanic spit, almost a seared collective memory, no matter the circumstance, no matter the season, no matter the weather. Less than a year before the big quake, Garson had been no exception.

On the island's snow-dusted tarmac, the DC-6's quartet of engines roared deafeningly before the props whirled to a stop. Wind howled outside, and ice pellets pecked ravenously at the windows. A rolling stairway thumped into the fuselage. Garson and Vandy, adjacent to one another on the harrowing flight from Kodiak, had been all but mute during those long hours, withdrawn into private thoughts and apprehensions. Garson's rotund buddy had nearly buckled when he'd been added to the transfer list from NAS Whidbey. Now, they released aircraft harnesses and gathered themselves. Just then, the cargo hatch flung open. Every eye turned to the doorway. Shoved by cruel wind, a ghostly wraith entered, draped in a snowy hooded parka that fell below his knees, his shoulders sparkling with icy epaulets.

"Rime on the Arctic Mariner." Garson screwed up his face quizzically, not understanding Vandy's parodic Coleridge reference. The navy greeter stomped snow from outsized rubber boots and peeled back the hood to reveal the cap of a chief petty officer. For a few seconds, he grinned wolfishly at the impatient human cargo. His words, Garson thought, bore the taint of inter-service antipathy, remembering the Boot Camp inculcation that Marines and sailors weren't even of the same species.

"Welcome to Adak!" the CPO announced, mock eloquently, "the Playground of the Bering Sea, the Golden Link in the Aleutian Chain!" Garson shuddered. He and the others had reached the virtual end of the world, almost as far west as it was possible to travel – four thousand miles from home, in the middle of nowhere, the frozen wasteland of his fears and premonitions for the past year.

Eight hours before, the navy cargo plane had powered through the turbulent leaden sky from Kodiak Island off the coast of Alaska Territory. But even above the thick cloud blanket, the aircraft had been buffeted by perpetually churning drafts, jostling Garson and other passengers like a cheap carnival coaster. He and his buddies had been wedged side-saddle along the window line, mere feet from massive cargo containers strapped down the middle of the deck.

When they'd reached altitude and crossed the continental peninsula, the cargo plane struggled over the cruel Bering Sea thousands of feet below. Ominous black and gray clouds, unlike benign pillowy cushions Garson remembered from flying movies, boiled outside, buffeting the aircraft; these were hard, angry formations that, Garson had suspected, might plunge the insubstantial DC-6 into the vicious waters below. The aircraft's metal fixings had trembled and rattled. Once, he'd unharnessed and stood wide-legged, unsteadily snapping photos with his tiny camera, barely maintaining his footing in the effort. The developed images would later be but blurs.

Garson had flown, not counting the journey from Seattle to Kodiak Island the day previous, only once in his life – when his father purchased him a giddy glider flight at postage stamp Aero Park Airport west of Milwaukee the summer after he'd graduated from ninth grade. The memory of those 30 airborne minutes, buoyant, nearly weightless, soaring and silent save for the rush of air outside had often been recalled. It had been thrilling and invigorating. But this flight from Kodiak was no airborne idyll.

The deafening drone of the cargo plane's engines had obliterated nearly all verbal communication less than a shout, so Garson and his fellow travelers had been wrapped in their own thoughts, fears and regrets. He recalled that the initial leg of the long journey the day before, west across the Gulf of Alaska from Seattle had been less worrisome. At the Kodiak naval air station where the dozen or so Marines in the transfer contingent had overnighted in a barracks that reeked of disuse, mildew and vermin, Vandy had told Garson that the Navy DC-6, their transport west into regions unknown, was powered by four Pratt and Whitney radial engines, each with a four-bladed prop. The buddy was conversant even with such details.

"We'll fly at about 30,000 feet," Vandy had averred confidently, "maybe 300 miles an hour." While they'd served together at NAS Whidbey, and Vandy helped doctor Garson's ID card, they'd never been close. Pudgy with a slightly protruding belly, short legs and small feet, Vandy displayed one jutting incisor, giving him a half vampirish leer. He'd used most weekend liberties to bus home to Spokane.

Some at NAS Whidbey had whispered that there was something not quite regular about him. While gregarious and sometimes comical, Vandy had never mentioned girlfriends, even eschewing typical boasts about getting his "ashes hauled." They'd never taken liberty together, except when a group trooped to downtown Oak Harbor for movies or an evening at The Canteen. Even then, Vandy had never been seen drinking beer or alcohol. More, unlike others, he'd not flirted with Flo, the comely cashier who'd won the eye of many NAS Whidbey Marines.

Steeped in such thoughts during the troubling journey, Garson had concluded it would be hours before reaching the dreaded destination – more than a thousand miles from Kodiak to Adak, his final destination, half a dozen time zones and four thousand lonely miles from home. His troubled mind was interrupted when word was shouted above the rattling and growling engine din that the plane had passed over Dutch Harbor on Unalaska Island. Over the Bering Sea now, the aircraft struggled southwest against prevailing westerly winds toward the halfway point in the thousand-mile scimitar of Aleutians. Still, 450 more miles to travel in this jolting journey into *terra incognita*, Vandy had noted. Garson had been tempted to pray that the navy crew would bring the Boeing plane to safe harbor, to prevent it from being swallowed by the ravenous sea below. He'd again thought of the old saw of former Adak Marines:

"There's a woman behind every tree," they'd universally chorused, always following with the caveat. "Ain't no fuckin' trees though!"

The aircraft had shuddered anew, interrupting Garson's reverie. He'd gripped the restraining harness with both hands. The voluminous cargo containers shifted inboard, and he'd pulled back his knees nearly to his chest. He'd craned his head toward a window to see thick vaporous formations swirl about the plane like wolves circling a dying prey. Ice had pelted the window. Engines wailed as if in pain. Hydraulics juddered and avionics beneath him whined and whirred. In the anxious moments of descent, he'd seen ailerons dip. Buffeted ceaselessly, the aircraft labored through the angry vaporous masses. When a tiny vista opened between the overcast, Garson had spied a craggy, snow-capped prominence, Great Sitkin, he was later told, an active volcano on a neighboring island. On occasional clear days ahead, he would witness its steamy exhalations.

In minutes, the plane had descended toward Adak over a jumble of hills, the most prominent of which was benign Mount Moffett, the island's tallest point, shrouded like old Grandma Servais's thick gray shawl. Garson's heart had tattooed until the fuselage's fishtailing, yawing attitude finally aligned with the runway. Engines labored loudly when it thudded onto the tarmac, the aircraft bouncing once before settling. Brakes had howled as Garson's body was wrenched sideways until the plane slowed in its approach to an unassuming rectangle that served as a terminal. It was less substantial than Curtiss-Wright airport back home. Garson's heartrate slowed. Then the naval "Ancient Mariner" had opened the hatch.

When the new arrivals filed outside, they were peppered with stinging frozen pellets driven horizontally by a gale. Garson squinted. There wasn't much to see anyway. He and the others were ill-prepared for the blast, wearing only dress uniforms and raincoats that flapped about their legs. The navy CPO who'd welcomed them stood below, gazing at each new arrival in turn, like a headsman at the block, Garson later reflected.

Loaded into a converted ambulance splattered with mud, they rumbled over rutted roads, and bounced around a traffic circle at the center of which rose a tall, colorful wooden totem of recent vintage – the creation of some derisive craftsmen in the manner of a Pacific coastal Indian effigy. Topped by a grinning, winged bomb, the carved icon included images of a bear, a wolf and a comic dual-headed duck (or was it a ptarmigan?) configured in the imperial Russian style.

The vehicle jerked and juddered its way on, over chuck-holes and rutted tracks toward a plateau upon which was arrayed a neat rank of concrete billets, all of contemporary concrete construction. Before, Garson had feared they'd be billeted in the dissolute World War quonsets he'd spotted that were scattered in the surrounding undulating landscape. At roadway's end, they pulled up beside a grimy cinder block garage, its oily parking area bearing ancient military vehicles – scarred jeeps and pickups and another personnel carrier — the Marine motor pool. It seemed to confirm the Corps's vision that the United States Defense Department placed Marines in low esteem since former President Truman's devaluation attempt.

"Last Chance Gas Station," a large sign proclaimed. "Cheapest Gas West of Kodiak." There were many ironists on this island, Garson thought.

He and his fellow travelers reluctantly exited the conveyance and shouldered seabags. Garson pulled his neck into the collar of his battle jacket, holding his garrison cap in place against the whistling wind. As he trudged dejectedly toward what was to become his home for a twelve-month eternity, a bare-headed Marine with an impressive jaw and broad grin flung open a third story window.

"You'll be *sorr-ree!*" he shouted, leering like some movie villain. Garson soon met the greeter, "Big John" Ringer, a mountainous, muscled Marine from Ohio, who, he'd learn in time, had been offered a Notre Dame football scholarship. But he admitted "knocking up" a "loose-limbed toots" shortly before graduation, and decided to flee responsibility into the Corps. He wasn't proud of that abandonment, and belatedly determined to rectify the situation. "Might write to the mother of my little shaver. He's two now. Maybe put things right."

From Ringer, a nine-month resident of NAS Adak conversant with such things, Garson quickly heard of potential seismic paroxysms that sometimes visited all along the thousand-mile curve of the Aleutian chain, from seabed fissures that eons ago belched up magma to form these insecure, craggy bits of Bering Sea firmament.

"If a big enough quake hits us up here," Ringer amplified, "it might dump us into this freezing drink." Garson uncomfortably visualized an unstable rocky isle slipping beneath the waves – one more worry that would plague him on nights when his unquiet mind revved like a racing engine that wouldn't go into gear.

"Why, we're so far west, we're almost East," Ringer mused. "You know you'd be a day younger if you got that far." Jovial and gentle, the impressive Marine had a square block of a head, outsized jaw and wide mouth, reminding Garson of the Sunday comic character "Alley Oop." Ringer usually parked a tobacco plug behind his lower lip. His breath was fetid.

Adak was not a typical Marine duty station. It was a world apart, isolated from the "real" one. Garson wasn't certain if he'd assembled other facts from barracks wags like Ringer, read about them in base library books or gathered them decades later while fitfully scribbling notes in preparation for an eventual memoir. Part of an island group identified as the Adreanofs, Adak, like its neighbors, had heaved out of the sea by volcanism. It was a large island, over 30 miles long and 20 wide, the naval base occupying its northeast corner.

"We're up here watching Russkies," said Blake who some called "Shaky" behind his back because of his oblique demeanor. Garson was privy to later whisperings about some squirrely-eyed behavior. Some tempted the fates by erroneously informing Blake that the Top Sergeant wanted to see him, just to watch the twitchy private almost convulsive reactions.

"Man, Shaky talks about 'gazarians' sometimes," related another observer. "It's some kinda bird, I think, like a ptarmigan. Only Shaky can see them. He's not even a boozer!" The company clerk, Sergeant Lewis, would later identify the mysterious creature as "Blake's *rara avis*." That drove Garson to his paperback dictionary.

"Shaky needs a fuckin' Section 8, a discharge, I tell ya'!" was another barracks assessment. "Seen guys like this before. I know a thing 'er two 'cause I seen a thing 'er two." Blake was a "slick sleeve," a base private, meaning something — court martial, captain's mast or untoward behavior — had blocked promotion. Here was more evidence for Garson's despond over another consignment to a duty station of lesser Marines – common fodder in a war against the Russkies.

Still, Blake was articulate and knowledgeable, and, like Garson, a reader.

"These Pribilof Islands're spittin' distance from here, a few flying hours to the west," Blake put in. "You know, Japs invaded up here, taking Attu and Kiska in '43. That's why the army air corps established this base. Fly boys bombed the Hell out of the Japs, and eventually drove 'em out." Adak Island had been transferred to the navy after the war, he added, to accommodate aerial patrols toward the Soviet Union. He'd read a lot about this, that seemed certain.

"That's why you see all these derelict quonsets round here," Shaky said, his right arm sweeping at the scene through a top floor window. Indeed, the undulating landscape was populated with a dissolute collection of corrugated half-circles, rusted, weather-worn and wind-blown. They'd been hastily constructed for the army and navy during the World War, but not neatly arrayed as at San Diego Recruit Depot or Camp Pendleton. On Adak, they'd been plunked down helter-skelter wherever a suitably level rectangle of surface was available. Most billets featured wooden decks, but some were erected on concrete foundations as Garson would discover.

"Only three ways you're gonna get off this here Rock," proposed heavy-jawed Ringer, ever seeing the glass half empty: "Serve your time (he meant a year on Adak), leave in shackles after court martial or..." – he paused to make certain Garson fully comprehended the import – "zipped up in a body bag."

"Kinda a cold weather Alcatraz, huh?" Garson added, again recalling scenes of Burt Lancaster in his favorite prison movie, "Brute Force."

Save for its dangerous, rocky shorelines, much of Adak's acreage had been denuded and scarred by military habitation, Still, the island flourished with sub-Arctic foliage — low shrubs, lichens, mosses, and long, entangling sedges that tore at boots and legs during training exercises through the uncompromising terrain. In the teaming Bering Sea, Arctic mammals — walruses, seals and whales — might be seen, some said. But the island itself was home to only one indigenous life form – a species of grouse called the ptarmigan. The island's "national bird" changed plumage, from winter white to mousy summer brown, and its feet were protected with absurd feathers. It shared the island only with interloping rats that had come ashore with the military, and grown fat and sassy — targets of sport for some Marines.

To Aleut Indians, the word "*adaq*" meant "father." Garson thought the male designation appropriate because of the old saw about no women or trees. Army fliers stationed on Adak during the World War had planted a copse of 14 fir trees in the under-nourishing soil; after a dozen years the lonely stand had grown no taller than three feet. Later, when the navy took charge of the island, some satiric sailors or SeaBees, had erected a sign that proclaimed: "You are now entering *and* leaving the Adak National Forest."

"Think the sun's gone away for good?" was an oft-heard query. "It's like the earth somehow wobbles when the sun's about to shine on Adak, turning away so not one ray reaches the island," was one unscientific riposte. The feeling of utter isolation was compounded by the oceanic climate whose moderate temperatures were countervailed by incessant precipitation, infernal fog and mist, often driven by gusting winds the Aleuts called *williwaws*. Atop 400-foot Mount Moffett, one-third of the days recorded snow, totaling one hundred inches a year. With sun an uncommon commodity, dampness insinuated into billets and bodies.

Garson never fully adjusted to insinuating daylight that lingered late during "summer" and into early fall, until well past "Taps." He burrowed under his blankets most nights to escape illumination flooding the squad bay through tall unshrouded windows. Occasionally, he arose to study Mount Moffett, virtually aglow in moonlight.

Not surprisingly, Garson yearned for the change of seasons, a comforting feature back in Wisconsin. He missed the spring renewal of trees transformed from barren brown to leafy green, creating virescent vaulted arches over city streets and avenues; grass, budding shrubs and plants erupting in color, and sighing breezes instead of raging tempests; the return of robins and songbirds, flitting butterflies, the nightly thrum of insects and amphibians, and scampering squirrels and rabbits released from winter torpor. Summer radiance had always lifted Garson's spirits.

The advice that Adak had no women, Garson discovered, wasn't accurate; but females were precious few and unavailable out here.

It was a worse circumstance, Garson felt, because he saw them. He could look but couldn't touch. A handful of officers and senior NCOs who served at NAS Adak with wives and families were billeted in segregated base housing. Some wives found work in the base exchange, the laundry and elsewhere, supplementing husbands' military pay. But no girls older than ten were evident. As time passed, even the less comely women grew more attractive. Like a typical 19 and 20 year old, Garson's hormones raged and colored perspective.

"You *cow*-casians," smirked "Red" Bolden, one of the guard company's Negro Marines "ain't gettin' much sun tan up here, huh?" Strikingly, the color of his cork-screw curls determined his sobriquet. Slender with dark patches under his eyes and jowly cheeks, his skin bore the hue of russet leaves; his eyes were disconcertingly obsidian, reflecting light, Garson was reminded when he saw Ridley Scott's film "Blade Runner" decades later, almost like Replicants. Bolden's demeanor was usually prickly. At first ill at ease around him, Garson concluded that the Missouri Marine used racial references as prods; when Garson came to ignore his buddy's reflexive goading, he penetrated the defensive shell, developing a passable relationship. Still, Bolden preferred the clannish association of fellow Negroes.

But because Garson's bunk was proximate to the glowering PFC, he overheard conversations between Bolden and his buddies. More, Garson affected an air of obsequiousness around Negroes, thinking that might foster their tolerance, even permitting him to become privy to privileged exchanges and repartee. Thus, he gained an understanding, even an appreciation of their backgrounds and situations.

As at NAS Whidbey, guard company duty watches were 24 hours on and 24 off, with four-hour gate watches and roving patrols, a schedule with which Garson was accustomed, having served the previous two years in such routine. The on-duty company on NAS Adak was housed on the lowest deck of Marine barracks, along with supply and storage. Off-duty guards were billeted on the main barracks deck. The second level housed Marine headquarters and clerical offices as well as non-guard personnel — Headquarters & Services "pogues." Vandy, a clerk typist at NAS Whidbey, was assigned to similar duty.

The NAS Adak Marine guard company to which most were assigned was responsible for security at the island's naval installation. But this was no spit and polish outfit as at NAS Whidbey, where guards wore dress greens, white helmets and braided brassards. Instead Garson and others donned no more than dungarees and, when typical weather demanded, heavy below-the-knee parkas, cold weather vests and the ludicrous, outsized "Mickey Mouse" boots issued upon their arrival. Garson recalled such clothing from Korean era training films, newsreels and movies.

Moreover, NAS Adak had but one "gate" – entry and egress to the expansive fuel and ammo dump. It was said that storage facilities were scattered about the northern reaches of the island, but Garson's memory after so many years was indistinct about such details. Marines at the gate certified manifests and other documents, and maintained logs of all the tanker and truck traffic that trundled through. More important, it seemed to Garson, were the roving patrols that circuited and crisscrossed the base around the clock.

Marines also guarded the same aircraft, sleek P2-V Neptune bombers, as at NAS Whidbey, that were nightly tethered to the tarmac against frequent gale-force winds, their blue underbodies and stinger tail radar housings and bomb pods reflecting runway illumination. The rakish aircraft daily patrolled Bering Sea waters for Russian submarines.

Ever muddy Marine barracks' Jeeps were shrouded in canvas with isinglass sides and rear windows; the vintage vehicles were heavily sprung, and sentinels were wont to mutter that the Adak uniform issue should have included kidney belts. Save for the landing strip and macadam roadways, island passages were mazes of muddy tracks, laden with ruts and crater-deep pock marks. Shot-gun passengers – Garson's typical assignment – operated windshield wipers manually. Worse, vehicle heaters provided no more than tepid comfort against the damp cold because Jeeps had no blowers, meaning that when the stubby vehicles slowed or stopped, not a thermal of warmth issued forth.

"Got a driver's license?" Garson was asked. "'Course," he lied. He'd driven only sparingly before – illegally when he'd briefly owned the lemony Chevy convertible at NAS Whidbey. Of course, the car's three-gear steering column shift and soft clutch bore up to his heavy-footedness. Marine Jeeps, in contrast, featured floor gearboxes; clutches that strained calf muscles and short wheel bases that made steering a chore. The few times Garson was permitted to drive, gears screeched excruciatingly, and the vehicle lurched and bucked each time he released the clutch. Even double clutching failed to smooth gear changes. One of the final times he drove, Garson nearly lost control, veering from the muddy track toward a ditch.

"Whoa, man! Whoa! Stop!" Falson shouted. Garson braked, his neck snapping. "You tryin' ta fuckin' kill me and Deets here?" Garson was relieved of driving duty that night, and after. Word passed of his pitiful skills, and he was permanently relegated to shotgun or the jolting back seat.

"Look at them ugly fuckers," PFC Deets said. He flashed the headlights on high beam, scattering a covey of fat brown rats that scurried among the hulking mounds of garbage and debris. During that roving patrol, Deets took the steering wheel, his clutch foot dexterous and shift changes smooth. They veered off the usual rutted track during the midnight to four tour, bucked up a pitched draw, through (Garson borrowed another writer's phrase) "chassis-deep mud the consistency of horse glue."

Called "Josh" by white Marines and "Lone Star" by Negro buddies because of his home state, Deets's true name was Joshua Dietrich. Tall, blocky and muscular, his skin was the color of mahogany, and he displayed a smile as broad as his home state. He was invariably sociable with nearly everyone in the Marine Barracks. Garson would in time learn that he also possessed an unerring sense of direction and distance.

Riding "shotgun" in the Jeep that night was Falson, the Negro corporal whose hometown, he was proud to proclaim, was Haines City, Florida. Of average height and physique, his facial features reminded Garson of Africans — eyes glossy, skin nearly iridescent blue-black; his nose was broad with flaring nostrils, his lower lip blubbery. Garson regarded his personality and demeanor as neutral. They first met playing pool in the Marine Barracks rec room.

"Name Folsom?" Garson queried. "Like the prison?"

"Naw, man, that's Folsom, in California. I'm Fall-*son*." The NCO, like others in his narrative, grew in memory.

Haines City, Garson learned from various conversations direct and overheard, was initially known as Clay Cut when the railroad came through early in the century. Falson's forebears were citrus pickers who'd migrated from elsewhere in the South. He confirmed information that Garson's MCRD buddy, Liska, had related about the deadly Jim Crow plight of Negroes: There've been more lynchings in our so-called Sunshine State than in any other state of the old Confederacy, Falson said matter-of-factly. He was the first Garson heard spew the term "pecker woods" at Negro-hating white folks.

"Fuckin' rats! Hate 'em!" Deets grumbled that night on roving patrol. "Heard some Jarheads come out here nights, flashin' spotlights, an' poppin' them with pistols." Garson said, though he didn't credit that as anything but scuttlebutt. How would a Marine account for missing ammo and having a dirty pistol bore? he asked himself.

From information gleaned during his months in the guard company, he discovered much about Deets, Falson, Bolden and a few other Negroes. Deets, for example, had actually picked cotton; his father had been a sharecropper who, confirming other stories Garson had overheard, had been unable to break free from a system, lifting himself only a small step beyond shackled servitude.

"Got two brothers," Falson revealed during a pool game with Garson. "When we was kids, my pappy went north before the war" – he meant the World War. Falson surprised Garson with his candor. "Said he was looking for work and better things for us. Never came back. Many years later, a colored woman came to our house, askin' if our mama was Donita Falson. Claimed she was from Kansas City. Name'a Estelle Holloway, she said. 'We're related.' Seems, when he went north, pappy changed his name and made more babies with that woman, Donita — two girls, our half-sisters. Never knew 'em before and never met 'em since."

The NAS Adak Marine guard company was also, of course,

responsible for operating the base brig, a dank segregated space on the lowest deck, divided into no more than a half dozen barred cells. As at NAS Whidbey, prisoners were minor offenders who'd been sentenced after a captain's mast or summary court martial – adjudged guilty of sleeping on post, insubordination, failure to obey lawful orders and similar minor misdeeds whose penalties did not exceed 30 days of brig time. AWOL, the most common offense, was virtually impossible on the Bering Sea island. What was more, much to the guards' delight, sailors usually comprised the majority of the population, and miscreant airdales and SeaBees were ready targets for invective and ill-treatment that rarely rose to the level of physical cruelty.

"Mind the step, you fuckin' clowns," Garson and other Marine chasers shouted as they marched prisoners to chow and to work details. "Fuckin' dipshit Deck Apes!"

Garson never conducted a census of Marine Barracks personnel, but he judged the total complement numbered not many more than 50. As at NAS Whidbey, most were white, of course, but perhaps a third of the company seemed to be comprised of Negroes, Mexicans, Puerto Ricans, Pacific Islanders and Americans of color. Initially Garson worried that he once more served with misfits, Marines of limited potential and prospects, serving out on the Cold War's front line. He was soon disabused of such jaundiced judgements, and became confident in the fighting readiness of every Adak Marine.

Prematurely during Adak Island's abbreviated "summer" season, the Marine Barracks commanding officer ordered half of the company on a day-long exercise, a typical combat "problem," as it was known. The second half of the company would replicate the situational later in the season. Both units were to simulate cold weather battlefield conditions with the added benefit of providing rigorous physical conditioning for Marines with limited physical activity. The exercise also afforded an opportunity for Garson and others to explore a new and raw part of Adak Island, the authentic Aleutian boonies. The unit donned the full panoply of cold weather gear that included cumbersome Mickey Mouse boots and parkas. Garson's unit shouldered M-1s and BARs, and boarded a pair of ungainly flat-bottomed craft in Sagak Bay (or so Garson later surmised) on the island's west coast. The boats did not venture far from shore, remaining mostly protected from the dangerous gray-green sea.

Still, Garson worried. He'd somehow avoided the Marine requirement for swimming proficiency. Even though life preservers had not been issued for the excursion, danger lurked in his mind. The day was uncommonly clear albeit blustery wind-buffeted the ersatz defenders. They spilled over gunnels at Three Arms Bay on the Yakut Peninsula, not like charging Marines at Iwo or even on mock Mediterranean landings, but like disorganized stragglers over the stony beach where they ate a cold and cheerless midday meal. Garson dined on packaged cheese of unknown vintage, an unfulfilling concrete cereal bar washed down with metallic canteen water. He was mesmerized by the pulsing surf that clawed up the beach incline, bearing detritus – sea-scoured driftwood, tiny bones of dead fish and sea life, riven fishing nets and ruptured buoys. Variegated pebbles and stones swirled and swished like a myriad susurrating sirens.

With a fresh-faced Lieutenant Hildebrand in the lead, the unit afterward set off through tall tundra grass that swayed like waves in on-shore breezes. The island vegetation grasped and clutched at heavy boots and legs like tentacles of giant octopi. Progress over the undulating landscape was glacial; ranks grew ragged. Pack straps and rifle sling dug into Garson's bony shoulders despite the thick parka. They'd trod for an hour, maybe more. Garson groused silently. He sucked for breath and flagged; perspiration welled in his armpits and dribbled down his spine, his forehead slick beneath the steel helmet.

Garson's fantasy pried its way forward in his mind: Here he and his buddies trudged in the desolate environment, weapons at the ready, preparing to counterattack Russkie invaders. Emulating the Japanese strategy early in the World War of landing up here to attack America, the dastardly Reds were now attacking from nearby Pribilof Islands. NAS Adak Marines were front line defenders of the nation. He gripped his M-1 tighter, right index finger edgy on the trigger lock. Were he and his buddies up to the task? But these invaders were no mere play-acting Camp Pendleton Aggressors. This was the real deal. The fantasy was quickly swept away by the wind.

At intervals, the unit maneuvered in various formations, on command flopping to the sodden ground. Garson rolled the rifle butt into his shoulder, inserted a clip of eight blank rounds into the receiver and rammed a cartridge into the chamber.

"Commence fire!" the lieutenant barked. The fusillade spit impotent red sparks into the gloom until empty metal clips clanged free. Garson gripped another eight-round clip from his cartridge belt, preparing to thumb it into the receiver when the "Cease fire" command aborted the action.

The unit arose, cleared and slung weapons and labored for fifteen minutes up a clingy rise. When he gained the summit, a knifing, icy wind scoured Garson's face, tearing his eyes.

"Holy fuckin' shit, what's 'at?" someone in the lead rank shouted. Garson and a few others stumbled, gape-mouthed gazes fixed a football field distant just beyond the craggy bay's verge where a phenomenon churned the gray-green waters.

"Some kinda fuckin' midget sub. Soviet, likely," another voice added.

"Shark!" a third Marine declared.

"Ain' no shark," yet another voice contradicted. It was Deets. "No sharks up here in these waters." A huge dorsal fin poked above the surface, tall, like the black mast of a strange sailing ship. A second fin crested nearby, spouting vaporous breath from a blowhole. The pair seemed to gambol just beyond the frothy surf line.

"Close ranks. Keep moving!" Lieutenant Hildebrand growled.

"How far you make 'em, Deets?" Falson asked. Deets squinted, calculating that the creatures were probably 60 or 70 yards away.

"Maybe it's some kinda sea monster, or a dragon, something like them things that hide in Scottish lakes," a recently-transferred Marine conjectured.

"Don' think so," said Deets. The sleek and shiny creatures circled one another, roiling the sea, creating foamy wakes. Tail flukes rose and hammered the water. White undersides flashed. Then one whale breached, lifting itself almost entirely free of the water, crashing back to create a tidal wave.

"Killer whales," clarified Blake, "Orcas," he said, again exhibiting impressive knowledge; cousins to whales, dolphins and porpoises, he later imparted, carnivorous mammals that hunted seals and penguins in packs, like wolves. By the size of those jutting dorsal fins, almost like piratical sails, the creatures must measure 20-feet long or more and weigh thousands of pounds. Garson was flabbergasted, his mouth hanging open. But when the Marine contingent trudged nearer bay's shore, the whales submerged and were seen no more.

The unit thereafter was arrayed in more and various battle formations, and conducted live firing exercises until late afternoon. They once again tramped through the grasping wavy tundra, and returned to the flimsy boats. Garson and others were amazed that the sun remained high so late in the day, brighter than the end of June in Milwaukee.

Several months after joining the guard company, Garson had been transported by Jeep to Sweeper Cove on the island's northeast coast. Dropped off at one of the weathered wooden piers, he relieved "Shaky" Blake for the four-hour duty, midnight to four. His buddy appeared like an olive-drab wraith wafting in the dark night.

Garson had been apprised of the duty: Guard against any untoward activity from a Jap fishing boat that had developed engine trouble and put into the island for repairs. The shabby vessel carried two augmenting masts with fore and aft sails. Even the freshet off Kuluk Bay couldn't clear the boat's fetid fishy odor. Armed with his M-1 and a .45 sidearm belted about the bulky parka, he suspiciously watched crewmen at their work; only a few more than a half dozen comprised the vessel's complement, Garson judged.

As chilling dampness seeped through his outer garments, a random thought came to mind, about imported ten-cent tin toys that appeared on store shelves some years after the World War. "Cheap Jap crap," his boyhood pal, Toby, had crabbed because the insubstantial metal playthings quickly chipped, bent and fell apart. It had been the defeated nation's initial effort to recover its economy, producing such shoddy export goods. Toby had it on good evidence that the tiny, hollow cars, trucks and boats were fabricated from reclaimed soup and C-Ration cans, swearing he'd spotted American lettering and logos inside.

Garson was pulled back to the present as ponderous mooring ropes groaned and squeaked against the pier's bollards, the ship rising and lowering with the bay's swell and decline. Then he recollected scenes from a motion picture, "Captains Courageous," that he'd seen at the Ritz back home; it was one of those so-called wartime "re-releases" first screened during the late 1930s. He'd detested the rich and spoiled pantywaist portrayed by Freddie Bartholomew whose character found himself on a Gloucester fishing boat. Garson was especially put off by the kid actor's patrician affectations, pronouncing Spencer Tracy's "Port-a-gee" name as "Man-*you*-ell." He visualized the claustrophobic below-deck scenes on this Japanese schooner, slant-eyed sailors swaying in hammocks after grueling and dangerous labor on unpredictable northern seas.

During a later late-night watch, Garson observed a young boatman climb onto the deck, stretching and exhaling blooms of misty air. He turned, and after a pause inclined his head in what Garson interpreted as an acknowledgement. Garson had lived his youth with the Pacific war in the foreground of life, in Hollywood movies and in newsreels that had engendered antipathy, even hatred that still pulsed viscerally. Japs had invaded these Aleutians before, remember; perhaps they'd try that again.

On Garson's next duty, the youthful sailor reappeared. He wore shapeless trousers and a canvas jacket; in the gloom, Garson discerned only that the crewman seemed about his own age. He again acknowledged Garson's presence. Marines with daytime watches had reported that most of the Japs were an older set, middle aged, some gray haired.

During long dockside hours, with damp cold penetrating multiple uniform layers, Garson recalled the collection of prurient artful prints and garish black and white photos that O'Toole had proudly displayed at NAS Whidbey – nude women, geishas he'd said, shamelessly baring their breasts and furzy pudenda. Might, Garson wondered, the young fisherman, so far from home, carry such images? he wondered.

On deck on another night appeared an older man coiling heavy rope. Of course, Garson spoke no Japanese, but somehow he gained the crewman's attention, and through gesture and pantomime, asked if the young sailor with whom he was familiar might come up to converse. Suspicion was evident. Still he walked to the below-deck hatch.

"Toshiro," the man called. "Toshiro Mifune!" After long minutes, the young crewman, rubbing his narrow eyes, climbed onto the deck. He met Garson at the stern where ropes snugged the boat to the dock. He set down a small propane lantern that under lit his sleepy face with bluish shadows. He bowed once more. Though he felt foolish, Garson reciprocated. Again, using the paltry communications available to him, Garson asked if the young crewman possessed any images of women, naked women, or "fuckey-fuckey pictures." He tried an array of gestures, removing his mittens and poking his right middle finger into the "O" of his left hand. Still unable to break the communication barrier, he paused in frustration. Then the older man returned, apparently having overheard Garson.

"No fuckey-fuckey pitcahs, *Ma-leen*," he glowered. Turning to Toshiro, it was obvious that he summarily ordered the young man below deck. Garson was deflated for the remainder of his watch. He was jostled in his bunk an hour after returning from duty that night, poked awake by the corporal of the guard.

"Lieutenant wants to see you, chop, chop." Garson unsteadily arose, donned his wrinkled dungarees and strode apprehensively to the Lieutenant Hildebrand's desk, standing unsteadily at attention.

"You were guarding that Jap fishing boat on Kulak Bay last night, right?"

"Sir, yes, sir!" Garson's muddled mind remained fogged, filled with the recollection of his encounter with Toshiro and the older boatman, of his untoward request for the nude images. Was he guilty of fraternization with the "enemy?" Worse? He grew faint, and his legs weakened, threatening to collapse under him. The room blackened.

"Push up," the officer's voice urged, "push up hard. Against my hand." Garson found himself slumped in a chair, head bent forward, the officer's hand pressed on the nape of his neck. Slowly he roused. Gaining sufficient equilibrium, he staggered to his feet, standing at wobbly attention. The officer studied him for several moments.

"You all right there, Marine?" Garson nodded.

"Get back to your rack then," he ordered. Of course, ever the worrier, Garson fussed over the ramifications of the incident for several days and nights. Another captain's mast? Court martial? Losing his PFC stripe again? But he heard nothing further of the incident — except Garson had long cause to wonder whether his transfer from the guard company the following month was opprobrium for his fraternization with Toshiro, an enemy. He was shortly thereafter assigned to the top floor of Marine Barracks, to Headquarters & Services, pogue heaven, Bolden and others called it.

"'Ol' Corps's dead now!" The emphatic statement from the bar stool next to Garson was a pitch or two high, certainly not that of a hard-bitten Marine. Garson grunted in agreement despite being unsure of the meaning. He continued to sip his cherry-red cocktail, the first high ball he'd ever tasted, a Singapore Sling. He stared at the framed charcoal sketch of the recumbent nude that hung above the Marine Club back bar, an amateur charcoal rendering, he surmised, head and upper torso turned away, leaving little more than fulsome buttocks to titillate the viewer.

"Yeah, McKeon was finally let outta the brig after all these months, but the Corps'll never be the same. We'll get soft like the army, navy and flyboys because of liberal newspapers and whiny civilians." Now, Garson understood the statement's import: The controversy had bubbled all year since the accidental drowning of six Marine recruits at Parris Island the past spring. Drill Instructor Matthew McKeon had been brought up on charges of homicide and drinking on duty. The public was enraged. The Corps's harsh training regimen must be modified. Even court martial testimony of the legendary General "Chesty" Puller, the Corps's most decorated combat veteran, wasn't enough to forestall punishment – demotion from staff sergeant to private, hard labor brig time, forfeiture of pay and a bad conduct discharge. Then, after long months of controversy, the Secretary of the Navy modified the punishment, releasing McKeon from the brig, rescinding the fine and returning him to duty.

Garson was visibly startled when he turned to the Marine on the barstool next to him. It was Rufus, the NCO that some in lower ranks called "Rufus the Doofus," the staff sergeant in charge of supply; a loner who Garson had occasionally noticed sitting solitary in the mess hall, nose poked in books. He also recalled him from his first days on Adak, when he drew cold weather infantry gear and an M-1 from the dank, dungeon-like room in Marine Barracks basement.

Other than this, Garson had never before interacted with the peculiar sergeant. He'd no cause to do so. But he'd heard stories about staff NCO, about his unusual proclivities. Scuttlebutt had it that Rufus had extended his time on Adak. Another year on "The Rock." Unthinkable. Who in his right mind would do such a thing? There may be one other reason, a rational one.

"He's *non compos mentis*," Blake declared, hardly an authority, like burned chocolate pudding in a Marine mess hall calling the skillet black, Garson thought.

Rufus's body was lumpy, misshapen, shoulders slumped like some Dickensian "clark." Garson stole a description from the lauded Irish novelist Sebastian Barry to note that the staff sergeant had "hair on his face not quite a beard, more like the patchy heather on bogland;" and he displayed slightly mossy teeth. Some in lower ranks called him "High Pockets" because he wore his trousers above the natural waist line.

"'I'll buy the drinks,' he says." Bolden had mimed the superior by reaching his right hand over the shoulder to extract an imaginary wallet from his back pocket. The sergeant's quirks were the stuff of barracks scuttlebutt. His battle jacket sleeve bore three hash marks, indicating he'd served more than a dozen years in the Corps; he'd enlisted during the World War. Battle ribbons revealed combat in the Pacific and in Korea as well as the Purple Heart. His sideburns were tinged with gray, and Garson concluded that Rufus was in his late 30s.

"Bet Rufus liked it better before, when the Corps didn't mix us coloreds and you '*cow*-casians' together," Bolden groused, face typically sour. Eight years had passed since the Marines and other services were integrated. Other suppositions about Rufus were legion. He was a souse, had been captured by North Korean Gooks, been subjected to dreadful interrogation.

"So who'd you vote for, young Marine?" Sergeant Rufus asked at the Marine Club on that most auspicious date on the calendar – November 10th, the birthday of the United States Marines in 1775 – one year before the nation's founding. DIs and instructors were never at a loss to proclaim that. Organized at a Philadelphia tavern by sea-going fighting men, the cutlass-swinging boarding parties battled the British navy and Barbary pirates. Sharing places of prominence with the charcoal nude above the crude Marine Club back bar were portraits of the Corps Commandant Lemuel C. Shepherd and flamboyant "Chesty" Puller, the most decorated Marine in history. Chesty's pugnacious portrait contained a famous quotation:

"Damnit, give my Marines booze and broads," he'd howled when underage combat veterans had been denied both in Japan.

Garson set down the tall glass of red liquid, and turned his head.

"Not old enough yet," he said of the recent national election that had reelected General Eisenhower. "Turned 20 in September," he admitted.

"No election next year," Rufus snorted. "Gotta wait two years when we vote for Congress and some Senators." Not attuned to every political whirl, Garson at least knew that much.

"Well, I voted for Ike, I can tell ya," Rufus announced. "That Stevenson's a real liberal egg head. Ran twice. Lost twice. Who could vote for a man named Adlai?" Garson wasn't certain if the sergeant referred to the Democrat's intelligence or to his balding pate. He wanted to retort that President Eisenhower was bald himself. Four years past, the army general had been the first Republican elected to the nation's highest office in Garson's lifetime. His parents were loyal Democrats, laboring people who revered the fallen Franklin D. Roosevelt.

On other Marine Club walls hung large artful prints of the First World War and Pacific War battles – Belleau Wood, Tarawa and of course the iconic flag raising on Iwo Jima's Mount Suribachi. Garson had recently learned that one of those half dozen Iwo heroes had been a navy corpsman from Wisconsin.

Garson, still a year away from his majority, gave little thought to celebrating that august November Saturday until buddies howled, "Don'cha know, anyone wearin' a green uniform drinks tonight!" So he'd donned his dress uniform and cadged a Jeep ride into the boonies where the reclaimed and refurbished quonset sat in solitude on a prominence above Marine Barracks.

Staff NCOs managed the rough-hewn bar exclusively for enlisted Marines; the Spartan facility was devoid of beer taps and other typical amenities; its dented and vintage refrigerator, a 1940's Westinghouse painted in Marine yellow and red with a Corps emblem on its door, was stocked with cans of "Ollie," Olympia and Rainier beer. A limited array of booze bottles lined the back bar, and most Marines, Garson assayed, were given to brandy or bourbon, neither of which he'd ever tasted. Celebrants tended to be NCOs. Fortuitously, Garson had earned his promotion to corporal the month before. He wondered why no Negro Marines were present. Maybe they're all on guard duty, his addled mind concluded.

When he initially slid onto an unvarnished stool, Garson was uncertain what to order. He'd only once before tasted booze, and that rock and rye whiskey he'd purloined from his father, poured into a quart mason jar and consumed on a hay ride. That recollection had been interrupted by a PFC carrying a colorful red concoction.

"I'll have one of those," said Garson, swiveling to point a finger at a passing frosted glass.

"Singapore Sling. Comin' right up, young Marine," promised the smiling NCO bartender, apron girding his belly, khaki shirt sleeves rolled on his forearms, and shirt collar and tie loosened. The gin and cherry brandy was delivered in a frosted glass sprouting a sprig of limp leafy garnish. Garson had second thoughts: The drink looked flossy. But he discarded the straws and sipped over the rim. It tasted like a cherry coke, no hint of booze at all. Nothing to it, he convinced himself.

"Better be careful with those," Rufus nodded when Garson signaled for a refill. "Those'll creep up on you." Garson waved him off, alcohol already insinuating its way into his brain.

"Well, here's to the Corps," the staff sergeant toasted in his constricted voice, "to General Shepherd and "Chesty" Puller, to Sergeant Dan Daley and the 'Devil Dogs,' to Tarawa and Iwo, Inchon and the Chosin, to the 'Old Corps' and to and every swingin' dick Marine who ever served." The four-striper raised his glass to the framed portraits and to the charcoal sketch of the teasing nude hanging to the right. Garson raised his glass and sipped.

"You in the guard company?" Rufus questioned.

"Who? Me?" Garson felt a bit thick of tongue, but he responded that he was in H&S and worked at the base laundry.

"Oh, so you're up there with 'The Champ'." When he turned, Rufus must have read his face. "You know, 'The Champ. Joe Louis Lewis. *The* Buck Sergeant up there. Chief clerk." Garson detected a note of envy, but concentrated on his drink. Rufus swallowed the final dregs of his brandy and wash, and called for another.

Garson studied the odalisque now: She lay amid a mass of soft cushions, wearing only a Turkish head covering, its tassel brushing perky breasts that seemed to quiver. He blinked when her head slowly turned toward him, her "Mona Lisa" smile inviting. He'd seen only one girl completely *au natural*, the Mexican tart he'd named Catana; but that had been in a dim Tijuana whore house cubicle. Slowly now, the Marine Club seemed watery to Garson, like the surface of a lake from below. He felt a silly smile on his face.

"You know," Rufus broke the silence, "W.C. Fields claimed he never drank." Garson had seen the bulbous-nosed actor in several movies, and was aware of his Hollywood reputation for imbibing. "Claims he only carries a hip flask of liquor in case of snake bite. And he says he always has a small snake in his pocket." The sergeant guffawed, but it took several heartbeats for Garson to understand the vignette.

Garson noisily sipped the dregs of his saccharine libation, his head swirling, ears buzzing with bees. He tried to blink away floating white spots before sliding from the bar stool intent upon the head. He staggered only three or four steps before everything around him dissolved. The next he remembered he was sprawled on his bunk back at Marine Barracks, his jacket unbuttoned, tie loosened and shoes removed. Opening his eyes, the ceiling revolved like a careening carnival ride. His stomach churned. He staggered to the head, supporting himself with hands along walls.

Reaching the first crapper, he kneeled and embraced the porcelain with both arms. His stomach erupted like Vesuvius, tiny orts and alcohol splattering. He groaned, as he retched repeatedly until only stomach spasms remained. The taste of lima beans, hamburger and gravy seemed distinct. His throat tissues were raw, his head hammered and tears cascaded down his cheeks. He staggered back and onto his bunk.

Reveille bugle notes blared from the stairwell on the first floor. Garson rolled into his blanket, brain mushy, head and eyes painful. Minutes later "Spike" Ungar's the morning "Reveille" notes blasted louder from the second floor, more penetrating. Finally, the Field

Music flung open the third floor squad bay doors, blowing the daily call right into Garson's ears, or so it seemed. But it was Sunday, he realized, and Ungar's harsh notes had been but a figment of alcohol-induced imagination.

"Fuck me," he murmured.

"Hey, man, you had a night last night," chortled Sergeant Lewis as he passed Garson's bunk. They'd been billeted together in H&S for a few months. Lewis was the indispensable Marine, the essential cog of NAS Adak Marine Barracks, the chief clerk responsible for records and record keeping, appointments and scheduling — day-to-day functioning and operation of the island's guard and security company. To Garson, he appeared as vital as the commanding officer. But he wore his responsibilities without superiority or arrogance; that coupled with his ordinary manner set him as a Marine apart.

Garson hadn't realized until the comment by Rufus that Sergeant Lewis had a middle name, Louis, after the great heavyweight boxing legend, the mighty "Brown Bomber," who, despite his race, had won the hearts of Americans black, brown and white in the ring but especially when he'd enlisted in the army. He'd served honorably until war's end. Garson regarded Louis as humble and soft spoken, and recalled his discomfort watching "Jersey" Joe Walcott and, later, Ezzard Charles, pummel the aging champion on television's "Gillette's Friday Night Fights" after the World War.

Sergeant Lewis, who bore the even coloration of his namesake, was tall and square shouldered; tightly-coiled hair was worn in Marine trim. His head was pumpkin-shaped with tiny ears like a seal's; his eyes were the color of cocoa, and his face sometimes seemed cartoonish behind round, owlish plastic-rimmed glasses. Easy to laugh, he unwaveringly presented a smiling countenance to match his convivial demeanor. As far as Garson knew, he'd never betrayed a trust. With his university background, the three-striper reminded Garson of other college-educated Marines he'd met – intelligent, knowledgeable, insightful and broad-minded. He even brought to mind Charles Hill, Garson's bright grade school protector. He, too, became a model Garson hoped to emulate.

"Ever box, Sarge?" Garson once asked. Lewis smiled broadly at Garson's question, shaking his head.

"No, no. My folks wanted me to be an educated man." From a small Missouri town, he'd graduated from Fisk University the all-Negro school in Nashville, Tennessee.

"How come you never went to OSC?" Garson asked. Lewis paused, considering his response.

"How many Negro officers do you know in the Corps?" His grinning reply hung in the air. Garson was left to wonder why Lewis even enlisted. He would learn over time that the NCO was a well-informed conversationalist who stoked Garson's inchoate knowledge about the Civil War. It may have been Sergeant Lewis or someone else who told Garson that men who volunteered were required to have a full set of real teeth.

"Yeah, they had to be able to bite through paper cartridges to pour powder down the barrel of their muskets." Garson was adding more information to his growing store of knowledge and detail about that war.

Garson had first met Corporal Falson over the nearly bald baize of the Rec Room pool table. Garson had never mastered the game; he only played at it, a pretend Willie Mosconi, deftly curling left index finger and thumb about cue in the classic fashion he'd seen in movies. But he knew nothing about applying English, ball placement and positioning, or other subtleties. Falson, on the other hand, had the full panoply of skills. Yet in their games of Eight Ball, Garson was simply preternaturally lucky, sinking solids or stripes willy-nilly, without strategy or design.

"You kin beat skill, but you can't beat slop," Falson fussed, sometimes slamming his cue into the wall rack on his exit from the room. Finally, Garson made excuses for not playing more games after fortune finally abandoned him.

Unfortunately for Garson, the unimpressive base theater never screened one first-run movie. For ten cents, the fare reminded him of unscrupulous independent Milwaukee movie house owners who foisted fourth-run titles and battered old prints to Saturday kid matinee audiences. It was a frustrating reality that Garson confronted since, for at least ten years before his enlistment, he'd sat through literally thousands of movies, sometimes six in a week, in hometown venues. But on reflection in the fullness of time, he admitted that the majority of movies he'd seen had been only hackneyed Hollywood dross and midden.

Two or three times while Garson was island-bound, the miniscule base movie theater provided a stage for traveling USO shows, largely amateur performances, pale reflections of the star-studded World War extravaganzas featuring Bob Hope, Betty Grable, Francis Langford and others. While unimpressive traveling acts by comedians, magicians and jugglers failed to generate interest from jaded Marines and sailors, female dancers and singers perked up audiences. The performers were invariably young and pretty, curvaceous in abbreviated costumes, drawing applause and response disproportionate to their talents.

"Man, can't get into any fuckin' crapper after these shows," some Marine groused, "all the Jarheads're beatin' their meat in there!"

The wind-scoured island in the middle of nowhere offered few diversions for Marines, sailors and SeaBees. One large and dowdy quonset hut contained a roller rink, but Garson and several buddies were ejected after a brief Saturday foray. Having rarely skated before, Garson was unable to negotiate turns; he simply caromed into corner railings to redirect himself. A few times, small dependent children were nearly run down by raucous Marines. The duty navy chief demanded they turn in the skates.

In Garson's fallible memory, he and a few buddies occasionally trudged into the surrounding boonies on rare days when *williwaws* eased to ordinary on-shore wind, just sufficient to brush away the infernal fog. The scavengers probed several abandoned half circle habitations. Doors hung loose, and windows admitted insistent Bering bellows; plywood decks and interiors were swollen by damp and mold. Garson felt like an archeologist, picking through the ruin of recent war. In one hut, flapping calendar pages of saucy pinups clung desperately to a wall, displaying upturned skirts and stockinged legs that Garson remembered from youth, bringing to mind titillating boyhood era renderings of Vargas, Elvgren and others his mother had detested. He thought to tear off a vintage month, but the pages were brittle, faded from their former gaudy relevance, a testament to a time gone by.

"You know Dashiell Hammett, the author of *The Maltese Falcon* and Thin Man mysteries was up here during the war," Sergeant Lewis informed Garson. "Yeah, he was an old man in his 40s when he volunteered. Shipped out here to Adak to start a newspaper when the Japs invaded the islands. Wrote a book about it. You can read it in the library here." He was also conversant with Hammett's time afterward the war experience.

"Accused him of being a Red. Investigated by a congressional committee a few years back. Never charged with anything, but was black-balled. He's kind of a recluse now, an alcoholic, they say." Lewis agreed with Garson that "The Maltese Falcon," the Bogart movie made from Hammett's most famous novel "was great. Bogie was a perfect Sam Spade. And Bacall was beguiling." Garson made note of the alliteration.

"Yeah, liked those other actors, too, Peter Lorre and Sidney Greenstreet."

"'Here's to a plain speaking and clear understanding. I distrust a closed-mouthed man.' Remember corpulent Gutman said that?" It was obvious the sergeant was a fan of the film.

"And that guy, Wilmer, the gunsel," Garson said. "'The cheaper the crook, the gaudier the patter.'" Lewis identified the actor, Elisha Cooke, Junior. "And Miss Wonderly or Brigid O'Shaunessey."

"Mary Astor," Lewis said. "Fine actress from the 40s."

Garson also mentioned Bogart as the detective Philip Marlowe in "The Big Sleep" — the seductive glances of Lauren Bacall, batwing eyebrows and plumy lips telegraphing such promise. He'd long intended to read the novels that had been the sources of those movies. But he was attracted of late by Mickey Spillane, whose private eye, Mike Hammer, offered more intensity and whose lurid pocket book covers promised more titillation.

Sergeant Lewis was often given to more pithy observations and analyses. When Garson reiterated some of the movie information he'd recalled imparted by Boot Camp mentor, Ridley, Lewis shared singular expertise. He was knowledgeable about *film noir*, the deeply shadowed post war movie style that dealt with dislocation and ennui. Garson recalled his discomfort with the denouement of "The

Killers" and similar movies — "The Blue Dahlia," "Criss-Cross" and "The Asphalt Jungle." Garson's new mentor also explained details about behind camera credits – the Best Boys, Key and Dolly Grips – and shared information about editing, rear screen projections, wipes and dissolves, cinematography, camera angles that held clues to plots. Garson was impressed.

Typically, as at NAS Whidbey and earlier, movie discussions failed to rise above "what happened next," or who was the best swordsman – Flynn, Power or Stewart Granger. Garson always opined that the latter actor whose performance as "Scaramouche" would win every duel. Was John Wayne superior to Joel Macrae or Randolph Scott? Garson nodded. Was the West of John Ford or Howard Hawks more authentic? Garson invariably preferred "Red River" to the former director's cavalry trilogy, at least until he'd viewed Ford's iconic "The Searchers."

While he contributed to such ruminations, Garson was reticent to reveal his attraction to movies he'd viewed alone at the Ritz Theater, away from Milwaukee pals who likely regarded his favored fare as saccharine and "girly." But such screen stories had energized Garson's romantic sensibilities: He'd anguished at the loss of love in "Roman Holiday," "The Red Shoes" and "A Place in the Sun." More, he'd been troubled by the implications of "The Third Man," "Sunset Boulevard," "M" and "Black Narcissus."

It was during one of these wide-ranging exchanges that Ungar, NAS Adak bugler, revealed that his father's second cousin, Trixie Firschke, had once been in the movies.

"Yeah, had a part in 'Broadway Melody of 1940.'" Garson recalled that movie from some Saturday matinee at a cheap Violet showhouse on the west side that typically screened old movies for kids. Garson had been smitten with leggy Eleanor Powell, who, partnered with Fred Astaire had mesmerized his boyish self. He'd forgiven her wooden acting ability because of the dazzling dance numbers — shapely legs busy and acrobatic, feet tapping staccato, tireless pirouettes, fiery eyes, Clara Bow lips and sensational smile. He'd been nearly breathless by the climactic "Begin the Beguine" number with Astaire, ten or more minutes of perfect harmony and synchronicity.

"Remember that scene in the waiting room," Ungar continued. Trixie had been the comely acrobatic juggler in the agent's waiting room. "She threw balls, batons and other things at Astaire. That was the Ungar family's only claim to fame." Garson was one of the few who recalled the sequence. Ungar, who most called "Spike" because his short blonde hair jutted out in every direction, was compact with regular features, eyes the color of pea soup and a ready dimpled smile. From Covington across the Ohio River from Cincinnati, he was classified as Marine Barracks Field Music.

"Red" Bolden was also conversant with movies, and provided a different slant on Hollywood.

"You *cow*-casians think you know everything," said Bolden sometime later, typically caustic. Garson was often surprised that Bolden addressed him as frequently as he did. "You think your favorite Hollywood stars're white when they're not. Take Dorothy Lamour. You think she's Puerto Rican or Mexican er somethin' when she's really colored. So's that yellow gal name'a Dinah Shore and lots a' others. They all got dingy daddies." Startled, Garson harked back to the movie "Pinkie" with Jeanne Crane and Ethel Waters, whose story had troubled him. After seeing it one night at the Ritz Theater with a sparse North Milwaukee audience, he'd afterward suspected that pretty, red-haired Crane might have been a mite swarthy, tainted perhaps.

As weather eased toward Adak "summer," Garson won the top M-1 rifle medal that had eluded him for three years. On the windiest range he'd ever experienced – some moments the Baker red flags at the edges of the range blew in opposite directions. But fortune favored him, and he scored 41 points at 200-yard off-hand, his weakest position; that and two "possible," 50-point scores propelled him to 221 total in the qualification match — three points higher than Boot Camp. Now his uniform jacket carried Expert medals for both rifle and pistol. And on the third anniversary of his enlistment, he was awarded the Good Conduct medal. His future brightened. Only one more year remained. Perhaps he'd ship over for four years more, perhaps even six.

The October elation was only momentary because he realized that his Milwaukee pals, Preston and Rusty had been discharged, having served their three-year enlistments. He recalled that long ago ill-considered conversation about enlisting for 20 years to improve career prospects. But because of a misunderstanding with his pals, and to his parents' everlasting dismay, he'd signed on for four years.

He'd exchanged no more than a letter or two with his old Villard Avenue pals over time, recalling only that tall, angular Preston had determined to remain in California, to live in San Pedro, the southern Los Angeles community on the curve of the bay, where he hoped for employment at the busy port.

Semi-weekly mail was carried to NAS Adak by a Reeves Air service, aboard an old DC-3 that flew in every Tuesday and Friday from Kodiak. He was proud to boast an FPO – Fleet Post Office — address. It meant he was "overseas," somewhere on or near the front line. Friday deliveries usually brought the prior Sunday's "Milwaukee Journal" newspaper; he'd imposed upon his mother for the subscription. While he rarely perused the entire, bulky publication, samplings reminded him of home.

Letters from his parents, usually a page or two, were fitful, arriving no more than once a month. Garson observed that his mother's handwriting, once classic school cursive, had grown less legible with the advance of arthritis in her hands after all of those years plunged into dishwater. Frequently, she lamented losing the family house in foreclosure, and complained of his father's declining confection business. Occasionally, she coaxed her husband to append a few labored lines, in which he sometimes reiterated the hope that Garson would "take over the family business" when he returned. Garson shuddered at the prospect. His mother's lifelong argument in favor of college was beginning to win that argument; and the examples and influence of Ridley, G. D. Coleman and now Sergeant Lewis were gaining sway.

"So you plan to become a newsy, huh?" the articulate Negro Sergeant opened an exchange one afternoon. "Heard of Nellie Bly, the muckraker?" Garson's silently confessed to his deficient knowledge, but nodded in assent to his current mentor. Lewis offered a thumbnail verbal sketch about Bly, whose true name was Elizabeth Seaman, and her ground-breaking newspaper career — solo around-the-world tour in the previous century, emulating Jules Verne; and her reform-minded exposés of political corruption and industrial monopolies. He went on to mention other famous muckraking newspapermen – Lincoln Steffens, Ida Tarbell, Brad Whitlock and others.

"We need more of that kind of journalism these days," Sergeant Lewis proposed. The information further fostered Garson's dream of pursuing such a noteworthy career.

Garson still maintained correspondence with Nola, the pretty, athletic blond he'd dated while at NAS Whidbey. He maintained keyboard skills typing letters to her and others on weekends in the Marine Barracks administrative office. He was certain Nola still liked him, perhaps even cared for him because she often enclosed photos of herself and her parents. He'd always got on well with them. Nola looked sunny wearing tasteful outfits and swimsuits. Still, he felt occasional pangs of guilt because of his engagement. But, he rationalized, they were so far apart. Who knew what his future held.

His putative sister, Lana, also remained a faithful correspondent; she kept him apprised of news of North Milwaukee chums. Sadly, Garson had lost contact with Karen Sisko, the smoldering girl from

Montebello with the succulent, honeyed kisses. He still castigated himself for sharing her address with the predator Moldy, hoping she hadn't succumbed to any untoward blandishments.

Most important of his correspondents was Betsy, of course, the girl to whom he'd pledged his love and fidelity. The fact that she'd accepted his proposal after only a few dates while he'd been home on leave now seemed curious. He questioned and considered the situation on many troubled nights. He was 20, after all, old enough to marry. It was the "thing" men of his age did. His buddies Mellish and Toby back home had wives and children already. Lana wrote about friends' engagements. Garson's mother had readily expressed delight at the prospect of Betsy as a daughter-in-law. Her framed graduation photo, prominently placed in his wall locker, continued to draw admiring comments from buddies.

"She's a beauty," remarked Sergeant Lewis among others. Indeed, Garson's narrow chest puffed out at such comments. He'd often gazed at the colorized portrait, admiring her short, tight black hair, shapely ruby lips and dark intoxicating eyes. She'd even shipped him a handsome leather-bound writing portfolio and high-quality pen; he faithfully eschewed the typewriter when composing weekly missives filled with ardor and pledges of love.

She was attending Milwaukee Downer College, and working part time at Schuster's Department Store. She wrote of studying psychology and literature, thinking she might like to become a teacher.

"I got a letter, I got a letter. Hope ta' hell you got one, too!" sang Ungar, mimicking Mail Call bugle notes. "Gladsome tidings, Garson. Think you got something from 'you know who' today," he announced as he waved an envelope in front of his nose. Betsy always scented her letters, and jotted "Tiny," above her return address. It had been more than two weeks since the preceding letter; inveterate worrier that he was, Garson had given in to anxiety as days passed. The envelope felt uncommonly thin, not like the usual multi-page missives he'd received before.

A "Dear John" letter was classic, the dreaded bane of any Marine or serviceman who was away from home. Even a lugubrious country-western tune had been composed about it.

Dear John, oh how I hate to write
Dear John, I must let you know tonight
That my love for you has died like grass upon the lawn
And tonight I wed another dear, John.

Typically, the new "John" was some civilian who'd avoided military service, now trolling around hometown while others served. It had been a wartime Hollywood movie trope.

It was as if Betsy knew the song because that was the substance of the note. The single sheet shook in Garson's hand as he read hurriedly, then perused Betsy's words once or twice more, hoping to change their meaning. There were no details, there was simply someone else now, she'd written. But Garson read between her few lines. She was in love – truly, madly and deeply, likely with some handsome college guy, older, wiser with a great job and a shiny convertible, with unlimited prospects.

Was there something he'd missed in previous letters – a hint of ebbing ardor? Thinking back to his leave the year before, had Betsy revealed anything? Had he missed some sign? His face and ears were hot, pulse pounding violently in his neck. He crushed the page in his fist, compressing it into a tiny ball, a Black Hole, wishing to obliterate it completely. His breathing labored.

In his rage, he thought to fling Betsy's portrait out the window, into the grey gloom and isolation of Adak Island. Sitting on his bunk for half an hour or more, he calmed and considered. Perhaps this was some kind of cosmic retribution after all, as he'd carried on simultaneous correspondence with two others – Nola and Lana. He guiltily dismissed an urge to renew correspondence with Karen

Sisko.

In Garson's early draft of his Marine memoir, he wrote of re-reading Betsy's final letter numerous times, of retaining the missive for weeks, trying to change its substance before discarding it. As an octogenarian, his recollections contradicted themselves.

No, he'd simply remove her photo from its place of prominence in his wall locker, and store it in a dark foot locker recess. Perhaps he'd return it to her. None of his buddies mentioned Betsy's missing image, and he spoke to no one about the end of his engagement. Likely, he wrote to his mother about it, but couldn't be certain. Only days later, he wrote a multi-paged missive to Nola, redolent with endearments and promises. He planned to stop in Washington to see her when his NAS Adak tour ended.

While Garson was anxious to expunge the name Betsy from memory, her tantalizing succubus visited him in vexing dreams. During dull laundry work, his mind wandered as he began to reassess their relationship. They'd dated only four or five times, and they'd had no carnal knowledge of one another. Actually, he concluded, he'd barely known her despite vivid, hopeful yet unrealistic expectations. Slowly such recollections grew hazier; even his rancor faded.

(He'd see her once more when he returned home after discharge, returning her high school portrait and fawning over a cherubic infant daughter. She'd had to quit college, she said; her husband "John" worked at a bank, having had to curtail his university studies. Ironically, Garson felt release from a life of narrowed potential had they married. He'd enrolled at Marquette University only days before seeing Betsy. He demurred when she tried to return the engagement ring.)

When Garson composed this story after decades of reflection, he was conversant with classic war literature and movie memes that discouraged men in the military from deepening acquaintanceships to friendships; avoid bonding too closely, it was advised. Still, he found that the very impermanence of many of his Marine associations somehow intensified in recollection. It amazed him that memories from many decades past produced clear portraits of former buddies. However, he did admit that as he wrote about some characters, they literally became unruly, uncontrollable and unrealistic. The scurrilous O'Toole and Gunter the German at NAS Whidbey; Rufus the Doofus on NAS Adak were ready examples; even the good Sergeant Lewis grew more impressive on the printed page.

Time weighed as heavily on Garson and his buddies in the Aleutians – at least excepting Sergeant Rufus.

"Geez, can't even go AWOL up here," the hulking Ohioan Ringer groused, "'less ya' got wings." Heads nodded in agreement. Oddly, the isolation suited one of Garson's characteristics. As an only child with working parents, he'd long ago grown accustomed, even comfortable with an interior life of solitude. He thought he coped better than most. Still, that Sweat Sheet calendar tacked to the cubicle wall was a constant reminder of the glacial speed of time on Adak. Sands in the imaginary hourglass drained grain by grain.

"Here's another thing," "Big John" Ringer continued, finding it amusing that young Lieutenant Hildebrand appeared every payday accompanied by a sullen armed escort. On a Marine green blanket laid over a Rec Room pool table, he carefully confirmed identification of each enlisted man, even though he knew everyone by sight. Dipping a thumb and forefinger onto his tongue, the officer counted out crisp, recently minted bills.

"Geez, man, why's he need the armed guard? Who's gonna steal that money out here anyways? An' if they do, how they gonna get it off this Rock? Stow it away on Reeves mail plane or on a Jap fishing boat, paddle an Aleut kayak or something'. Don't make sense," Ringer snorted. There was a lot on NAS Adak that didn't seem to make sense to enlisted men, or in the "real" world.

After earning his second stripe, Garson's monthly pay for a corporal with more than three years in service, including $60 in overseas duty, jumped to $177 a month. For him, there was little on which to spend such a staggering sum, so he decided to draw only $15 each semi-monthly payday, leaving the remainder "on the books." He was astonished that by the end of his NAS Adak tour, he'd saved well over 500 dollars, a princely sum, despite accruing no interest. Sergeant Lewis told Garson that he'd extended his tour for another year to save money for graduate school at the University of Chicago. But Garson dismissed that as an option.

Occasionally, Garson and others eschewed the mess hall on weekends to eat at the base exchange lunch counter whose limited fare featured overcooked hamburgers, lukewarm hot dogs, chips, soft drinks and cellophane-encased brownies as durable as Civil War hardtack. But the true attraction was "Spike" Ungar.

"You know what happens when he sees hair in his chow," Blake reminded buddies. Indeed, it was no secret in H&S that a single wayward strand caused Ungar's stomach to revolt and appetite to flee. He would summarily depart, leaving sandwich or other food behind; some Marine was always ready to consume it.

During some exchanges, Garson was prompted to ask Ungar the meaning of curious words that larded his speech. "Gobsmacked," the Field Music explained, meant astounded, and a "doss," as he called his bunk, was a rough accommodation. He grew up in a neighborhood of Kentucky "Irishers," he said, who used peculiar words like "betimes" – before something was expected. He referred to Sergeant Rufus as a "bowsie," a boozer. His personality was pleasant and voluble, and he was ever ready with joke or quip.

"Do you pronounce the capitol of Kentucky as *Louis*-ville or *Louie*-ville?" he'd ask some unsuspecting new arrival who'd invariably reply "Louie-ville."

"Naw, man, don'cha know it's Frankfort?" Ungar chortled that he'd tricked someone else with the same verbal trap. Even Bolden lauded "Spike" Unruh's rousing Dixieland renditions using only a bugle mouthpiece.

After one payday, Garson carried a handful of coins into a poker game with penny-ante stakes — nickels, dimes and occasional quarters thrown into the pot. Garson's mind wandered occasionally when other players contemplated their hands, recalling the telling description of a game in Walter van Tilburg's novel, *The Ox-Box Incident*. He remained in the game for less than an hour, losing over $6, nearly half of his by-weekly draw. When he walked away, he vowed not to engage in such foolhardy play again – a pledge never broken.

Invariably, on days money was distributed, a different crowd collected in a second-floor corner where Negro Marines "got up a game" of craps, attracting as many spectators, like Garson, as players. He found the fast-paced gambling contests energetic and animated — in many ways creative, more performance than contest, like something out of Damon Runyon. Stakes were eye-opening, betters clenching fistfuls of currency while the floor was littered with singles, fives with an occasional ten dollar bet thrown down. The action swirled among players, the air alive with incessant banter and braggadocio.

"Come on seven, mama needs a new pair a' shoes!" shouted Deets, blowing on dice cupped in his hand, snapping fingers as cubes rattled into the corner. "Oohhhh," several groaned while winners snatched currency and hooted in pleasure.

"Hey, dice, don't fail me now." Even losers, Garson thought, found pleasure in the action and interaction. He enjoyed the flair and flamboyance, the verve and swagger as dice snapped and rattled.

In contrast, Garson occasionally participated in a card game peculiar to Wisconsin called *Shafskopf* or Sheepshead, a contest similar to skat and bid whist that required a minimum of three or more players. Garson had learned the game during his youth, watching his father unsuccessfully attempting to ingratiate himself with testy in-laws.

On Adak, for the only time in his Marine years, Garson joined the minimum number of players from his state to organize a card game. One of these was Litke, a handsome, dark-haired school drop-out whose parents owned a tavern on Milwaukee's Polish south side. The Old Place, it was called, and, as Litke enthusiastically described, it featured polka music jams every Friday and Saturday night. He claimed that famed accordionist Frankie Yankovic had even dropped in one weekend. Milwaukee Poles loved him.

Litke, taller than Garson, readily admitted that he'd been forced by his father to join the Marines. His speech was peppered with "youse guys" and similar stereotypical "Milwaukee-ese." Garson began his friendship by asking if his family name was the German — "Luedke." No, it was Polish.

"We was lake rats." Litke's prominent pale eyes flashed at several points in the story he told one afternoon. When school ended in June every year, Litke's parents closed the tavern for two weeks and took the family "up Nort'," to Three Lakes, a five-hour journey in his dad's Chrysler New Yorker. "They packed all of us, me and my four sisters in the back seat, an' we pushed and shoved one another all the way. Ma'd always turn her head to the back seat an' yell: 'Don't make me stop this car, 'ey!'"

They traveled in tandem with their Uncle Lenny, an unassuming and gentle man who'd been widowed; after a few years of solitude, he married a woman named Dell, who, after consuming a few drinks, became obnoxious and profane. "One time Ma even kicked her out of the tavern because of her potty mouth, 'ey?" Litke laughed. Even so, Lenny adopted three children from Dell's first marriage. When the families arrived at the rented Three Lakes cabins, "us kids had to unload the cars while the adults sat in the tavern drinkin,' 'ey.

My oldest sister didn't have to because she was a star. She played accordion and was the favorite." On one trip, Litke thought to clandestinely "borrow" a boat from a neighbor.

"Paddled it out a ways, thinkin' to start the motor without them hearin' it, 'ey? Must'a been ten 'er so. My sister Cheryl, the youngest, threatened to squeal but I shook my fist at 'er." Finally, Litke reached a point off shore that he thought was safe to start the motor. But when he braced his foot for leverage to pull the cord, he shoved the motor into the lake. The owner hadn't locked it in place.

"So I grabbed the oars, 'ey, hopin' to get the boat back to the pier. I braced my feet on one seat to start rowing. The fuckin' seat broke, an' part the board smacked me in the face. My nose broke and blood flew all over the place. Tried to row with one hand, but you know how that goes, 'ey? So I stopped and waved my arms. Cheryl said she thought I was just wavin' at 'er, and didn't notice all the blood until I got near the shore.

"'Why, your poor nose is smashed on the side of your face,' she said an' laughed." Litke turned a profile to his listeners, and fingered the hump of his nose. Garson sniggered. This and similar adventures reminded him of a childhood pal, Mellish, whose yarns of mischief and misadventure were similarly enjoyable.

Litke's bedroom, another tale began, was in the tavern's basement adjacent to the storeroom where cases of beer and booze and half barrels were stacked. One night, determined to purloin beverages for his pals, he clandestinely unlocked the window that opened to the sidewalk. He handed out several six packs.

"'Hurry up,' I said, 'before my Old Man finds us, 'ey. I handed out another six-pack, but everybody got quiet. I knew something was up.

"'Your Old Man's here right now,' my dad said from the sidewalk. Had'a empty out the bottle chute and clean the tavern for weeks after that caper, 'ey." Litke reflected that such hijinks were one of the reasons for enlisting.

"One time me and my pal Wolowicz borrowed, well, OK, stole, a car from a sout' side used car lot, B. S. Wisnewski's, I think. Actually, we did it lotsa times, hot-wiring 'em an' cruisin' around, to Leon's Custard stand on 27th, and to Pulaski Park where our pals and gals hung out. Well, we allas' took them cars back with no body the wiser, 'ey." But one night, Litke lost control of the stolen vehicle driving across the long viaduct that spanned the city's industrial valley, crashing into the guard rail, gashing his forehead on the steering wheel. He and Wolowicz abandoned the car, and hobbled home afoot.

"Well, my head bled like Billy be Jesus, and the cops followed the drops across the bridge right to Ma's tavern, 'ey. Judge gave my old man a choice: Join the service or go to Juve hall." His father insisted upon the Marines, to "teach him some sense, and make him a man." Garson knew that Litke's reason for enlisting in the Corps was common. Likeable, Litke readily regaled buddies with more stories of youthful adventure and hijinks.

"If youse guys ever visit Milwaukee, come to Litke's on 14th and Rogers, an' we'll hoist beers all round, 'ey."

Garson often felt inadequate when captivated by Litke and other adept yarn spinners. While he acknowledged that such tales were likely hyperbolic and exaggerated, he envied their bases in reality. As an only child he couldn't recall any drama and adventure in his life; even if he could, he lacked necessary oral skills. He seemed to be only an audience for these Marine Barracks fabulists.

Garson only rarely detected animus among white and Negro Marines. They were all in this thing together. They agreed without stating it, that contentions would threaten the Corps's need for unit cohesion and combat readiness. "You're only as strong as the Marine in the next fighting hole," was a principle military law.

Personal antipathies were usually set aside.

"Got any *members* up there?" Bolden had asked Garson after the transfer to H&S. Interaction between the Marine guard company's second floor and so-called pogues up above was limited, as much by choice as circumstance.

"Members?"
"You know — *'members'* — colored guys like me?"
"Sergeant Lewis is in H&S."
"Oh, you mean, 'The Champ?'" Bolden sneered. "He's more like you *cow*-casians than us."

Garson considered that he was generally tolerant and fair-minded, having had rewarding associations at Camp Pendleton and NAS Whidbey with buddies like "O.D." O'Donoghue, G. D. Coleman and others. He still proudly wore the dark green woolen dress shirts and glossy boots the Chicago Marine had given him when he'd been discharged. He'd been attracted as a child, even while his grandfather wasn't, to the little Negro girl named Sally, in kindergarten. He remained grateful to Charles Hill, his playground protector at Holy Redeemer Grade School who kept playground bullies at bay. More, he'd been smitten with Lena Horne, the sultry light-skinned singer and Hollywood actress with the seductive smile and flashing eyes. And, he felt accepted by Sergeant Lewis, Bolden, Deets and others.

When previously billeted in the guard company, Garson's cubicle had been proximate to Bolden's where other Negroes often congregated for conversation and kibitzing. He'd overheard candid exchanges about "cuffies" and "fancy maids" – shackled slaves and Negro women sold for sex by white owners.

"Great gran-pap was stolen in Virginia by a Mississippi slave man," Bolden claimed, "an' sold to a Louisiana slaver, then shipped to Texas. Deets here knows 'bout pickin' cotton in Texas, don'cha Deets? My auntie said that some married coloreds back then found out that they was actually related, even brother an' sister sometimes." Garson's was shocked by such revelations, and shaken from his insular assumptions and narrow social frame.

"You *cow*-casians," Bolden once prodded Garson. "You're ridin' a gravy train on biscuit wheels. Y'all allas fall into a bird's nest on the ground." Garson had heard similar Negro aphorism from a kid whose father collected rent from a Bronzeville barber shop; they often lingered to listen to the pontifications of a street philosopher and hustler named Luster Dapp.

"When I get outta here, I'm gonna get me one a' them high yella gals, and slow walk her." The voice was Falson's, the pool shooter whose skills were nonpareil; their matches had attracted audiences and became the stuff of barracks legend. "Gotta have a big behind, nice hocks." Many decades later, Garson could almost "see" Falson's eyes roll and toothy smile white against coal black skin. "Gonna slow walk 'er 'til she say, 'yeah, baby.'" There was a burst of guffaws.

"You tell it, Sea Breeze!" an unfamiliar voice rejoindered, using Falson's fanciful name.

"Naw, man, you all's got it wrong," someone else said. "Don'cha know what they say: 'Closer the bone, the sweeter the meat.'"

'Naw, man, only a dog wann'a bone!" Laughter erupted anew, and Garson heard hands slapping. Obsequiously, he eavesdropped on uncommon stories like none he'd ever known before.

"My auntie had a friend once, name'a Sipsy." The voice was Falson's. "She was some kinda herb woman who cured fevers and such with special brews and potions. Used things like jimson weed and jalap. Can't credit it but they said she could cast spells and even help folks fall in love — or out. Her man – can't say they was married — name'a Rollie was no-count, folks in Haines City said, free with the bottle and loose with his coin for anyone but Sipsy an' his kids."

Sipsy moved out, and days later Rollie was found dead in their wormy shack. When the sheriff came, he discovered animal bones beside the body, bundles of twigs and a pile of "goofer dust" under the bed.

"Everybody in Haines City said good riddance ta' Rollie." Voices in the cubicle murmured.

One transitory remedy for boredom – Vandy called it "Adak ennui" — was AFRS, Armed Forces Radio Service received in the mid-Aleutians. Weekly programming ran the gamut of popular music.

"White guys borrowed a lot from black music, you know," Waldron put in. He was a recent transfer to NAS Adak, a smallish Hoosier with "trick baby eyes" and coffee skin. "The Gershwin's and others got inspired by gospel an' low-down blues – Witherspoon, Redding, even the old Delta cats like Muddy Waters, Howlin' Wolf and Lil' Walter, an' such. Heard a' 'Blues Boy' King?" Waldron asked; Garson had to say he had not. "That's R an' B, man. Presley and Haley an' them new cats made the blues popular with white folks. You know what they say: 'White folks just listen to the blues. Black folks live 'it.'"

"Remember what Moms Mabley say on her party records? Them good old days? I was there. Where was they?'" Laughter rose.

"That cat up there, that Field Music, Ungar, think his name is, can play some mean, low-down licks on that bugle a' his," said Waldron. "We heard him couple a' times.

AFRS also broadcast a weekly jazz hour, and Garson was introduced to salient musicians of the day, some probing daring forms – Miles Davis, Thelonious Monk, Charlie Mingus, Charlie Parker and others. While he often failed to "understand" or appreciate the more outré and experimental performers, his exposure laid a foundation for a future passion. The Columbia Record Company advertised special discounts and free shipping for military personnel stationed overseas, so Garson ordered discs in the new long play format, and presumed upon Vandy's insubstantial player to listen.

In Sergeant Lewis, Garson found another confident and counsel who helped shape world views and challenged shibboleths.

"I see you read Civil War books," Sergeant Lewis remarked one Sunday afternoon when he noticed Garson rummaging through his foot locker. He'd retained the pocket book of Fletcher Pratt's *Ordeal by Fire* purchased years earlier at the Oceanside bus station, now dog eared and worn. The little paperback with its striking cover sustained an inchoate interest in that nation's seminal conflict.

"Been to the library here on Adak?" the erudite chief clerk questioned. Garson hadn't. "There're some books you might find interesting." It became apparent during his months in H&S that the tall, college-educated Missourian was conversant with wide variety of topics. Garson often compared Lewis to his admired Boot Camp buddy, Ridley, the former Southern California University student from whom he'd learned much about movies.

As was the way of most barracks discussions, Garson came to realize, one tidbit of information spun into another, often wandering off in tangents and trivialities. Conversations with the tall chief clerk were different. The three-striper seemed to avoid predictable scuttlebutt and cant, bent more on imparting and extracting substance from interchanges.

"Know how Decoration Day started?" Lewis's voice was calmly modulated. Garson knew only that the May holiday Lewis mentioned involved visiting the graves of fallen soldiers, planting flowers and flags. Lewis's information was new. He explained that colored people, freed slaves, initiated the solemn observance in Charleston, South Carolina. At war's end, after Lee surrendered, they disinterred the bodies of more than 250 Union soldiers who'd died in the Reb prison and were unceremoniously dumped into unmarked graves at an old race course.

"A memorial celebration was held, May First in the city – it was three weeks after Lee surrendered at Appomattox. New graves were dug and decorated at an old race track, and a special burial place designated as 'Martyrs of the Race Course.' They say ten thousand marched — black kids from freedman's schools and white missionaries. Colored infantry regiments joined the parade, including the famous 54th Massachusetts.

"The former slaves were Gullah people, West Africans, who believed honorable warriors deserved proper burial, part of the cycle of souls that entered and departed the world." According to Lewis's disquisition, it wasn't until three years later when a former Union general proposed designating a day every year to honor war dead." In time, Garson learned that the officer was "Black Jack" Logan, the head of the post-war Grand Army of the Republic

Over time, Garson fingered over the spines of library books Sergeant Lewis mentioned, reading *Mr. Lincoln's Army*, the first in what was to be a trilogy about the great Federal army in Virginia. The author, Bruce Catton, was a newspaperman, and his stylish

prose and brilliant characterizations had captivated critics. Garson finished the first of the volumes before he departed Adak.

He'd also stumbled upon an obscure book of fiction set during the war. The book's flyleaf claimed that Joseph Stanley Pennell had labored for years bringing his opus to fruition. Garson sometimes struggled through the artful prose of *The History of Rome Hanks, and Kindred Spirits,* that had garnered wide acclaim even from the famed writer Maxwell Perkins. The book had been withdrawn from the NAS Adak library only twice since World War's end.

Diversions on the Bering Sea island were spare, and even the most inconsequential of events generated attention and conversation.

Top Sergeant Orville King drove a boat-length 1947 Packard Super Clipper, the legacy from his predecessor, it was said. Atop a gleaming grill swooped an elegant swan hood ornament that contrasted with gaudy, "audible" livery of yellow and red with outsized eagle, globe anchor emblems on its side doors like some kind of Marine Viking ship plying Bering waters. How and under what circumstances the heavy four-door came to the island in the first place was invariably the topic of speculation. More, the lead Adak enlisted Marine also had a pet, a feisty German shepherd named "Chesty" after the legendary general. The mascot even had an official dossier, and wore a coat adorned with sergeant's stripes. Unfortunately, the canine's reputation was besmirched by unbecoming behavior when it was discovered in front of Marine Barracks locked back-to-back with a mongrel bitch of no account. After being hosed apart from the female, "Chesty" was ignominiously "court martialed" and reduced in rank from sergeant to private. Sailors rarely lost opportunites to hoot about the disgrace.

"Ain't that a bitch?" chortled Phipps, the SeaBee seaman second who worked in the base laundry with Garson. Tall and gangly with a long neck and protruding Adam's Apple that reminded Garson of his Chicago cousin Bob, Phipps exhibited a similar shambling gait. Droll and quick witted, he was a member of "MOB" 43, one of the navy's Mobile Construction Battalions created during the World War to erect and maintain physical facilities – fuel and ammo dumps, docks, depots for supply and storage; they dredged harbors, lay concrete and tarmac runways and more. To Garson's eye, SeaBees wore peculiar attire, nondescript shirts and trousers with baseball caps, all in olive drab, and heavy work boots. Most were uncommonly scruffy, almost unmilitary, like denizens of the Marine Barracks motor pool.

"See your city's in the majors now," Phipps observed during an early conversation. The Braves had moved to Milwaukee two years before. From eastern Ohio, Phipps was a Pittsburgh fan, but it was evident his roots were pure West Virginia. "We're gonna be competitors for the National League pennant." Garson had only fitful interest in baseball. Each morning, Phipps greeted others with "What's cookin', kids?" Passé expressions, arcane and archaic words tripped from his tongue: "Okey doke," "Bugs in a rug," "whole shebang," "thick as thieves," "jabberwocky" and "toff."

He claimed his family ancestry traced back to Ashkenazi Jews in Bessarabia who'd immigrated to the United States when his mother, like Garson's, was a child.

"Know what 'Bessarabia' means?" the droopy-eyed SeaBee asked rhetorically. Garson, of course, did not.

"Means no Arabs." The land of his forebears, he explained, no longer existed. "Like Armenia." Before its dissolution, the former nation had been located between the Dniester and Danube Rivers contiguous to Romania.

"My gramps was a round, barrel-chested man with a wiry Santa Claus beard. Wide gap between his front teeth. Wore a yumalke and phylacteries, strings hanging from his belt." Garson remembered his mother cleaning well-appointed houses of Jewish lawyers and doctors on Milwaukee's west side before the war when, as a child, he'd accompanied her, curious about brass menorahs, and tiny mezuzahs affixed to doorways.

"You a Jew then?" Garson asked. Phipps's smile revealed he didn't practice that faith.

"Gramps was disgusted when my mom married a non-observant Jew, my dad. They didn't speak after. He died disappointed," Phipps said.

The base laundry was staffed with, in addition to Phipps and Garson, about a dozen or more airdale sailors and two women, enlisted men's dependents. Maggie was short, a beach ball with legs, as Phipps characterized her, married to a navy chief. "She ain' no spring chicken," the SeaBee said.

Animated and funny, Maggie contrasted with Billie, her comely counterpart with short black hair, narrow dreamy eyes and dark penciled brows; her voluminous white blouses could not completely disguise generous breasts or slacks hide her "Apple Cheeks," as Garson's mother might have called them. Invariably reticent, she became an object of Garson's Aleutian fantasies. She and her husband were from Atlanta, she said. When Phipps prominently posted a voluptuous Vargas nearly-nude pinup on the laundry wash deck, Billie frowned. "It's only a Toots," the rangy Buckeye laughed. During his final days at NAS Adak, Garson once pointed his camera at her but she shielded her face.

Garson found another opportunity to get "down wind" of women when he volunteered to sing in the Catholic Church choir for Christmas services despite his uninspiring voice. His purpose had nothing to do with renewed piety. He was singularly motivated by the proximity to females. He and two other Marines were the only males in the chorus whose majority was composed of navy officers' wives who were decidedly more mature and sophisticated than the laundry women. They wore tastefully tailored attire, were prettily coifed. While he found their appearance and conversations fascinating, what singularly invigorated, even sustained him during

December, were the heady feminine pheromones that wafted about them.

A decade later when asked what'd he'd done for a year in the middle of the Aleutian Islands, Garson glibly quipped: "Shoot pool and go to the movies."

"Hey, Garss," observed Vandy a few weeks after the cataclysmic March earthquake. "Slept right through it, huh? Nobody saw you move that night when the rest of us were running for cover."

"Naw, man," Garson admitted. "I was fuckin' frozen in fear. Couldn't fuckin' move." He didn't mention that he'd somehow grabbed the rosary.

"How'd you get past that big ironing table," Vandy turned to Blake who hunched his shoulders.

"Musta jumped, I guess," Shaky responded, squirrely eyed. "Maybe flew!" He did complain of a sore knee afterward. The heavy table, four-foot square and as tall, virtually blocked one aisle along the windows. In the immediate aftermath, many trudged the stairwell, fingering the jagged crack that descended all the way to Sergeant Rufus's Supply Room dungeon. Some Marines claimed they'd seen the Great Sitkin volcano belching out a mushroom cloud of steam and ash.

Garson was awakened and gripped with renewed terror by late night aftershocks and persistent tremors that continued for weeks. None registered as high as the 8.3 Richter Scale as the dark Thursday morning paroxysm, but the almost daily roaring and crackling in the boonies, the shuddering of Marine Barracks and ominous sway of long ceiling light fixtures in the cavernous laundry unnerved Garson.

"Hey, when this here Rock sinks, maybe we can surf all the way to Hawaii and some good liberty," the SeaBee Phipps grinned.

Garson failed to appreciate the gallows humor. During ensuing days, Garson cadged Jeep rides to view damages to the base: Several insubstantial buildings had been jarred from foundations, the pier where Garson had guarded the Jap fishing boat had collapsed into Sweeper Cove. Several concrete runways and stretches of macadam roads bore dark chasms. Like a seismologist, Garson snapped several photos, preserving them in his tattered album.

When Garson wrote of these days in good time, science had identified the subduction zone between the Pacific and North American tectonic plates grinding against one another, building up unrelenting pressure along the Aleutian Trench. The late winter earthquake created a tsunami of over 50 feet that crashed into Oahu 2500 miles west, causing millions of dollars in shoreline damage; in the opposite direction, the wave swept all the way to Monterey, California. The Adak quake would be listed as one of the strongest of the century. Garson never tired of recounting his fear and trembling, even recounting the detail of his end-of-the-world thoughts.

Aftershocks struck several times during ensuing weeks. At the laundry, the earth's contortions were announced by groaning and rumbling that rolled down from the hills. Long ceiling light stanchions swayed, and their metal shades rattled; several bulbs shattered. Garson spread his legs and braced himself, expecting the worst. Shouts and murmurs pumped his pulse. Falson and other roving patrol Marines described SeaBee crews furiously repairing roads and structures all over the base.

The existentially threatening earthquake and its aftermath had occurred at an inauspicious time for Garson's psyche, coming, as it had, on the heels of Betsy's "Dear John" letter. Despite subsequently renewing correspondence with Nola, there was nothing tangible to which he could cling. Months of his duty at this craggy and insubstantial island still remained. But then, a relieving surprise occurred.

"Top wants to see you," Vandy announced one day after Garson had torn loose another month from his "sweat sheet" calendar. The Aleutian spring, such as it might be on this desolate duty station, seemed to stir.

"I see by your record here," the foremost Marine Barracks enlisted man began, "that you've qualified Expert with the .45 every year. The Western Division Rifle and Pistol matches're scheduled for Camp Matthews soon. Want to compete?" This was a question Garson had never hoped to hear, to represent NAS Adak.

"Means you can get off this here Rock early. Spend time in sunny, southern Cal, soak up some rays. But, more important, you'll compete with the best from the West." The burly and florid sergeant-major's eyes demanded a response.

Garson did not hesitate, even though he considered himself unqualified for such competition. Yes, he'd had no difficulty in firing Expert at NAS Whidbey and here on Adak. But he'd shone brightly in a poor class of competitors. The Western Division matches were another matter. But it required no more than a handful of seconds for him to agree to the transfer. And, thus, orders were cut for early May departure. His mood lifted and stride lengthened over the remaining weeks.

Sometimes, sleep still eluded Garson, his mind dazzled with disparate worries and concerns about his future. Lately, of course, it had been Betsy's "Dear John," that troubling missive that had wrecked plans and prospects. Never mind that he'd exchanged missives with Nola at the same time. Around midnight near his departure date he arose to gaze once again out of a window, at glowing, moonlight-bathed Mount Moffett to the west, a scene that he thought many decades later was worthy of a Robert Glenn Ketchum photo — an almost sainted sight, the prominence virtually aglow in its snowy mantel. It seemed to settle his mind.

He began gathering uniforms and impediments over ensuing weeks, reclaiming never-worn civvies, AWOL bag and other personal items from Sergeant's Rufus's storage dungeon. He packed his seabag a day early, contemplating some dramatic departing gesture, a statement by which they'd remember him. His Boot Camp buddy, Hal Faltschaft, came to mind, and the impression he'd made three years before after MCRD Boot Camp. Plagiarism, Sergeant Lewis had told him, was the sincerest form of flattery.

"Heard a' *'déjà vu?'*" Garson asked that morning, waving his transfer order alongside his ear as Sergeant Lewis, Ungar, Blake, Vandy and one or two others gathered to wish him bon voyage. It was a script he'd used before.

"Sure," the chief clerk instantly replied. "Means you have a feeling you've been to a strange place before."

"Know what *'vuja de'* means then?" No one replied.

"Means you never want to come back to this fuckin' place again!" Garson hoisted the bulky seabag onto his shoulder, grabbed his gripsack, smiled and saluted with his left hand. "Semper fuckin' Fi, you fuckin' Jarheads!" His buddies grinned.

CHAPTER 6

OSCAR COMPANY

"Short Timer"

It was like one of those memorable scenes born from a lifetime with movies – like Flynn and de Havilland in "The Adventures of Robin Hood," or Lancaster and Kerr in "From Here to Eternity." Garson preferred Kerr opposite Mitchum in the more recent, "Heaven Knows, Mr. Allison." The Marines, you know! Just now, no cloaked gallant clung to a castle turret, pledging love to his fair Maid Marion, no illicit lovers glistened in a surging Hawaiian surf. Without swelling orchestral strings, woodwinds and reeds evoking emotions, the scene played out on a gravel parking lot outside a Marine sentry gate at Camp Pendleton. Still, as was his wont, Garson found romance.

When he and Piccolo arrived at the guarded portal, she was

leaning against a miniscule convertible — sea green with a white top and broad white side wall tires. Garson was given momentary pause because this tiny single-seater seemed insubstantial, too timid for traffic during the hour or more drive north to Los Angeles.

Long, shapely legs descended from bleach white shorts, feet strapped in sandals. The edge of a colorful sleeveless blouse was knotted under her bosom, revealing inches of flat diaphragm below folded arms. Not what Garson's buddies regarded as "chesty," her lithesome body was what *he* regarded as perfectly proportioned — a classic California girl, athletic, fit from tennis and swimming, callipygian, as he would often describe her. Yet, she displayed only minimal tan. Of course, her hair was shaded ash blonde to gold, banded in a ponytail that fluttered in August breeze rising from San Onofre Beach. Her welcoming smile could serve as a perfect dental advertisement.

"Zephyr," Pico introduced, nodding to her. "And this is Corp..., I mean Garson," he said. Of course, Zephyr — like a balmy Pacific breeze. But this was Garson's recollection, after all, and he was free to shape it as he pleased, even to her name.

"My next door neighbor. Known each other since we were kids." She smiled at that. "Went all through school with her since third grade. Well, I was half year ahead." She was several years his junior, Garson quickly calculated. He couldn't of course foresee that the nubile girl would soon have his measure – even though she'd never realize it.

When, in the fullness of time, Garson wrote of these circumstances, he worried that readers might regard him as a callow Marine with a girl in every port. Guilt occasionally tugged at him, as he'd once carried on simultaneous communications with three correspondents, including the fiancé he'd believed had been faithful; but why should Betsy have remained true when he hadn't been? Nola, the Whidbey Island blonde, had sent fetching photos to

NAS Adak, poses in a hugging one-piece swimsuit that he'd pasted in his album. But Garson's attempt to revivify communication with her after Betsy's stinging "Dear John" had been unsuccessful; he surmised that Nola had somehow suspected his lack of fidelity. Now, the proximity to Montebello and Karen Sisko reawakened that memory of scintillating hours in the balcony of the Coliseum movie palace downtown. He still carried guilt that he'd given her address to Moldy while at NAS Whidbey; who knew if the sinister scarred Marine might have seduced the *café con leché* girl. In the end, then, he'd been left with no one – a situation that, he'd confessed to himself, was fair recompense.

When Garson returned to southern California in early summer, the steady sun was a golden tonic for his chalky Aleutian pallor. Several times he slumbered between quonset huts during off-duty afternoons soaking up Pacific sun and warmth. Those weeks at Camp Matthews rifle and pistol range in the spring of 1957 had been invigorating, firing a .45 automatic pistol each morning in preparation for competition in the Corps's Western Division Rifle & Pistol matches. But while his mood was ebullient, having only months to serve in his enlistment, he was frequently fraught by dilemma: Should he re-enlist for four or six more years? He'd passed the promotional exam to sergeant and was slated to earn his third stripe in November. It would translate into a substantial pay raise, nearly balancing the loss of the overseas stipend he'd earned at NAS Adak. More, he'd wear one of the Corps's respected enlisted ranks — buck sergeant.

Still, he'd often boasted, even as far back at MCRD Boot Camp about plans after discharge: With a GED in hand, successful completion of correspondence courses and auditing classes at Oak Harbor High while at NAS Whidbey — all proof of academic abilities; and with the G.I. Bill, he might fulfill his dream of studying journalism. He'd invariably imagined himself in the Ben Hecht drama *Front Page,* "Press" badge parked in his fedora, peppering politicos and the powerful with questions as flashbulbs popped – an idealistic reporter informing citizens and earning newspaper by-lines.

Buoyed by his early departure from the unstable, storm-lashed Adak Island confinement, he recalled little about the return flight east. Certainly, it had featured the tortured departure through roiling gray overcast, the DC-6's four prop motors howling, avionics groaning, fuselage metal creaking as he sat sidesaddle in the largely empty cargo bay, Bering Sea turbulence tossing the aircraft like a toy. At the midway stop of Kodiak Island, he clearly remembered seeing the movie "Giant" at the base theater, an overlong melodrama he disliked. He'd been unconvinced by James Dean's mumbling portrayal of Jett Rink. My god, he remembered thinking, the actor was an urban persona not a ten-gallon hatted Texas wildcatter. Within months, the actor would be killed in his Porsche racecar. More, Rock Hudson and Elizabeth Taylor hadn't seemed compatible.

From Seattle, he'd detoured to Whidbey Island for a brief visit with friends, Rollie and Georgia Mae, married now and living in a single bedroom walk-up near downtown Oak Harbor. He slept fitfully on a lumpy living room sofa draped by a chenille comforter.

Garson seemed to be unwinding the direction of his Marine Corps travels, like a feature film spooling backward, he reflected while constructing the chronology of those distant days, something like the movie "Memento."

"Nola's in school now, at Northwest College in Seattle," Georgia Mae related. He recalled the saucer eyes behind those large academic spectacles, thinking she'd been an unusual confidant for gregarious Nola. "Haven't talked to her much since graduation. See her once or twice, at Christmas and such. They say she's dating some guy from Wenatchie." Garson deflated, recalling some promising nights on her living room couch.

Despite uncommon prowess with the .45 pistol, Garson's performance at Camp Matthews during the May competition was a disappointment. He easily earned another Expert medal, his fourth, with a fresh-out-of-the-grease pistol that the range armorer, a typical rumpled Old Corps gunny, had tuned to Garson's specifications. But he was well out of his league, no match for the "professionals" – staff NCOs, mustangs and officers who regularly competed in national and worldwide matches. He salved disappointment with the thought that the assignment had freed him from the "Aleutian's Golden Link" a month early – before another quake could topple the barren island into the sea.

In June, he was transferred to Pendleton's Camp San Onofre's advanced combat training battalion. Called "Oboe" in the old phonetic designation, the Third Battalion company was now identified as "Oscar." Garson never warmed to the designation; in fact he considered the old Able, Baker, Charlie, Dog, etcetera more manly and virile than the new Alpha, Bravo, Charlie, Delta. And Foxtrot replacing Fox? He also grew disconcerted by other changes in the Corps: The World War's classic dungarees had been replaced by darker-hued issues made to be worn tucked at the waist. Chevrons were no longer stenciled on jacket sleeves, rank now designated with small brass emblems on collar points. Did more spit and polish improve combat readiness? he fussed.

Too, the natty waist-length battle jacket and green wool dress shirts he favored were no longer part of the dress uniform. Scuttlebutt, like a low-level hum, also suggested a new enlisted grade between PFC and corporal would soon be introduced: "Lance" corporal, it was to be called, along with three more grades above master sergeant. While these were intended to increase pay for enlisted men, Garson thought the plethora of new stripes smacked of a Gilbert and Sullivan opera. More insult was in the offing as military service numbers would give way to common Social Security numbers. No matter, 1427801 would be his indelible identity.

Garson also fretted about the new squads drill manual being introduced — more peacetime parade ground movement than practical linear marching with which he'd been trained. He grumbled that some recently minted major at Marine headquarters on Washington's 8th and I Streets must have concocted the maneuver to earn promotion to colonel. But he was to be disabused of that speculation when he learned that the "new" formations and movements had actually been the standard before the World War erupted. What he'd been taught at MCRD had been a simplified expedient drill regime necessary to quickly train tens thousands of volunteers and draftees for service.

Most troubling of all, it appeared that the classic tactic of amphibious assault that defined the Corps in the Pacific seemed to be losing its prominence. No longer would Marines gloriously splash ashore as they had on Tarawa, Peleliu, Iwo Jima, Inchon and elsewhere; now, in the tactic called "vertical envelopment," fighting men would descend from the belly of choppers. Somehow, it all lacked the heroic imagery he'd harbored since childhood.

Like all Camp Pendleton companies, Oscar was comprised of four 60-man platoons that slogged for a dozen weeks over Camp Pendleton's precipitous coastal hills, carpeted with sage and chaparral, cut by dry water courses, arroyos, canyons and draws. The landscape was greened only by a few pitiful oak woodlots. As a young Marine who'd completed advance combat training years before, Garson had found the terrain taxing.

But now he was a salty "veteran," not quite "Old Corps," but one of the base's permanent duty personnel assigned as a Troop Handler, a curious designation, he thought. Carrying 15 more pounds than he had at enlistment and a bit more muscle, he was sinewy and cocky. Buddies came to call him "Bandy Corporal." But to the company's Top Sergeant Peckem's dismay, Garson exhibited less than exacting Marine demeanor.

"Don't appreciate your 'short timer' attitude," he once pointedly fussed.

"Don't mind him," Corporal Bischoff commented. "He's married to the Corps." Peckem had never had a wife, it was said.

Garson, emulating Oscar Company's peerless Corporal Deal, stood out in starched dungarees, glossy boots and shined brass. He enforced discipline and reinforced lessons in Marine Corps lore, and directed physical drills and obstacle course exercises. He marched the entire company to the chow hall, and to open-air classrooms in the rolling Pendleton boonies where instructors conducted lessons in combat tactics and battle formations, care and maintenance of small arms, personal hygiene and more, preparing trainees for the expected hot wars ahead.

When leading his platoon or the entire 200-man company, Garson wore only starched dungarees, a helmet liner and carried a broom handle walking stick that one trainee had carved and decorated for him. He set blistering paces, especially into the hilly boonies, amused that the fresh-faced Marines, burdened with steel helmets, marching packs, M-1 rifles or BARs, ammunition belts and canteens, flagged and straggled. Garson caught many hateful glances.

Typically, Oscar Company NCOs did not long serve as Troop Handlers; they were either, like Garson, short timers soon destined for discharge or Marines moving up in rank and on to promising duty stations. Hence, most associations were transitory and lacked substance. Among most memorable was the unit's bellwether NCO, a tall, rigorous corporal named Deal, characterized by large, rarely blinking blue eyes, impeccable discipline and flawless comportment. Sergeant Bischoff, the Negro from East St. Louis, called him "Big Deal" or "Real Deal," even "I-Deal," sometimes teasing that the Illinoisan was bound to be a Corps lifer like Peckem. Garson doubted it.

Deal had studied at his hometown's Northwestern University for a few semesters, and articulation and erudition were readily evident. In some ways, he reminded Garson of his Boot Camp mentor, Ridley, the Southern Cal college boy, and the "Champ," Sergeant Lewis.

While Garson and Deal found occasional consonances, they were often diffident and competitive with one another. Almost prudish at times, the Illinoisan eschewed crude humor.

"Heard the one about the Jarhead on L.A. liberty...?" Deal began, large light eyes wide.

"One about the Catalina Island Ferry, you mean?" Garson returned abruptly. Deal nodded quizzically. "You're *thpeaking* to him?" Garson lisped the punchline. "Yeah, that's so old Columbus got shot in the ass for tellin' it ta the Indians," he snapped. Deal glowered. "Matter of fact," Garson lied, "read that even Mark Twain told it to his wife during some world tour or sometime." Competitive tension simmered, born of scuttlebutt that the steely, self-contained corporal would soon earn a meritorious advancement to sergeant, something Garson coveted. Yet, to Garson's pleasure, Deal was conversant with movies. Idling one afternoon while trainees perched in the bleachers of an outdoor classroom, the Illinoisan dispensed his knowledge.

"During the war, they shot several motion pictures (he preferred to use that phrase instead of "movies") around here," he said with a sweep of his arm. "I believe they included 'Wake Island' in '42, and during '43, 'Guadalcanal Diary,' 'Gung Ho' with Randolph Scott, 'Salute to the Marines" with Wallace Beery as the old sergeant, and then John Garfield's 'Pride of the Marines.'" Garson had seen many of those as a youth. When he'd turned 13, he'd applauded John Wayne's portrayal of hard-bitten Sergeant Stryker in "The Sands of Iwo Jima" that had also been filmed at Pendleton's tent camp. The actor became Garson's personification of the Corps, and he often averred that Stryker had been his Marine recruiter.

"Read the pocket book of *Battle Cry*," Garson boasted. "Huxley's Whores and all that."

"Yes, Leon Uris," Deal nodded. "That motion picture was filmed here at Pendleton, too."

"Liked the book better than the film," Garson replied. "Movie was a little syrupy. Dorothy Malone, you know."

Bischoff, as tall as Deal, was similarly slender and willowy with angular shoulders like coat hangers. Despite sleepy eyelids, the Negro NCO was energetic and active with an acute sense of humor. He was in the final months of his enlistment, having resisted the "shipping over lecture" from officious Master Sergeant Peckem. Bischoff was determined to take his discharge and return to family and friends in East St. Louis. Garson envied his stack of long-playing jazz records, and listened to tunes spun on his tinny portable player.

Bischoff's eclectic collection included recordings by Stan Kenton, and hard bop players like Miles Davis, Art Blakey, Cannonball Adderley and others. He especially enjoyed Davis's nonet on an LP titled "Birth of the Cool," the dozen tunes arranged by Gil Evans, Bischoff explained; it had been recorded years before when the group played at an intermission of a Count Basie concert. Garson enjoyed the lush brasses and urgent reeds, the sound softer than the aggressive style Davis had usually played. Garson listened intently to both music and Bischoff's commentary which was the equal to Garson's Boot Camp buddy, Heissen.

"Got some cats wailin' out here on the Coast now," Bischoff opined, "cool jazz types. Chet Baker, Jerry Mulligan, Phil Woods." Bischoff's recordings also contained cooler and less aggressive performances by pianists Ahmad Jamal and George Shearing.

"Some who enjoy hard boppers back east don't much favor the Pacific Coasters because they're not as 'out front'. They play with more shading and subtlety." He went on to explain that Jamal's "Live at the Pershing" had been a top seller for many weeks. "Critics say he and others like him are just noodlers playing soft pitch stuff. But that's the beauty of jazz. It's not just 'one size fits all.' You hear lots of influences – classical, blues, standards."

"Name like that — he Moslem or something?" Garson asked.

"Yup! Changed his name from Fred Jones years back." The Negro corporal also spun records by Errol Garner and Thelonious Monk, and, of course, Charley Parker. Garson was being weened away from rank popular music of the day.

During one of Bischoff's disquisitions, "Pigeon," the company clerk drifted through the quonset. After pausing briefly, he blurted. "Jazz! Don't like it. Sounds like a bunch of unconnected notes. Guess maybe I just don't understand it." With Sergeant Peckem, Pijanowski was the other long-serving Oscar Company enlisted man. He was responsible for record keeping, official communication and mail; his milieu did not include marches in the boonies. Large "porthole" glasses reinforced a youthful, studious visage; his chest was as narrow as Garson's. He seemed not to resent being called "Pigeon." A few muttered that he might be the Top Sergeant's toady, but Garson doubted it. The clerk bunked with the Troop Handlers.

"Well, Pigeon, you're young yet," replied Bischoff. "Jazz ain't chaotic at all, ya' see. It has defined structure just like all music." The Negro corporal went on to describe that a jazz tune had a statement or theme, and everything emanated and revolved around that. "Soloists use the theme as a basis to interpret and articulate, dropping or adding notes, 'commenting' on one another, sometimes adding phrases from other tunes." Pigeon just shook his head, no more enlightened than when he entered. Garson wasn't certain he understood everything either. But it sounded right.

Master Sergeant Peckem and PFC "pigeon" were the exceptions to the transitory character of Oscar Company's personnel. Because of Garson's early antipathy to the superior, he wasn't interested enough to determine how long the six-striper had been assigned to Camp Pendleton; but his sleeve bore five service stripes, indicating more than 20 years in the Corps. The sergeant's chest was laden with rows of ribbons from battles and duty stations virtually around the globe.

Save for a slight midlife bulge above a glistening brass belt buckle, Peckem was sinewy; tightly-cropped sandy hair was threaded with gray; his ears were disconcertingly large and his mouth virtually lipless; wrinkles radiated from the corners of dark eyes that penetrated like a dental drill. His gravelly voice sounded as if it was somehow constricted in his throat.

Like every platoon Troop Handler, Garson was also responsible for selecting trainees to serve as squad leaders. As new companies were organized, he and other NCOs perused Boot Camp personnel records, and observed their young subordinates, searching for candidates with potential. Those selected for leadership wore distinguishing armbands, and assisted Troop Handlers in daily routines. Trainees failing to measure up were "demoted" and returned to ranks. Since, in this "new Corps," Marines were rarely advanced in rank after MCRD recruit training, Garson also recommended names for promotion to PFC at the conclusion of Pendleton training.

Piccolo, the light-hearted Angelino, was not considered for promotion. One of the rear-rank short rounds in Garson's platoon that late summer, he displayed prominent chisel front teeth that dominated his visage. Barely reaching the minimum Marine height and likely not weighing 130 pounds, Piccolo's steel helmet seemed outsized, virtually rattling on his small head as he jogged. Yet the trainee's compact body and short legs were indefatigable. He smiled through physical adversity, even buoying buddies with infectious humor. He was, of course, called Pico, after the famed Los Angeles Boulevard that cut across the city from Santa Monica. He'd enlisted shortly after January high school graduation.

Garson rarely slackened the pace or discipline, kept his distance from subordinates and avoided fraternization. Pico was one of the few with whom he found affinity. They affected a tentative acquaintance, occasionally conversing during off-duty hours when Pico talked effusively about his hometown. Save for night marches and three-day training exercises called "problems," trainees and

Troop Handlers, unless they had the duty, were free evenings and weekends.

"Takin' liberty home, to El Monte for the weekend," Pico told Garson about halfway through the Pendleton regimen. "Got a ride comin' ta pick me up next Saturday mornin'. Want to come up for the weekend?" Garson set aside his reluctance, tempted by the invitation. He'd been off base sparingly in several weeks.

Taciturn, demur and undemonstrative, Zephyr was clearly unlike most other girls Garson had met. Sunny and virginal, she, like Nola, tested his growing preference for smoldering brunettes like Karen. Surprisingly, no photos of Zephyr graced Garson's old album. Thus, only a sketchy residual recollection remained that he fortified with wishful fancy. Their meeting became one of his rarified "memories."

She drove up the Coast Highway north to Los Angeles for over an hour that afternoon. Garson half curled on his side on the ledge behind the single bench seat and against the isinglass rear window. His head was pleasantly close to Zephyr's. Breeze from the half open side window whisked her ponytail and bathed him in her subtle scent. He marveled at her driving skill, clutching and shifting the tiny Nash Metropolitan's gears with aplomb, ignoring blaring horns and reckless passing by male drivers. Their eyes met at intervals in the rearview mirror, like one of a half dozen times in Garson's life when he thought he detected an instant connection. Like Saturnian rings, her pale eyes shaded from hazel centers to yellow outer edges; thin brows arched provocatively. He was willingly beguiled.

"You know they make cars like this in my hometown – in Milwaukee," Garson offered. "Got, ah, we have a big Nash plant back there. This one was made there, I bet." Zephyr seemed unimpressed.

"One night before I enlisted, me and a bunch of pals spotted a tiny, little car, like this, at a curb on our block. Only it was a Crossley — British car." In telling the tale, Garson suppressed the guilt he'd felt back then as a member of marauding baboons bent upon deviltry. "We rocked that car back and forth, and worked it from the street, over the curb and across the sidewalk, right onto the house's front lawn." He recalled their raucous laughter. "Never found out what the owners did when they saw that car there next morning." Pico chortled. Zephyr raised an eyebrow.

Intent on the wheel and thickening traffic, Garson's small talk garnered only nonverbal responses from her. He turned his attention to the freeway ahead, to the zooming multi-lane traffic that threatened to devour Zephyr's little convertible. She evinced no nervousness, saying little during the journey, announcing only: "We're almost in El Monte" as they approached the mountain foothills.

"Usta be lotsa orchards around here in the San Gabriel Valley – oranges and lemons mostly," Pico related, a proud tour guide. "Most were bulldozed and made into subdivisions ages ago. What few're left will be big time 'burbs soon, they say." Garson gazed north to the crest of the broad mountain vista, perhaps a dozen miles away, prominences like Mount Wilson and its observatory jutting up six-thousand feet.

"That the observatory in the Jimmy Dean movie?" Garson queried.

"'Rebel Without a Cause,' you mean?' Naw, that's Griffith, near the studios and Hollywood," Pico corrected. "Maybe we can go see it sometime."

"Us kids always used Zephyr's pool," Pico said as she parked in her driveway next door to his house. Their El Monte neighborhood, Garson observed, was composed of new but unremarkable single-story residences with garages and carports that sprawled on looping courts and *cul de sacs*.

"I watch her swim sometimes," Pico admitted. "Looks great in a two-piecer." Garson soon readily agreed. But he was torn. With no suitor evident, she sometimes seemed to enjoy his attention. Still, he eschewed all but the gentlest flirtations because she so young, fresh and, he assumed, virginal. He even found her a little intimidating as though she was pleased with his ill-ease and hesitancy. Perhaps she was physically too perfect. He'd never dated a girl so beautiful. If feelings such as he'd had for Betsy ever materialized, how would he channel them? Would he remain in California after the Marines, find a job and live here? The thought of his mother intruded. His mind too often raced well ahead of events.

More than once, Garson strolled next door to Zephyr's pool when she languidly swam free style and back stroke laps, water sheening her toned torso. She seldom spoke or even looked at him during her routines, emerging from the water after perhaps 20 minutes, like Esther Williams or shapely Sophia Loren rising from the Ionian Sea in "The Boy on a Dolphin," a movie seen that summer. He often hurried to the poolside ladder and offered his hand; their eyes met as he gently pulled her up, thrilling to her grasp, and handed her a towel. She wrapped it about her body and smiled demurely. "Thanks" was all she said.

During weekend liberties, Pico assumed the role of impromptu tour guide. He drove a sparkling powder blue '56 Chevy coupe for which his father had co-signed; Pico remitted semi-monthly installments every Marine payday.

"Nothin' much downtown anyways," Pico replied when Garson asked about the famous intersection. "Hollywood 'n' Vine's just two roads comin' together. Oh, they might gussy up a sidewalk there with movie star names on it, maybe a thousand of 'em, to bring yokels down here, Zephyr says."

Garson was frustrated, long hoping to see a roller derby game. He'd been fascinated since youth at the disreputable rough and tumble "sport" broadcast on television — Anne Calvello with her gnarled, oft-broken nose and the Thunderbirds, triumphant against all comers at the Grand Olympic Auditorium in downtown Los Angeles. Pico demurred traveling to such déclassé spectacle – no more real than professional wrestling grunt and groaners.

"How far's Montebello?" Garson asked during one of Pico's junkets.

"South a' here by a bit," his buddy responded. "Why? What's there?" Garson explained that years ago, when he was a Pendleton trainee like Pico, he'd had a date with a dark-eyed senorita who'd nearly won his heart.

"Montebello — Italian word for 'beautiful mountain,' you know." Pico doubted they'd find Garson's sweet chiquita, Karen Sisko. "Probably a fat mama with a dozen squallin' niños by now."

During other drives, Garson gaped in fascination at the ever-surging parkways and freeways and snarling spaghetti interchanges, thinking his dowdy hometown would never construct such thoroughfares. He hoped to see Beverly Hills, the famed thoroughfares of Wilshire Boulevard and Huntington and Mulholland Drive he knew from movies, the Le Brea Tar Pits where bubbling ooze belched up fossilized prehistoric remains. He hoped to see other sites others as well — Angel's Flight incline railway, Echo Park lagoon and Pershing Square where impromptu speeches were delivered by ordinary even addled orators, pontificating about omnivorous topics. But distance and time always precluded such treks. Usually, Pico was content to cruise local El Monte streets, eliciting admiring glances at his gleaming new Chevy.

One Saturday evening, they flowed along a four-lane commercial strip, perhaps Valley Boulevard, in a bumper-to-bumper caravan of gleaming vehicles and custom rods, burbling mufflers, driven by youthful drivers with girls. Curiously, Garson thought, Pico had installed tiny blue bulbs in his wheel wells; the lights were reflected in swirling chrome hubcaps of adjacent cars. At one stoplight, a long, sleek four-door sedan sidled alongside, refulgent paint mirroring sidewalk storefront neon; the car's candy-striping accents were flamboyant, and the chassis barely clearing the pavement. Growling mufflers threatened. Garson turned to look: Four swarthy faces glowered.

"Hey, hombre," the narrow-eyed driver snorted, nodding at Pico's decorative lights. "Do them things down there make it go faster?" Intimidated, Garson slid lower in his seat, deigning not to respond. Some hard-bitten Marine, he castigated himself silently. Mariachi music thundered from the car. After several dangerous minutes, the traffic light blinked to green, and the sedan screeched, slithered and launched forward like a rocket in a cloud of acrid tire and exhaust fumes. Pico didn't bother to trump the accelerator, aware that his Chevy was impotent to the challenge.

"Cholo punks!" he muttered. They drove in silence for many minutes.

"Gotta see this," Pico announced during another weekend liberty. Garson had been turned around by the raceway traffic and direction changes in looping, multi-leveled freeway connections.

"Man, it's fantastic," Garson blurted, aghast at the view as Pico crawled around the Los Angeles site off Santa Ana Boulevard. "Look at that, man!" Garson said, gazing at the phantasmagoria. "Spires're look like they're made of steel rebar wrapped in wire and cement or something." The tall curved towers, one rising a hundred feet, and other structures were studded with a carnival of ornamentation – ceramic plates and tile, damaged pottery, glass bottle bottoms, all in a rainbow of colors glistening in the afternoon sunlight. A terra cotta sign proclaimed "Neustro Pueblo" – our town, Pico translated. Garson was disappointed that they couldn't gain access.

"Guy named Rodia built it — by himself," Pico offered. "Italian immigrant. Took 'im 30 years, they say. Found all of this junk an' stuff at an old pottery factory and along the railroad tracks hereabout. Few years back he gave up an' moved away, disgusted at politicians and neighbors who complained it was an eyesore. They want to tear it all down. Who knows what'll happen now." Garson was mesmerized by the site.

"This is Watts, a colored, er, a Negro section. A little dicey around here now." Many decades later, Garson was reminded of the unique site when he climbed into the unfinished Gothic towers of Goudi's Church of the Sacrada Familia in Barcelona.

On his final weekend liberty with Pico, they were joined by Zephyr and another neighbor, her doll-like friend, and journeyed over an hour south to the recently opened Disneyland Park in Anaheim. While in his youth Garson had been captivated by the studio's animated screen adventures, memorably "Fantasia." He'd also found fascination with carnivals, seedy midways, sordid tent shows with tattered trappings that evoked the milieu of the movie "Nightmare Alley." But Disneyland was nothing like those; instead, the fantasy park was clean, precise and orderly — unreal.

Even while the amusement park lacked his preferred tawdriness and grittiness, Garson was giddy, childlike, swirling in Mad Tea Party cups and flying Dumbo cars, King Arthur Carousel, rocking on the Space Mountain coaster, sailing languidly on Davy Crockett canoes and Mark Twain riverboat. The four revelers also dived in Captain Nemo's submarine. When he later realized his near obliviousness to Zephyr, he repeatedly butted her bumper car.

On the drive back, at least to his selective recollection, he inched closer to Zephyr in the backseat, holding her hand, perhaps draping an arm about her shoulder. He certainly regretted his inattention to her during the outing. Did he ask if she had a good time? Had he even expressed his hope to see her again? He ached to give her some unambiguous indication of nascent affection but all he could muster was asking if she'd write to him. She turned to face him and responded only with another inviting golden-girl smile. Had he correctly interpreted her expression? The answer would remain one of Garson's late-life surmises.

Garson, of course, could not suppose he'd pass this way again. But in less than a dozen years he'd return to Southern California with a wife and children in tow, spending a week with his old Boot Camp mentor, Heissen, then a graduate student at the University of South California, and his family. Garson visited Disneyland again. Zephyr came to mind briefly, but the confected memory of the golden California blonde and their brief, sunny "romance" had grown fainter with each passing year.

"This's the same fuckin' shit they gave us here when I was a trainee," Garson groused, opening a hot olive drab can of hamburger patties, lima beans and gravy just retrieved from the boiling ten-gallon drum of water. "See here," he held up the container, "February 1950. From fuckin' Korea." He was sharing noon chow in the field with other Troop Handlers.

"Man," he said as they munched on the hard-as-cement dessert crackers, "even these Lucky Strikes're wrapped in World War green." He held up the compact box containing four cigarettes. "Bet they're dry as hay." Later conversation permitted Garson to display his tiny "war wound," his "red badge of courage" — the L-shaped white scar at the base of his left palm. A little less than four years before, he described to fellow Troop Handlers, while trying to open an obstinate ration can, he'd pounded the edge of a bayonet into the sliverous opening; miscalculating, he'd gashed the meat of his hand and blood geysered. After a huge hypodermic fit for a horse and yards of catgut, a navy corpsman had summarily stitched him up in the field.

"Didn't even get a Purple Heart for this," Garson self-deprecatingly noted to guffawing buddies.

In another of those expected starless nights, Garson snorted awake from the cramped and dewy fighting hole, wiping his eyes to clear the blur as "Willie Peter," white phosphorous shells bloomed in the inky sky, bathing the rolling landscape in flickering, ethereal light — déja vù from his own training days. He slammed the blue helmet liner on his head. While stationed here nearly four years before, a smoky sagebrush fire propelled by dry Mohave winds (Los Vientos dos Santana, his fellow trainee, Cortes, called them back then) had swept down from the eastern mountains, unleashing a retreating carpet of the furry tarantulas.

As a Troop Handler now, he'd drawn another duty during the three-day combat problem; Garson and PFC Backus, the new man, were responsible for Oscar Company command, marching the unit from one field classroom and demonstration area to another, and insuring the daily rendezvous with meal trucks. Most onerous, Garson and ruddy Backus were assigned to overnight security, especially to steady the Main Line of Resistance when ghostly enemy tried to infiltrate or penetrate the perimeter in darkness. Aggressors still discomfited Garson a bit. Adorned in camouflage dungarees and peculiar helmets, faces swathed in Halloween paint, they play-acted as enemies, mimicking Gooks, North Korean and Chinese soldiers, who'd confronted Marines fighting on the Asian peninsula. For young trainees, the unnerving experience was effective.

As the black sky illuminated by glowing Willie Peter shells, horns howled and drums thudded. The Aggressors' script was familiar:

"Hey, *Ma*-lenes, come on oh-ver! Got lotsa brew for you!" Voices reverberated from loudspeakers in the hills beyond. "Soft place to lay down. Get some shut-eye. Pretty fucky-fucky girls here, too. Come on oh-ver, *Ma*-lenes," they teased, attempting to seduce stuporous tyros to quit their MLR. Daring Aggressors were known to creep toward the defensive position, dragging off fresh-faced privates, caging them on the enemy hilltop eyrie like the Gooks had done. Captives were returned on the third morning, sheepish and derided by superiors and buddies. Garson would experience such scenarios with four companies during his final months of service.

Some weekends just before paydays when money was short, four or five Oscar Troop Handlers remained on base. They tossed coins to determine who among them would don dress greens to drive off base – Basilone Road to the San Onofre gate, and a short distance to a Taco Bell stand; the "runner" carried back bags of Americanized Mexican food — *barritos, tamales, chimichangas, tacos* and more. Food and drink seemed to stimulate chatter.

"What's the largest organ in the body?" Deal asked. Lungs? Heart? Stomach? Other surmises were offered.

"You're all wrong," smirked the corporal nonpareil. "It's the skin."

"Skin ain' no organ," Backus rejoindered. A reservist, the stout PFC had joined the regular Marines the year before and been assigned to Pendleton after advanced combat training. Deal countered, producing convincing evidence to his assertion.

"It's another of those facts hardly worth knowing," Deal added, attesting to a typical ephemeral exchange that often passed for enlightened conversation.

"What's this fluted depression called?" he asked, touching an index finger beneath his nose. When no one offered an answer, he responded to his own query: Philtrum, he said.

"You gonna be a doc 'er somethin', then?" Deal only scoffed and smiled at Backus's question.

"Here's another one," Bischoff offered quickly. "What're the hard little ends of shoe laces?" He surveyed the blank faces before chortling. "An aiglet."

"Dumb," Backus snorted distastefully.

Often discussions meandered into movies, and just then Jimmy Stewart's "The Spirit of St. Louis" was playing in San Diego.

"How many sandwiches did Lindbergh take flying across the Atlantic?" Garson queried.

Someone recalled Stewart munching on one in the movie.

"Five," Garson said smugly. He was asked where he learned that.

"Read up on it somewhere."

"How come we always read *up* instead of readin' down, er, better yet, read across," commented Bischoff, "like we really do." No one offered an opinion.

Contrastingly, occasional conversations took serious turns before veering back to the trivial.

"Y'all heard a Dien Bien Phu in French Indochina. Couple'a years back. Frog army weren't worth a fuckin' shit. Got beat by the Oriental Commies. Wait an' see, sump-un' gonna pop there one'a these days, I'm sure of it." Such was Backus's prognostication; it was obvious he was conversant with the situation in Southeast Asia. Some accused him of an attitude that was too "Gung-Ho;" he invariably trimmed his hair Boot Camp close. His face was dominated by large, rarely blinking eyes and thin lips. He sometimes exhibited a bellicose bent, expressing hope to "see the elephant." His home was El Dorado in southern Arkansas, not to be confused with the well-known Texas town, he always insisted.

Garson had no knowledge of the Southeast Asian battle against the Communist Viet Minh army fought at Dein Bien Phu two years before, about the time he'd arrived at NAS Whidbey. Beaten, the French army had subsequently withdrawn from all of colonial Indochina, and the country, like Korea before it, had been divided into two halves. Commies, Backus snarled, were on the march everywhere.

"Also, the stupid fuckin' Frogs're fightin' Algerians, and will probably lose that one too, the fuckin' bastards. Y'all watch: Us Jarheads'll be getting' into both'a them hotspots pretty damn quick," Backus fussed.

(Little could Garson or any of his buddies predict that in only a year, Marines would splash ashore in Lebanon; it would serve as an introduction of sorts to the Middle East where in due time at the beginning of a new century Marines and other fighting men would be presented with almost endless combat opportunities.)

Garson was torn, of course, still considering himself less than a combat-ready Marine. He was trained to fight, and his 0311 spec number designated an advanced infantryman. His skills with rifle and pistol were sharp. But, late in his enlistment, he remained a peacetime pogue, still craving battle as any true Marine must.

"You from Oregon, Garss?" Backus once asked.

"Naw, Wisconsin. Oregon town's spelled with 'ie,' not 'ee.'"

"Oh, yeah! Beer Town, huh? Great Lakes. Colder'n a whore's tit!"

"My town's much bigger, in Wisconsin I mean. When I was up in Washington, way I heard it, the place in Oregon was actually named after Milwaukee a hunnert years ago." In later conversations Backus, as did many Marines, shared his personal story.

"Tried tool 'n' die once, delivered Wonder Bread, worked at a printing shop and other places," Backus said. "Nothin' was ever steady though," he candidly revealed. "Pa was critical because I never measured up in his eyes, and to my brother's success." The older Backus was in a St. Louis law school. "'You're always doin' the right thing the wrong way,' Pa told me. It wore on me even though I graduated with B's. That's why I joined the Reserves, but even that didn't satisfy him." Tiny muscles above his eyebrows knotted.

"Hey, Verby?" Garson asked of the salty corporal who'd recently joined Oscar Company. If memory was reliable decades later, it was the final Camp Pendleton trainee company for which Garson served as Troop Handler. While not in appearance or manner, Verbinsky exhibited similar erudition as had Garson's Boot Camp mentor

Ridley and other educated buddies. Of medium height, Verby's was blocky, and his legs were slightly bowed; but he maintained his fairly toned torso and arms by pumping a weight bar. His face was long with a broad forehead that tapered down to a pointed chin.

"Heard of a guy at S.C. name'a Ridley?" Garson asked. Verbinsky had studied at Southern Cal, too.

"Can't say as I have," Verby wagged his head. "Was he a Greek?"

"Greek? I don' fuckin' know." The NCO gave Garson a narrow-eyed riposte.

"You jokin, right?" Verby retorted with obvious condescension. "No, man, not *a* Greek. Just Greek. Was he in a frat, a fraternity?" Mouth open, Garson nodded, but chastened by his lack.

"Top Peckem ain't gonna like that, Verby," Garson observed at another time when the corporal sprawled across his bunk wearing only colorful civvie briefs while strumming a guitar. His voice was tremulous and he carried a tune passably; when he played, his eyebrows danced with the beat.

"Good thing Peckem don't bunk in here then," Verby returned with a snap. He displayed an occasional corrosive demeanor and a compromised Gung Ho attitude.

"Well, Ridley told us at MCRD about his fraternity brothers drivin' down to T-Town, Tijuana, for the bullfights. Takin' off their shirts, slathering on suntan lotion and cheering for the bulls. Guess the Mexicans didn't like it much and a couple'a times they had to fight their way out of the *corrida* – that's what it's called, right?" Garson, of course, put a faster spin on the real story that Ridley had imparted.

He also widened Pigeon's eyes answering the company clerk's query about the great Adak quake.

"Thought it was the fuckin' end of the world," Garson began, describing the existential paroxysm with every adjective and adverb in his arsenal.

"Few years ago, they had big shakers up north of here about 200 miles," Pigeon responded, "near Bakersfield. And another one closer, maybe an hour. Six point four Richter that time. Something called the San Andreas Fault." Garson was unnerved anew; he feared living through another of such elemental episodes. Perhaps it was time to take his leave of California.

"Let's us get up a party for Garss," Backus suggested that fall when he learned of Garson's impending birthday. Thus, on a late September evening after duty, Deal, Garson and two others wedged in Backus's battered Buick; he'd driven it from Missouri to Camp Pendleton, and it wheezed, he said, coming in from San Berdo. They were intent upon celebrating Garson's signal day — "Natal Day," Deal called it. Verby had Oscar Company duty.

Garson was somewhat discomfited that Bischoff wouldn't join them. For he knew from past experience that friendships among most white and Negro Marines, especially while wearing civvies, often temporarily terminated at main gates; the public racial barrier had only been partially breached.

Their destination was a string of fabled coastal town gin joints perhaps as far north as Sunset Beach; they planned to drink at every bar. Heading north from San Onofre, their initial stop was an unimpressive Laguna Beach bistro. The revelers parked on backless stools. An owly bartender eyed them suspiciously. Deal ordered bourbon and water, Backus called for an Old Fashioned and the others (Garson's memory wasn't clear) opted for bottled beers. Recalling his lone experience with highballs at NAS Adak's Marine Club the year before, Garson ordered a Singapore Sling.

"See your ID?" asked the bartender. Garson confidently withdrew the card from his wallet. He'd long since "lost" the fraudulent one

Vandy had modified for him at NAS Whidbey. The replacement was bona fide, and he was confident. The heavy-browed barman scrutinized the card.

"Says here, September 24th's your birthday." Garson nodded with a smile. "Means you won't be 21 until after midnight today."

"Whatcha' mean?" Garson demanded, flabbergasted. "I turned 21 *last* midnight."

"No, no," the barman insisted, "you ain't of age til the end of today." Garson's buddies were also taken aback,

"That's not right, my man," said Deal. "Today's his birthday, not tomorrow. Give him the drink." The others closed ranks, attempting to reason with the surly server. But after a few retorts, he remained mute and unrelenting, arms folded about his chest like shields. Then he wiped his hands on the apron and ambled away.

"Let's blow this fuckin' pop stand," Garson groused. Their second stop that night was at Newport Beach, a larger seaside town with a nightclub virtually in surf. The interior was dark, elegant with a glossy, curved bar, small tables and a tiny riser with a piano. Many male customers wore white shorts, light sport coats and flowery open-collared shirts; handsomely-coiffed women were adorned with ankle-length skirts and dresses and filled the club with competing scents. Garson was once again carded, but the "inspector" returned his ID without question. He ordered the same cherry-flavored cocktail.

"Aw, come'on, Garss, that's a fuckin' pussy drink," Backus groaned. "Bourbon and branch. Scotch and water. At least a gin and tonic." Cowed, Garson ordered the latter.

After several sips, Garson swiveled his barstool to observe a singer with carefully-applied makeup and a Billie Holiday gardenia in her hair. Wearing a clingy, low-cut gown, she bowed to scattered applause before seating herself at the piano. A Negro bassist lifted his instrument. In a low-register voice she rendered several American Standards, evoking Peggy Lee's sultry styling. As alcohol insinuated itself, Garson tried to draw the singer's attention with broad smiles and robust applause, once lifting his glass to her in a toast. She paid him no heed.

During the set, he recalled that she sang the titillating tune that had been banned by the Catholic Church and eschewed by radio stations back home — Jeri Southern's provocative "An Occasional Man" with its double-entendre lyrics:

> *I got an island in the Pacific*
> *And everything about it is terrific*
> *I got the sun to tan me*
> *Palms to fan me*
> *And*
> *An occasional man.*
> *When I go swimmin'*
> *I'm always dressed in style*
> *'Cause I go swimmin'*
> *Wearin' just a great big smile.*

The nightclub singer and her songs were as intoxicating as his second gin and tonic. As on Adak the night of Marine Corps Birthday, a third cocktail wobbled Garson, spun his head and slurred his words. He withdrew from the milieu, descending into his stuporous self, critical of the chattering denizens who paid little heed to the entertainer. For him, music wasn't background, its purpose demanded attentiveness. His next memory was of slumping in the back seat of Backus's four-door while his buddies remained in the nightclub. He woke up the next morning sprawled on his bunk, clothed, parched and diffuse.

Once, when Verby rearranged the lower level of his foot locker, Garson noticed a cardboard box in which his buddy stored his books, paperbacks mostly. Curious, he asked the college boy what he was reading. He held up a volume titled *The True Believer*, described as a sociological study of mass movements and people attracted to them. It sounded a bit dry, but Garson listened.

"Author's an autodidact, self-educated, just a dockman here in L.A." Garson picked up the slender paperback and scanned the rear cover. "You should read it sometime," Verby said.

"And what's this about?"

"Oh, that's Kerouac, as you can see, Jack Kerouac," Verby replied. A New Yorker, the author, he said, was part of some new literary ferment. "He wrote the book in a matter of days. Used a seamless roll of paper in his typewriter so he didn't need to waste time changing sheets. He wrote in what's called 'stream of consciousness.' Few breaks and little punctuation." This was all new to Garson. The author had struck a chord for the new generation, Verby went on, and with Bohemians like Greg Corso, Allen Ginsburg and others "flailed at convention and social shibboleths."

"It was like that way with Hemingway, you know," Verby continued, typically building a head of disquisitional steam. Garson listened intently, anxious for more. "He wrote in a new muscular male prose style which was a dramatic departure from staid 19th century letters." Garson had found another mentor.

The final month of Garson's enlistment wound down rapidly, outside events seeming to close in.

"You hear about that governor, Faubus, think his name is. Said he wasn't gonna let Negro kids in Little Rock High." Verby had kept abreast of the Arkansas events. He displayed a newspaper's iconic front page photo of Elizabeth Eckford, the Negro girl and white female student snarling at her, and threatening to boycott the school. In days, President Eisenhower dispatched the 101th Airborne and federalized that state's National Guard to protect students. A Negro journalist was beaten and kicked during the melee; *he* was charged with disorderly conduct. Other newsmen were harassed and heckled. Bischoff said little about the incidents or the larger issues of the day. Later in the month dark headlines revealed that mob violence erupted in Nashville during the attempted desegregation of an elementary school. Garson was uncertain how to assess these tumultuous events.

The weeks of advanced combat training for Garson's last Oscar Company drew to a close, and with his trainees he sat on the sloping sides of a large natural amphitheater for the firepower finalé. He never seemed to tire of the thunderous pyrotechnics, the marshaling of every weapon in the Marine Corps arsenal — small arms, heavy caliber machine guns, napalm spewing tanks, artillery, mortars and more. Projectiles pierced bunkers, block houses and gun emplacements, rusted and charred vehicle hulks, landing craft and personnel carriers in a reverberating orchestral fusillade, an orgy of eye-opening destruction.

For him, the highlight of the demonstrations had been the appearance of the Ontos, a two-man self-propelled armored anti-tank vehicle — the "little engine that could." It was mounted with six 106-caliber recoilless rifles and one .50 caliber spotting rifle. Marines cheered as the agile little monster charged across the "stage," unleashing its devastating firepower. Garson was doubly proud because the Ontos, called "the Thing," had been produced by his home town's Allis-Chalmers manufactory. The thunderous conclusion echoed for miles and enveloped the scene in acrid smoke.

Still in a dilemma about his future, Garson learned that Corporal Deal had been meritoriously promoted to sergeant, an advancement he'd considered his. Deal was not near discharge. It was unlikely a second three-striper would be named in Oscar Company. Garson was devastated.

Three weeks before Garson's discharge, Deal, who also kept abreast of events of the day, related to his buddies that the Soviets had launched a satellite into orbit around the earth. All but Deal was incredulous that the Russians had beaten the United States into space.

"It's called Sputnik," Deal announced authoritatively, "about the size of a beach ball traveling 18,000 miles an hour." News reports broadcast the ominous pinging sound the object made on each hour and a half orbit. What might this portend for the United States, for the Cold War? Again, Garson was torn: Remain in the Corps for possible combat ahead or return to civilian life?

"Top wants to see you, Corp," announced clerk Pigeon during one of those final October weeks at Camp Pendleton. With his right index finger, the PFC nervously pushed outsized porthole glasses back up his nose.

Garson had avoided Top Peckem as much as possible, uncomfortable with his hardcore demeanor. Now, they sat across from one another in the Duty Hut for the proverbial "shipping over talk." The superior's pinched voice sawed at Garson.

The six-striper carefully laid out all of the benefits of reenlistment. There'd be a month's bonus pay, he said, an immediate 30-day leave, and the *possibility* of selecting the next duty station. Garson thought of assignment to Great Lakes, the navy's basic training facility in northern Illinois about an hour bus ride from home.

"Finally, you're slated for promotion to sergeant November One, a week after reenlistment," the Top Sergeant said. "Your new rank will earn almost one hundred and sixty dollars monthly – that's a 37-percent increase." One hundred and sixty bucks, almost 50 more each and every month, Garson reflected silently. It was a tempting inducement, like a slick used car salesman's deal-closing set of new tires.

"Well, Top, I really want to get that third stripe meritoriously, like Deal, *before* I re-up." He tried to don the neutral, non-assertive expression cultivated years before for his Boot Camp DI's:

Eyebrows half raised, narrow eyes widened slightly, lips relaxed. "I think I deserve it. Expert with M-1 and .45 pistol. Selected for the Western Division matches. Bettered myself – corporal in less than four years, Good Conduct medal." He also mentioned his GED, the completion certificates from the Marine Institute and United States Armed Forces Institute courses, as well as the high school classes he taken while at NAS Whidbey. "I was also commended for the Marine Barracks newspaper column I wrote there." Garson had his accomplishments memorized.

"But the difference between a meritorious and regular promotion is only one week, corporal," Peckem returned. Garson hesitated a few moments, then reiterated his position: He wanted the third stripe dated *before* signing on for six more years. Peckem exhaled slowly. At that, Garson detected an obvious change in his superior's demeanor, as though the sergeant considered further efforts at persuasion useless, possibly regarding Garson unworthy of continued service in his beloved Corps anyway. Peckem's eyebrows drew down and his verbiage became officious, devoid of contractions.

"When you are separated (Marines were never discharged, they were separated from Mother Corps; and thereafter they became not ex-Marines but former Marines) you will receive three months' pay for unused leave. (Garson had only used 30 days in four years.) You will further receive another two hundred dollars severance pay and the money remaining on the books." Garson had begun saving at NAS Adak, and money had accumulated to a mighty sum. Added to other end-of-enlistment payments, the total amount was nearly one thousand dollars — a staggering sum. He selected to receive the full amount cash in hand instead of a cashier's check mailed to his home in 30 days. He'd never seen such a mountain of real greenbacks, and smiled smugly at the windfall.

Finally, Peckem reminded that Garson was obligated to military service for eight years total: Having served four on active duty, he still "owed the United States government" four additional years of inactive duty. "This means that in the event of a national emergency like another war, you could be subject to a call back to active service again. Any questions?" Garson had none.

Interview concluded, Sergeant Peckem pointed his pen at the blank line on the DD-214 discharge document. Garson signed slowly, deliberately. The hand he then offered across the desk was returned with a lukewarm shake.

So here it was – *fait accompli*. It was late October. He'd soon be a civilian. Closing the quonset door behind him, his stomach soured and second thoughts crowded in. Had he done the right thing? Halfway down the company street, he slowed, almost turning on his heel in reconsideration. The Corps had been his "mother" for a long time, but now less than a week in uniform remained.

In subsequent days, he sorted through his uniforms, giving scratchy tropical trousers and shirts, dungarees, boondockers and other well-cared for items to Pigeon who was about his size; he retained cotton khakis trousers for possible civilian use, and packed G. D. Coleman's glossy combat boots and the favored "Old Corps" dungaree cap, for what purpose back home he did not know He rolled up the long panorama portraits of the four Oscar companies he'd led and mentored, stowing them with the carefully maintained photo albums and other incidentals. His seabag was only half full. In a garment bag he'd carry one set of dress greens, having long planned to reappear in Milwaukee resplendent in uniform bearing a four-year service stripe on his sleeves, a good conduct ribbon and expert shooting medals on his chest. He'd soon be a "conquering" Marine come home.

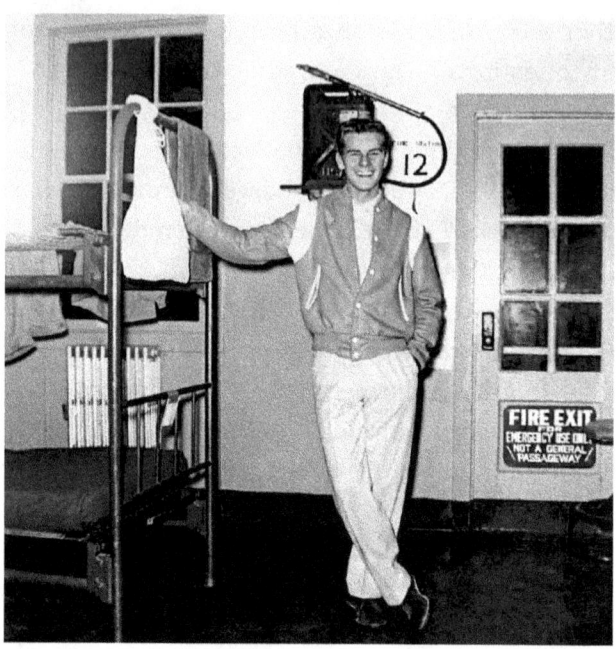

The other Troop Handlers were in the field with the new Oscar Company when Garson, seabag and gripsack in hand headed toward the San Onofre exit. In civvies and contrary to protocol, he paused to smartly salute the parade ground flag. The Marine gate sentry checked his documents and unceremoniously waved him out.

The cross country train retraced his route of almost precisely four years before. When it approached Milwaukee days later, he prepared to don his uniform as he'd envisioned. But he was crestfallen when he discovered the starched and pressed khaki shirt wasn't in the garment bag with other uniform components. His civvies were rumpled after the long rail journey east. No one waited at the train depot downtown anyway. He simply walked to Wisconsin Avenue and boarded a rattling yellow streetcar to the north side, and to his future.

*D*aughter's Reflection

"...always a Marine"

Was that a "Rosebud" allusion to his writing about the Marine Corps years – like the classic key to Orson Welles's "Citizen Kane?" Or was it something else, another movie reference that might hold an explanation – from Robert Rafelson's "Five Easy Pieces" in which Jack Nicholson's alienated character, pianist Robert Eroica Duprea, escaped from what he considered an inauthentic past?

Conversely, perhaps our Dad desired to overcome his unremarkable upbringing to seek something more genuine – an intellectual, cultured, even artful self that he'd envied in films (he often called movies that now – "films.") He admitted that he considered himself only minimally successful in real life, not having lived up to youthful fancies. Who among us did?

"Like many veterans, I felt out of step back home, missing the Corps's rigor and regimentation. I was caught in an existential eddy," he admitted to me.

Back home after four years away, he found kids gyrating with plastic Hula Hoops. Few radio stations featured the Great American Songbook playlist of his remembered mellow youth; now, Doo-Wop and other ephemeral musical forms dominated popular airwaves. More, grim newspaper headlines for months, revealed lurid details of an insane rural Wisconsin serial killer who'd stitched victims' skins into lampshades — a later-day movie would depict him as "Buffalo Bill." Newspapers feasted. What was happening now? What had gone wrong since his enlistment four years previous? Perversity seemed pervasive.

Only one event occurred that he'd envisioned, even before separation from the Marines: He donned his full dress uniform resplendent with stripes and shooting medals, and with GED and correspondence course completions in hand, he returned to his old high school, Messmer on Capitol Drive, hoping to obtain the mandatory equivalency diploma. His sights were clearly upon acceptance to Marquette University School of Journalism. But to his dismay, the high school's administration was adamant that he hadn't completed the requisite senior religion course to qualify. His impatience with petty religious considerations was reinforced.

Still, that November day, he visited the classroom of one of the nuns who'd been generous with encouragement and advice during the abortive years he'd attended Messmer. She'd apparently detected something in him that only his mother could see. Sister Immaculata remained as he remembered her – tall and angular with bottomless green eyes, expressive arched eyebrows, reminding him of the British actress who'd portrayed Sister Ruth in the movie "Black Narcissus." Even pinched by starched headwear, Immaculata's face, he'd long considered, would be attractive, save for a wisp of cosmetic enrichment and visible coiffure. The aura of intelligence beyond piety remained distinct. She smilingly reiterated her praise.

Such recollections our Dad imparted to me at long remove, when his contemporaries caterwauled that it was only yesterday that such events had occurred. But I countered that his life and times were now the stuff of actual history, not some simple recitation of contemporaneous events.

During those first months home, and in a gesture of uncommon boldness, he telephoned Betsy, the fancied fiancée who'd shaken him with a devastating "Dear John" letter delivered on the bleak, cruel, wind-scoured Bering Sea island. Married by then, she'd opened a bedroom door a few inches for him to see an infant swaddled in a crib — a girl. It was clear: There'd been someone else in her life when he'd been home on leave two years previous; she'd only indulged him, accepting the engagement ring. Decades later, however, he thanked her: Had they pursued their romantic course, actually *his*, to marriage, he might have been a work-a-day husband instead of a university graduate with a successful career and published books to his credit.

Our Dad tried to reconnect with former North Milwaukee pals and acquaintances. Many had dutifully joined the military after high school, and were still serving. Preston and Rusty had been discharged a year before, of course, after three-year enlistments. The former remained in southern California, and the latter had relocated to upstate Wisconsin. The trio, former Villard Avenue Musketeers, would have limited communication over the ensuing years. Meanwhile, Toby, his childhood pal, and Mellish were already married, both from "shotgun" circumstances.

Many girls he'd known were already engaged, married or decidedly settled and sedate. He and Lana, the youthful object of his fancies and currently a curvaceous high school graduate, reacquainted fitfully. To his delight, they set aside, at least for a few late evenings, the putative sibling relationship she'd foisted upon them. Only the keen ears of her widowed mother prevented more than occasional after hours groping on her screen porch. The past seemed to be present – he'd momentarily replaced Toby, Kawolski and many others. To his consternation, Lana continued to date widely with an array of suitors, some serious, others fitful, typically guys given to pink and purple, to sociability and ethnic dancing.

"When I married the first time," she would declare after shedding a third husband, "I was a virgin." Our Dad was ever dubious. But the unscratched Lana itch between them was never satisfied, he implied. I doubted that.

Then, he met our mother, young and inexperienced at the time, whose grape green, seductively-lidded eyes and buxomness beckoned him. I confess discomfort with these ramblings.

The year after his discharge, Marines and American military splashed ashore at Lebanon during a first foray into murky Middle East regional and religious rivalries. The invasion had a comic turn when children hawked Cokes to the well-armed invaders on the

Mediterranean beach. But 25 years later, agony arose anew as another peace-keeping force met a disastrous result when more than 200 Marines were killed in a terrorist Beirut barracks explosion. Younger Marines earned combat ribbons and Purple Hearts that our Dad had not.

Vietnam became another of the nation's ghastly, ill-considered post-World War conflicts that sacrificed tens of thousands of valiant lives with scant glory and billions in wasted national treasure. Only after his brother-in-law was killed and his name etched on the Vietnam Veterans Memorial, and after reading the trenchant memoirs of Tim O'Brien, Michael Herr, Philip Caputo and others, and viewing insightful films like "Full Metal Jacket," "Apocalypse Now," "The Deer Hunter" and others, did he gain perspective that had initially eluded him. He later disgustedly shook his head at the same ruinous American Middle East "strategy."

He found alliance with, among millions, the lauded British novelist, Ian McEwan who caviled: The "foe-of-convenience, the United States, barely the hope of the world, guilty of torture, helpless before its sacred text conceived in an age of powdered wigs, a constitution as unchallenged as the Koran. Its nervous population obese, fearful, tormented by inarticulate anger, contemptuous of governance, murdering sleep with every new handgun."

"Starting with Reagan," our Dad fulminated, "our nation's selfish moneyed cabal worked insidiously to limit democracy to any but themselves – the Kook Brothers, Sinclairs, Mercers, Waltons , Bradleys, the entire reactionary ilk. None of them ever gave a day of service or fairly supported our nation. They war against ordinary working people, plundering common riches; they seek to eviscerate or privatize government services, even replacing the military with mercenary armies," our Dad thundered. He couldn't mask his contempt. "They'll soon put a price tag on the right to life itself. Benighted bastards!"

Immediately after a four-year hiatus, our Dad never regained his youthful zest for weekly movie going. Hitchcock aside, he was discomfited by most current screen offerings: Too much Douglas Sirk and similar vapidity, too many Rock Hudson and Doris Day flummeries, epics without authenticity or humanity, he grumbled. Save for "West Side Story" late in the decade, he found a dearth of artful musical films and convincing dramas. With a few notable exceptions, our Dad found only a sad cinema wasteland.

Less than five years after our Dad returned home, I was born, the first of four. He and my mom were married in Holy Redeemer Church in 1960 after a two-year romance. At the time, he was an undergraduate majoring in journalism and history. My sister arrived after he'd completed his bachelor's degree and while he worked as a news writer for a local broadcast station. My brother was born after our Dad changed careers and near the end of his graduate studies. Our little sister, the "surprise child," arrived seven years after that.

He'd quit television when his boss proclaimed that "News is anything that's interesting," sacrificing significant reportage on the altar of visuals and ratings. It was prescient to our current age of what our Dad called Facebook PhDs and Fox News fantasists. "In my day, news was necessary to inform citizens to rationally carry out democratic responsibilities." "The film 'Nightcrawler' now typifies my chosen profession," our Dad lately averred; he'd become a heretical former journalist.

Still vital as a mid-octogenarian, our Dad reveled when our mother, his first wife, and others commented that he still strode like a former Marine.

Finally, our Dad was concerned that by committing his recollections to the printed page, he'd transformed them from reality. He sometimes confused what he'd written with what had actually occurred, confessing he'd shifted chronologies and circumstances in his writings to suit novelistic proclivities. Our Dad referred to his book as meta- or fictional autobiography. Maybe that's why he used the *nom de plume* "Garson."

Our Dad long hung in a spare closet his dress green uniform adorned with expert shooting medals, corporal chevrons, four-year service stripe and Good Conduct medal. He only once donned it for a Marquette University student veteran soiree. For years, he'd also retained some Corps paraphernalia and memorabilia, including the glossy boots given to him by his buddy G. D. Coleman. I might still have squirreled away that salty Old Corps dungaree cap he'd given me.

Over the years, our Dad circled every November 10th on his calendars — the date in 1775 when the United States Marine Corps, according to legend, first "came ashore" at Tun Tavern in Philadelphia.

After I reluctantly helped him complete this autobiographical memoir, our Dad mused that he might reminisce in writing about the years after the Corps — about college, marriage, children, career and more. However, I'm going to let my younger siblings decide about the considerable investment of time and spleen that'll demand. My brother and I have borne this burden long enough.

Semper Fi!

www.ingramcontent.com/pod-product-compliance
Lightning Source LLC
Chambersburg PA
CBHW071703160426
43195CB00012B/1560